FRANCE TO-DAY

Paul Sabatier

FRANCE TO-DAY
ITS RELIGIOUS ORIENTATION

BY

PAUL SABATIER

TRANSLATED

FROM THE SECOND FRENCH EDITION

BY

HENRY BRYAN BINNS

LONDON : J. M. DENT & SONS, LTD.
NEW YORK : E. P. DUTTON & CO. 1913

PREFACE TO THE SECOND FRENCH EDITION

WHY should I not confess that I was glad when I heard that this volume was to be reprinted a few months after its appearance? Did it not afford a striking indication of the new tendencies everywhere manifest in our country? Moreover, these pages had had the result I foresaw and desired; they had been criticised with equal vigour by every party and Church.

I thought at one time of replying here to all those criticisms. I have abandoned the idea, which would have swelled this book to undue proportions; but I wish at least to express my warm thanks to their writers. I am especially grateful to those teachers who have been so good as to write to me of their doubts, their hopes and endeavours.

If they will kindly continue to confide their experience to me, some day, perhaps, I may try to draw from it more precise and efficacious conclusions as to the evolution of moral and religious education.

PAUL SABATIER.

La Maisonnette,
    PAR S. SAUVEUR DE MONTAGUT,
        ARDÈCHE.

Oct. 1, 1912.

v

CONTENTS

INTRODUCTION

THE SPIRIT IN WHICH THIS BOOK IS WRITTEN

CHAPTER I

RELIGION AND RELIGIOUS ORIENTATION

CHAPTER II

WHAT IS AND WHAT IS NOT TO BE FOUND HERE

CONTENTS

CHAPTER III

CIRCUMSTANCES DETERMINING THE PRESENT RELIGIOUS ORIENTATION

CHAPTER IV

GRAVER AND GRAVER MISUNDERSTANDINGS BETWEEN CHURCH AND PEOPLE

CHAPTER V

DEFICIENCIES OF ANTI-RELIGION

CONTENTS

CHAPTER VI

CONTEMPORARY PHILOSOPHY AND RELIGIOUS ORIENTATION

CHAPTER VII

PHILOSOPHICO-RELIGIOUS VIEWS OF J. M. GUYAU AND ÉMILE BOUTROUX

CONTENTS

CHAPTER VIII

CHAPTER IX

CHAPTER X

CONTENTS

CHAPTER XI

ITS MANIFESTATIONS IN CATHOLICISM

CHAPTER XII

ITS MANIFESTATIONS IN PROTESTANTISM

CHAPTER XIII

ITS MANIFESTATIONS IN FREE-THOUGHT

CHAPTER XIV

THE CREATION OF THE UNDENOMINATIONAL SCHOOL

CHAPTER XV

MORAL INSTRUCTION IN THE SCHOOL

CHAPTER XVI

SCHOOL AND CHURCH

FRANCE TO-DAY:

ITS RELIGIOUS ORIENTATION

"None of the divinities successively created by the human spirit can satisfy it to-day: it needs them all at once, and something yet beyond, for its thought has left its gods behind."—J. M. GUYAU, *Irréligion de l'avenir*, p. 321.

B

INTRODUCTION

THE SPIRIT IN WHICH THIS BOOK IS WRITTEN

The phrase "religious orientation" not synonymous with religious
   affairs—Our object to make clear certain aspects of reality
   and of life—*Historia magistra vitæ*—The most important
   movements not always the best supplied with authorities—
   Inaccuracy of every historical picture—Can the historian be
   impersonal ?—The legend of the superficial Frenchman.

IT is long since religious matters have so continu-
ously occupied French public attention as in our
time. We are not here concerned with what the
Press calls religious affairs. The phrase, indeed, indicates what is most external in religious and ecclesiastical matters, what these become when they are
carried to political markets and utilised in party
quarrels.

If now and again we are compelled to mention this
utilisation, we shall do so as briefly as possible; our
title sufficiently suggests that we are not concerned
with the doings of Churches and Antichurches; that
is a chronicle which is written day by day, and is the
business of the Press.

We would attempt a somewhat novel essay : to see
whether, apart from any metaphysical thesis, in the
independent, disinterested spirit of scientific investigation, a kind of inquiry cannot be opened into

religious feeling, its presence or absence, its disappearance or re-emergence, and, in short, into the direction
of its evolution to-day.

Above all we must inquire whether, while still
remaining what it was in the past, it has not already
renewed and transformed itself; and whether, after
having, little by little, rendered age-long habits of
thought foreign to us, it does not tend to create a new
cast of spirit, and to open unsuspected horizons both
to individuals and institutions.

In other words, is there not a somewhat deep
religious feeling in our country, apart from any habits
of worship and traditional acts, apart from a language
that still subsists though the ideas and needs to
which it corresponded have passed away?   Is not this
religious feeling at the present time—and for the
generation to follow, does it not seem as though it
would be—an important factor in the history of
society?   Such are the two questions we would essay
to answer.

The reader has already been mentally asking:
Whither do you wish to go?   What is your object—
your interest in this question?   What God, what
Church do you serve?

Does the artist who instals himself on the borders
of a field to sketch a labourer and his plough dream
of increasing the money-value of the field?   What
he would seize and render are aspects of reality and
life.   Of us the same is true.   We shall pursue our
way, observing religious life and religious endeavour
wherever we think that we perceive them.

People who only understand or tolerate a religious
study if it be either for or against the Church, will
then be merely wasting their time if they come to

these pages seeking weapons for the struggles in which alone they are interested.

Here will be found—what to certain minds will seem a flagrant contradiction, and will greatly exasperate them—a kind of admiration and love, an ardent sympathy, going forth at the same time to each of the antagonists. The writer hopes that patient readers will quickly enough perceive that this attitude is neither affected, forced, nor sceptical; but that it is entirely natural when one puts aside the quarrels of everyday politics and takes the point of view of social history.

This book, then, is written in a spirit of deep gratitude for the past, of love for the present and faith in the future. History does not canonise the past, making it a sort of pattern that the future will but repeat; but discovers therein germs of life which the present has not created but among which it must choose—germs that will become the living seeds of a new era.

From this point of view the old formula *Historia magistra vitæ* takes on a fuller meaning : history no longer merely provides examples for individual conduct, nor does it merely point the nations to the sources of greatness and decay; it rises to a yet higher conception which reaches infinitely far into the past as into the future; and in making us witnesses of what is most intimate and mysterious in human endeavour, it teaches the present generation to enter into this harmony of eternal life, to become fellow-workers therein, first conscious, then deliberate, and at last inspired.

Thus there comes an hour when the contemplation of the history and toil of humanity may play in the

individual or collective life that moral and religious
part which was formerly played by metaphysics or
revelation.

.   .   .   .   .   .

Who says history says "document." Now the
reader must at once be warned that this volume,
being occupied with the present moment, will not
be documented like the study of a distant epoch.

It will therefore be possible to criticise many of
these pages for vagueness, lack of precision and
absence of justifying material. And with a good
deal of reason.

But this absence of authorities for events which
are going on around us and even within us, for an
evolution in which we are collaborating and of which
our vision can only be limited and incomplete, does
not constitute a reason for holding aloof. It is simply
a caution to proceed with prudence.

Moreover, the cult of the document and quotation,
which represents one of the best achievements of the
nineteenth century, should not degenerate into
idolatry.

How far the charlatan contrives to profit by the
tendency to regard the document as carrying with it
absolute proof may readily be seen in the Press.

People keep saying, "Where there are no documents, there is no history." And this is true on
condition that they add "for us." Without that
qualification the dictum would be as naïve as to
declare : "There are no meteorological phenomena in
countries where there are no observatories to record
them."

When we approach religious phenomena with
scientific and critical rigour we must bring besides

much tact and knowledge of the human heart and of the passions whose instrument it may become, if we are to judge truly of the value of documents.

Religious statistics, which ought to be accurate since they deal only with external facts, are falsified by party spirit. Before the Separation of the Churches and the State the latter had to abandon their ascertainment because it was impossible to place confidence in the sincerity of those who made either the declarations or the census.[1]

In studies such as ours documents are even more deceitful than elsewhere. They are the more dangerous because they commit errors without intending to; for it is far easier for the reader to guard against interested falsehood than involuntary error.

Abundance of documentation is often in inverse ratio to importance.

Thus it may be noted that, in the history of Christianity, there is only one small department in which the documentation suffices to give a comparatively adequate idea of the facts; and this relates to the question of rites, liturgies and customs.

The beginnings of that great movement are bare of any documentation properly so-called. Is this a reason for denying its actuality? Jesus seems to have written nothing. His friends, if they wrote, only did so long afterwards. For the reason doubtless, as has been suggested, that they expected the end of the world to come shortly : but also, perhaps, because a man rarely renders an exact account of the work he is accomplishing. One man, who will be quite forgotten before he is dead, thinks to move heaven

---

[1] See Arréat, *Le sentiment religieux en France*, p. 1.

and earth; another passes through life, unnoted by those who record the events of the time—both great and small—but the memory of those who loved him will raise him from the dead; a documentation will spring up about his life, lacking indeed to desperation in scientific value; and this documentation, feeble and replete with insecurity though it be, will become the life-programme for a portion of humanity. For centuries the flower of the civilised peoples will carry it in its heart as an image of the ideal.

Thus the most important for us among the religious movements of the past is destitute of all primitive documentation, whilst one can write volumes, bristling with references and authorities, on schemes that never saw a morrow. Public opinion is well aware of this, and regards without the slightest emotion, even indeed with a quizzical smile, certain religious founders who take great care to advertise through the Press the movements they are about to launch.

If we had to consider as belonging to our programme enterprises, like the *Cultuelles*, attempted towards 1905, this book would be ten times as big. Never was cradle surrounded by such promises; the favour of the ministry and of some of the most powerful papers was assured to the new Church; it had influential adherents, a clergy all ready, places of worship and its own organ. Should all these facts find a place in religious history under pretext of being well documented?

.   .   .   .   .   .

Should the difficulty of doing scientific work in the field of contemporary religious history make us abandon the task? Ought we to be persuaded to go on living amid incoherence, contradiction and conflict without seeing whither this agitation leads? That would be an impossible abstention: one need not abandon the effort under the pretext that one will never attain the goal. The human mind aspires to synthesis. If one is not satisfied to attempt syntheses that are incomplete and provisional but yet contain a core of truth, one will find a multitude of interested persons ready to fashion syntheses they will believe and declare to be definitive, though these will have only error at their core.

. . . . . .

Unfortunately, the historian perceives only a very small fraction of reality; the documentary indications that pile up before him, when he is dealing with modern history, are but a distant mirage, already falsified by incapacities, prejudices and passions; he is obliged to sort them through and only retain a minor part. Now whatever care he brings to his task, he is so far subject to the influence of a multitude of subtle preoccupations, often unconscious, that in the end his work will be far enough from attaining the value he would fain give it.

Certain historians do not choose to recognise this state of things. When one tells them that " to write history is to think it, and to think it is to transform it," they cry out indignantly [1] and remain persuaded

[1] The notion of the inevitable relativity of all historical narrative has lately made its way everywhere. Thus one of the editors of the *Revue Augustinienne*, Father Louis Talmont, admits as obvious in the issue of Aug. 15, 1910, that there can be no historical judgment without some principle of general philosophy to direct it,

that their interlocutor has decided to scoff at documents and to supersede them.

This is contrary to the truth. He is the true historian who, having done his utmost to reach historic verity, is aware of the incompleteness his work presents, and seeks to forearm his readers against the common tendency of accepting statements as unquestionable results.

We must seek to attain truth as circumstantially in the detail, and as completely in the whole as our intellectual powers and documentary resources permit; but to imagine that we can achieve a perfectly adequate picture of reality is to be the dupe of an illusion as mischievous to the writer as to his readers.

The historian, setting to work, must not fancy he can replace his own eyes; he cannot remake himself and become a man without either age, sex, country, or a soul whereon innumerable influences have left every one its mark. Absolute impartiality is a metaphysical entity, a sheer symbol. The idea should be kept as an ideal; but while seeking to attain it, one needs to have some notion of the distance that divides one from it.

What, then, we may reasonably ask of an historian is not that he should accomplish this impossible miracle of divesting himself of his own personality, but that he endeavour not to plead any cause, that he resolve to put his pen at the service of none of those grudges, hatreds and passions which trouble and divide his contemporaries. If he do this, he will thereby singularly deserve our esteem. He will very nearly attain to the perfection actually possible if, conscious of whatever may be limited and partial in his own view, he assist his readers to criticise it, and take pains sincerely to point out to them the tendencies that may have twisted his judgment.

. . . . . .

The writer of this book has studied his subject with too much enjoyment and enthusiasm to suppose that he resembles in the least degree that ideal historian of whom he spoke just now : but the attacks he will incur from every direction at once will sufficiently prove that he does not write to serve the passions of the hour. His attachment to Protestantism, the *milieu* of his derivation, his education and his thought, will not—at least he hopes it will not—have distorted his judgments on his fellow-believers, for as far back as he can remember he has sought to understand and love both Catholicism and Freethought.

If in this respect he feels himself to be without reproach, he wishes to be under no illusion, and not to let it be supposed he has written without a leading thought, without a deep faith which will inspire these pages.

This faith is first of all an intense joy not only of living in our age but of sharing the life of our age, of feeling that something new and ineffable is preparing, and that we all are preparing it : the persuasion that a new faith, whose germ was in the old, is being carried in the womb of contemporary society, and that to-morrow will be better than to-day. It even seems to him that we cannot truly behold to-day's crisis save on condition of considering it well; and that so to consider is already to love, already to desire to free ourselves from our hatreds and pettinesses, and to prepare for action.

It is obvious that these views exceed and bear sway over historic data; I realise this, and should have preferred not to have to make public confession of it here. But pray let those who may be tempted to cast too large a stone at me turn upon themselves and ask if they are without sin; if, when they have had occasion to deal with delicate matters of contemporary religious history, they have been able to do so uninfluenced either by dogma, or by the philosophic thought around which their intellectual life and activity has shaped itself, or by the tendencies which are so much a part of their moral being that they never even dream of acknowledging their existence.

The meekest realities escape from us on some side, and the sincerest efforts we can make to express them only end in subjective outlines.[1]

.   .   .   .   .   .

Legends are hard to kill : that of the superficial Frenchman has penetrated everywhere, and with

[1] If we are not greatly deceived the very title [of the series in which this book was published in France] " Library of the Social Movement " implies a sort of act of faith in this fact of experience that man exists no longer as an isolated individual—that that is a mere intellectual concept ; that he really is, willy-nilly, a *member* of an infinitely vast society, complex and ramified ; and that the effort of civilisation to-day ought to lead those who have already attained consciousness of themselves, as members of the family and nation, to complete another stage and attain consciousness of what they are and should be as members of society.

Here, as elsewhere, the inspired labour of scientific sincerity is no vain, random effort. It records experiences, persuaded they have not taken place for naught, and that their record may have its use. The publisher of this series [M. Armand Colin] has obviously desired to collaborate in his own way in the social movement by setting on foot an inquiry that may serve as the basis of fresh progress,

such success that some of our compatriots receive it as a kind of unquestionable fact, because it is un-questioned. Most foreigners, encouraged by this appearance of universal assent, judge us by what they gather of Paris in their hasty visits, glancing through some society papers, and seeing the kind of literature displayed on our railway bookstalls. If they read this book, they will recognise what is superficial in such a judgment. It is true that the importation of strange and foreign cults has upon the whole pro-duced deplorable results, and even that the efforts of some of our compatriots to endow the country with a brand-new religion by the cleverest maker, have miserably failed. So reformers of ancient cults and imitators of new, have alike gone away shocked, repeating the famous saying, "There is not religion enough in France to make two."

One may perhaps be allowed to question whether our country's very genuine disdain for what already runs to a long series of religious experiments is really the result of scepticism.

May it not come instead from a deep religious feeling much too exigent not to perceive the lament-able intellectual and moral gaps in the formulas proffered to it?

Nothing is more like religion than love. Is it from lack of heart or incapacity for the dream and desire of making a home that a girl dismisses one by one a whole series of wooers?

Very often her persistent refusals only show that she has set her ideal higher.

The religious expectation of France to-day is some-what analogous : her apparent scepticism may well be a faith ignorant of itself.

CHAPTER I

Search for a definition of religion valid for our age and civilisation
—Essentially ethical basis for which many simple minds are
looking in religion—Spontaneous and unconscious symbolisa-
tion in dogma—Religious change always achieved at the cost
of the Churches—The Catholic Church and her right to the
gratitude of France—Efforts of the Church to control public
opinion—*La Bonne Presse*—Uselessness of its activity—The
new religious orientation.

AT the outset it is desirable to determine precisely
what religion shall mean in these pages. Of attempts
at definition the latest to attract attention is that of
M. Salomon Reinach. For him it is "a body of
scruples that thwart the free exercise of our faculties," [1] or, in a word, a body of taboos. [2]

The introduction of this Polynesian term into our
current speech may be necessary in order to indicate
certain aspects of the Polynesian religion that could
not be rendered in the ordinary words of our language. But is it really scientific to write as though
this idea of taboo were characteristic of religion in
one of the countries in which religious feeling is most
developed, and in which it is, for most of those

[1] Orpheus, *Histoire générale des religions*, Paris, 1909, p. 4.

[2] " Taboo, in Polynesian, means, properly speaking, that which
is withdrawn from current use ; a tree one must not touch is
a taboo-tree, and one speaks of the taboo on a tree to indicate
the scruple which stops a man who is tempted to touch or fell
this tree."—*Ibid.*

associated with it, the very opposite of a body of taboos?

For a definition to be just, it must not only appear so to him who makes it, but it should satisfy those at whom it is aimed, or at least they should be able to recognise themselves in it.

One may admit that M. Reinach points out and throws into relief one element of religion as it exists amongst the most blunted spirits in our civilisation,[1] yet even for these it is but one element among many; and just in proportion as they emerge out of physical and intellectual destitution the part of the taboo decreases in importance.

In order that a definition of religion may apply to the whole past and to every people it must indicate the amazing plasticity of religions and the rapidity of their evolution in spite of all ecclesiastical attempts to keep them immutable; it must suggest their prodigious dynamism and creative power. Here, by way of documents, are some recent definitions:

"Religion is a *physical, metaphysical and ethical explanation* of everything by analogy with human society, under an imaginative and symbolical form. It is, in a word, a *universal sociological explanation under a mythical form.*"[2]

"Religion comprises all non-scientific knowledge and power."[3]

"Religion is the urge of the soul, that, reinvigor-

---

[1] M. Lévy-Brühl has recently published a work on primitive races, by no means for the exclusive benefit of specialists, in which interesting, new and well-authenticated suggestions are superabundant: *Les Fonctions mentales dans les sociétés inférieures.*

[2] M. Guyau, *Irréligion de l'avenir*, 1st edition, p. iii.

[3] Darmesteter, *Revue philosophique*, seventh year, Vol. II, p. 76.

ated at the springs of being, conceives a transcendent
ideal, and, in order to approach it, acquires a strength
surpassing that of nature.   It is essentially the
creator of patterns for life, and of strength capable of
realising them.   It is recognised by this sign, that it
moves from duty to power, not from power to duty.
Nemo ultra posse tenetur is the cry of mere nature.
What you ought, you can, is the good tidings that
religion brings us.   The activity of religion in society
is evidenced by the appearance of types and examples
of perfection which surpass the given forms.   And the
principle and means of propagation of these modes
of existence is the communion of men in God." [1]

    " Always and everywhere, religion has been under-
stood as the body of feelings, perceptions and voluntary actions occasioned in the individual or the group
by the consciousness of personal relations with the
higher sovereign powers at work in the universe in
whose midst it moves." [2]

    [1] Émile Boutroux, *Revue des Deux Mondes* for Sept. 1, 1910,
see below, Chap. VII, p. 115.
    [2] L'abbé Bricout, *Revue du Clergé Français*, Oct. 1, 1910,
Vol. LXIV, p. 15.
    There are several definitions of religion to which we would call
close attention because they spring from two sciences which are
in course of formation and will reshape many of our ideas : the
history of religions, and religious psychology.   In speaking thus, we
are thinking above all of Messrs. Flournoy and Marillier; but we
fear to spoil the thought of the eminent Genevan philosopher
by a quotation.   One must read him very slowly, live alone with
him, and let oneself be bathed in his thought in order to realise
its fecundity and life.   His pages do not lend themselves to being
parted from one another and sent wandering to and fro like the
pictures that travel from gallery to gallery.   His definition of
religion is to be found in a study entitled " *Les Principes de la
psychologie religieuse* " inserted in the *Annales de psychologie*,
Geneva, Dec. 1902, p. 44 *et seq.*

These definitions, and most of the others one could cite, leave still obscure the power of development that religion possesses, a power at once so striking and so strange. To take only the sacred books of Christianity, one finds prescriptions in these which are in absolute contradiction to one another. And yet they are not merely in the same collection—which might have been gathered by chance—they proceed out of one another: the God who in the Old Testament bids the Levites massacre their brothers and friends is the authentic ancestor of Him who, in the New Testament, commands love—love of one's neighbour and love of one's enemies.

Why should we not admit the impossibility of finding any single definition for religion? [1]

To-day, among those who seem its most authentic representatives, it has put off certain of the characteristics which in other epochs appeared to be essential to it. It has eliminated them by its own virtue. [2]

Leon Marillier, who has also directed his labours toward scientific history and experimental psychology, has said: "Religion is by no means a body of dogmatic affirmations, or ethical precepts, it is an ensemble of emotional states, feelings and desires which have their own originality."—In his preface to the translation of Lang, *Mythes, cultes et religion*, Paris, 1896, p. xxvi.

[1] American philosophers have well shown the uselessness of efforts to define the essence of religion. See in particular Professor Leuba's article *Introduction to a Psychological Study of Religion* in the *Monist*, Vol. XI, p. 195 (Jan. 1901). Cp. W. James's *L'Expérience religieuse* (translation of *Varieties of Religious Experience*, by Abauzit, Paris, 1908), p. 24 *et seq.*

[2] This may be remarked, for example, in the divinatory practices so strongly condemned by the Mosaic law. These were superstitious, according to the etymological sense of the word: residues of an ancient worship that the later religion endeavoured to efface.

C

Its word to-day may be the opposite of its word of
yesterday; yet this does not merely replace that, but
is its veritable sequel, or rather its legitimate heir and
child. All of which may perhaps be wanting in logic,
but it is true, and that is sufficient. Only by patient
observation, then, can we discover the succession of
religious facts.

And is it not observation that alone can show
that the winged butterfly of to-day, the chrysalis of
yesterday, and the caterpillar of the day before are
one and the same being?

Since we are concerned with contemporary history,
and our field is limited to France, it will be enough
if, without preconceived ideas, we seek to observe
religion as it exists around us.

And first, we must remark that, implicitly, most
religious men have two definitions for religion: one
which they learnt by heart in their infancy, or which
in later years they have borrowed from the doctors
of their Church; the other, a more or less deliberate
expression of their individual thought and experience.

Now it is very exceptional for these two definitions
to coincide. They may even be antithetical. A Protestant, for instance, who has learnt in the catechism
that, according to Schleiermacher's definition, religion
is "an absolute feeling of dependence," may end by
discovering in his faith an ineffable feeling of freedom, the possession of a limitless moral power and
of an inner law which he will apply to himself and his
surroundings, and transmit to his sons, stronger,
suppler and more effective.

The Catholic accepts with deference the official
definition given him by his Church; but even the
humblest peasant has a feeling that it requires com-

pleting by a more personal view. That is what generally happens to definitions in which the relation between religion and ethics is thrown into strong relief.[1]

May it not be said that, for our contemporaries, religion is the instinctive need by which a man is led to realise his better self, to unite with those who can serve him as guides or companions in that difficult task, and to endeavour to realise together with them what the inner witness prescribes?

In so far as man considers, reflects and discusses, philosophy exists. Religion exists when man, ceasing to be merely a witness of his own life and that of the community, throws his will into the balance, proclaiming himself a collaborator in the eternal task which he apprehends and to which he devotes himself.

But does not this definition exclude religions founded on revelation? In no wise: even the

---

[1] In the Cevennes, where I can closely observe the humblest social strata, discussions sometimes take place in the villages between Catholics and Protestants. The speakers never dream of claiming advantage from their Churches' divine origin. They always esteem them according to their moral efficacy and agree that true religion consists in loving one another. They regard the Churches as schools and homes of moralisation. For either of them, dogma plays an insignificant part. It is a flag which one is ready to plant at his window, or around which one may rally, at once a heritage and a symbol, nothing less, but nothing more.

Perhaps it may seem strange that a population which at first sight seems so religious should reach thereby a kind of symbolism. So it is, however. There is much to surprise one among these peasants if only one have patience to listen to their talk.

It may be said that in those regions in which the man of the fields sees especially the moral basis of religion, the townsman sees especially its intellectual and metaphysical systematisation.

Churches which claim such an origin, while they wholly deny man's right or power to criticise their claims, offer them, nevertheless, for his acceptance. There is an occasion on which a man gives or refuses his adhesion to them.

If he assents, it is because he thinks he will find in revelation a support, a concurrence, a light to guide him in his efforts. Revelation is above him, but in some way he confirms it, and thus re-enters into the definition given. When a believer says, " I am a Catholic because this is the religion which offers the highest ideal," he implicitly declares that he has made something like a choice.

On the opposite side, some will think this definition allows not only the most dissimilar forms of worship to use the name of religion, but even admits enterprises undertaken against it.

The contradiction is, however, only apparent.

In every epoch of history the most powerful religious efforts have been regarded in the hour of their greatest vigour as anti-religious. The first Christians did not escape this general law, and were accused of atheism.[1]

To cast down the statues of the gods is not always an act of unbelief. It is usually the proclamation of a higher conception of divinity.

From this point of view it may be said that religion

---

[1] M. Guyau has already said : " The irreligion of the future will conserve what is finest in religious feeling ; on the one hand admiration of the Universe and of the infinite powers therein displayed ; on the other, the search after an ideal not individual only, but social and cosmic, which surpasses present reality. . . . Irreligion, as we understand it, may be considered as a higher stage of religion and of civilisation itself."—*Irréligion de l'avenir*, p. xiv *et seq*.

presents itself as the human affirmation *par excellence*, the exercise of man's procreative will in the spiritual kingdom.   The religious man not only affirms what is good, he becomes its soldier, and despite all defeats, he predicts its triumph.   In the midst of ruins he catches sight of the future city, which he builds in advance, ideally, before he has yet power to build it in reality.   The great moments of his life are not those in which he pauses to rest and enjoy the verities achieved, but those in which he anxiously sets out again on a new stage, because the mysterious voice has said, " Get thee out of thy country and from thy kindred, unto a land that I will show thee." [1]   He seems to renounce himself when, on the contrary, he is finding himself : far from committing suicide, he is creating himself.

The cosmologies and doctrinal systems in which, from century to century, man has sought to express his faith, are not religion, they are but its necessarily imperfect and provisional language, eternally perfectible.

.   .   .   .   .   .

All the foregoing will make evident how far from synonymous are the two terms " ecclesiastical " and " religious."   Often confounded, this confusion is the source of numberless errors.

If our task were to study the ecclesiastical situation, it would be singularly easy.   What is ecclesiastical is to be seen and declared.   It would be enough to recur to the abundant and precise literature furnished by the Churches.   But the very fact that the Catholic Church of France, after so many centuries

---

[1] Genesis xii. 1.

during which, without a thought of its own life, or the need to realise its activity, it was yet the soul of the country, begins now, all at once, to review its work, to prepare the exactest possible lists of its organs and to take stock of its moral resources—is not this a sign of the times? [1] Does it not mark the close of a working year in the religious labour of humanity? There is joy on the farm when the last load of the autumn harvest comes in, but something of melancholy also broods over it.

The ecclesiastical situation of France must not, then, be confused with its religious situation; nay, more than this, the one is almost the antithesis of the other. The power that formed the Churches is also that which crumbles them. It is love which builds the nest, and love which bids abandon it.

At no period has the Catholic Church, to speak only of her, been more clearly conscious of all that she has done for her children. Advancing towards them with inexpressible sadness she asks, as on Good Friday: *"Popule meus, quid feci tibi? aut in quo contristavi te? Responde mihi."* [2]

O France, have I not tilled thy soil, and brought forth thy soul? Is it not I who proffered thee the ideal of the valiant knight; who opened thy universities, built thy cathedrals, wrought the sanctity and radiance of thy home, strewed all thy life with poetry, harmony and power?

France knows it all: she hearkens, deeply moved, grateful at once and embarrassed. She would kneel

[1] See p. 24, note.
[2] "My people, what have I done to thee? In what have I grieved thee? Answer me."—Chanted during the Adoration of the Cross.

down beside her old mother, and continue to let herself be lulled by the familiar croon. But she cannot.

She must arise, and forward; she must in her turn bring to birth.

It has been thus always. The Jewish Synagogue condemned Jesus to death, being unable to imagine that he, this rebel, this blasphemer, this impious man, this heretic, was about to realise the prophetic vision and make the tabernacle of Israel a Bethel for all peoples.[1]

. . . . . .

Never has the activity of the Church been so intense or its organisation so strong as in France to-day;[2] but the complaints and cries of alarm which

[1] Isaiah lvi. 7 : " Mine house shall be called a house of prayer for all peoples."

[2] To have some notion of ecclesiastical energies and the perfection of their organisation, it is enough to open, for instance, the *Guide de l'action religieuse* (Reims, Office of the *Action populaire*, published yearly), in which " religious " is, of course, constantly being confounded with " ecclesiastical." You are impressed by this immense effort, provided with infinitely complex agencies which penetrate everywhere, but which, almost ignored by our people, attain scarcely any appreciable result.

The multiplicity of the means only throws into stronger relief the exiguity of the results.

Among the forces enumerated in this book, there is one which for some years has been developed by predilection. I mean *La Bonne Presse*. No more methodical attempt has ever been made to take possession of public opinion.

Under this generic name of *Bonne Presse*, the Assumptionist Fathers have succeeded in giving to French Catholicism a body of newspapers and magazines answering to every need, which ought to relieve the peasant as well as the townsman of the slightest desire to read anything whatever that does not issue from their houses.

For the general public there is every day *La Croix*, with its six

arise on every hand tell plainly enough that it is uneasy, and realises the gravity of the present crisis.

When so vast a crusade has been set on foot in a country; when it has succeeded in turning aside to its own profit part of the moral inheritance of that country, and when, along with all this, it professes to have supernatural means [1] at its service, it is likely

---

pages, which, in spite of its illustrated Sunday supplement, has a lower subscription rate than most of the Paris dailies.

For dwellers in the country there is the phalanx of district and local editions of *La Croix*, with special ones for soldiers and sailors ; the *Noël*, for children; *Le Mois*, a large illustrated magazine, which deals with literature, art and music; and other monthly or bi-monthly publications which aim at special classes of readers— *Rome, Jérusalem, L'Eucharistie*. There are even those that touch on scientific matters : the *Cosmos* (Catholic review of the sciences and their application), and others which are propagandist organs, *Le Pèlerin, Les Conférences, Les Contemporains*, the *Vie des Saints*, the *Causeries du dimanche ;* or documentary bulletins, remarkably edited, which constantly place in the hands of lawyers and jurists such texts and materials as may be useful to them in defending ecclesiastical institutions, *e. g.* the *Revue d'organisation et de défense religieuse*. And there are even collections of authori-ties, like the *Questions actuelles*, which furnish on the one side the authentic and complete text of documents bearing on political, social and religious life, and on the other briefs and notes in which are to be found résumés and numerous references on all matters concerning the Church. I am obliged to pass over in silence many other periodicals—*L'Action catholique, La Chronique de la presse*, etc., etc.

One is stupefied at once by the perfection and the ineffectiveness of this machinery.

With a combination of such means it seems as though public opinion must be conquered : and all the more since this organisa-tion is as well administered from the technical as from the business point of view. But yet its ethical and religious results are as imperceptible as its financial prosperity is obvious.

[1] In the *Guide de l'action religieuse*, p. 387, " supernatural means " are indicated in the first rank of the means of propaganda

enough that its own failures may become defeats for the cause of religion which it professes to serve.

At election times, especially, how great an impression is made on the mind of the simple by the defeat of one who has been put forward as the candidate of " *le bon Dieu*," and the triumph of the candidate of " the satanic sect "!   When such coincidences recur over forty years with increasing frequency, the most pious countryman begins to ask if Satan be not stronger than the Almighty.   The artisan, meeting his parish priest, speaks in a tone at once commiserating and mocking of God's business, which is not going well.   Blasphemy! thinks our good priest.   But no; they only have blasphemed who taught him to identify a political party with religion.   His rudeness is not very different from that of Elijah, chiding on Carmel's summit the priests of Baal, who had been called together for the supreme trial between them and him : " Cry aloud," he said to these poor wretches who were dancing about the altar, gashing their bodies; " cry aloud, for he is a god : either he is musing, or he is gone aside, or he is in a journey, or peradventure he sleepeth, and must be awaked." [1] But this rudeness, like that of the prophet, disguises an outburst of religious feeling, still awkward in its manifestation, and even perhaps expressing itself by deplorable means—Elijah massacred the poor foolish priests, whose only fault was to believe too much in

---

in the Press.   A list is there given of the parishes in which a weekly Mass for the diffusion of *La Croix* is celebrated.   Elsewhere the priest says over a few prayers with the children of his catechism class, etc.   [1] 1 Kings xviii. 27.

their god—but marking, for all that, a development in religious consciousness.

.   .   .   .   .   .

We hope that what has gone before will have made clear the profound difference between Church and Religion, ecclesiastic and religious, and will thus have forecast the meaning we give to the phrase "religious orientation."

When we observe the currents of our time, we are at first struck by their diversity, but when we attain a certain elevation there comes a moment when we seem to see them meeting to mingle their waters at last in the same sea.

A survey of our religious orientation will not, then, consist in studying all that may seem important at the present moment from the religious standpoint. We shall doubtless pass before eternal palaces and definitive systems without so much as noticing them; because for us such palaces and systems appear as points of attainment, not of departure—summings-up of a proud and glorious past rather than endeavours toward the future.

That does not mean that we entertain equal admiration for every novelty. What is new is not necessarily fitted for life. The more reason we should lose no time on artificial novelties—the attempts of hindering personalities, eager to attract attention.

The programme of the religious movement is not outlined beforehand. It knows not whence it cometh nor whither it goeth. It is the work of no man. It is the property of no man, nor even of any community. Many collaborate in it without their knowledge or desire. Others lose their time and trouble going about the world if only they may discover where it may be seen and whither it is tending, that they may offer it their assistance and induce it to traverse their particular ground.

We wish, then, to study whatever is most dynamic and vital in the religious orientation of to-day, though it has scarcely yet dreamed of becoming conscious of itself, and is far from the hour when it will seek expression in a Church.

We are still in the period of origins: the period of most mysterious and perhaps most potent influence. Christianity was more vigorous in the centuries of gestation when it was seeking itself, inspiring visions, and spreading disquiet through Roman society, than when it came to rule over kings and nations.

If the present movement has not yet come to itself, or become incarnate, so to speak, in one of those founder-geniuses who are engendered by the spiritual urge of a whole epoch—and if, for that reason, it is more difficult to grasp—it is perhaps, for that very reason, neither less important nor less interesting; for it permeates the entire political, intellectual and moral life of the country like a spirit or a leaven, whose tendency is to transform the very foundations of society.

CHAPTER II

THOUGH preceding definitions have already implicitly
indicated the contents of this book, it may not be
superfluous to define it further.

The religious orientation of to-day is so complex
that several volumes would be required for a survey
of its entire field. It would have to be considered
in its psychological and racial origins, while its direction by intellectual, ethical and social needs, as various
in intensity as in manifestation, would have to be set
forth.

The religious instinct, which history has hitherto
discovered everyhere and at all times, is now brusquely
confronted with a humanity transformed by scientific
developments. Unexpectedly attacked on every side,
this instinct has offered resistance and upset every
calculation, losing battles where it seemed strongest,

and winning positions of which the day before it had not so much as dreamed, till one may venture to say that once again it tends to become the inspiration of the intellectual and moral life of our country.

To be complete, we should have to probe with absolute sang-froid, but yet with piety, into certain episodes in our recent history, and discover their significance and bearing.

The Dreyfus affair, for instance, was eminently a religious crisis; and here I need hardly say I am using religious in the strict sense we have given it. There were those on the Right who, unwilling to hear anything, and carried away by the advantages certain to accrue from it to their cause, would have erected the man's culpability into a dogma : while on the Left, certain of their antagonists proclaimed his innocence for a similar reason. So much is obvious. But what moved France—what forced her to suffer pangs which sent a tremor through the whole world—was not this; nor was it even a movement of sentimental pity for the victim of a judicial error. That undoubtedly contributed its part : but it was not the cause for which France arose, quivering with an emotion which put her beside herself and threatened us with a frightful civil war. Fundamentally it was a question of conscience, a religious resolution. Ought one to sacrifice everything in order to tell the truth as one sees it? Ought one to imperil the nation itself for a man who had only a shred of life left him? Those who asked themselves these questions felt indeed that every human power was confederated to counsel abstention, prudence, compromise; but a single voice that they would fain have silenced, said : " You have no right to love your life, your family, your land more than the truth. You have one duty—to be a martyr, if that is called for." [1]

I do not know of what our military forces may or may not be capable, but I do know that a country which faces crises such as this, by the mere act of facing them, manifests an indomitable religious faith.

.　　.　　.　　.　　.　　.

To be complete, it would be necessary to study the religious movement in its scientific aspect; to show, especially in the Catholic Church, an unexpected scientific awakening whose range no one as yet has ascertained.

In the field of history and exegesis not only have the labours of undenominational science been studied and equalled by men belonging to the Church, they

[1] M. Charles Péguy has thrown light on this side of the Dreyfus affair ("Notre jeunesse" [*Cahiers de la quinzaine*, July 17, 1910], pp. 210–12) : "We said that a single injustice, a single crime, a single illegality, especially if it be officially recorded and confirmed; a single injury to humanity, to justice and righteousness, especially if it be universally, legally, nationally, comfortably accepted;—a single crime is enough to break the whole social pact, the whole social contract, a single prevarication, a single act of dishonour suffices to ruin honour, to dishonour a whole people. . . . The greater our past, the greater precisely is our obligation to keep it great, to keep it pure. *I render back my blood pure as I have received it.* . . . Fundamentally, we were those who stood for eternal salvation, and our adversaries for temporal salvation. That was the true, the real division in the Dreyfus affair. Fundamentally, we were not willing that France should be forever established in a state of mortal sin. There is no doctrine in the world, in the modern or any world, that so deliberately, so totally, so absolutely as the Christian doctrine, counts temporal death as nothing, as a trifle, as zero compared with the price of eternal death ; and the risk of temporal death as nothing to the price of mortal sin, to the price of the risk of eternal death."

have often been surpassed. The annoyance, persecution, and excommunication which have overtaken certain writers ought not to be set against this. The measures taken by the hierarchy cannot rob these labours of their basic character, not only of having germinated on Catholic soil, but of having resulted from religious preoccupations specifically Catholic.

As regards the eager scientific development within the Church, certain of her adversaries would have us adopt as infallible the decisions of an authority that they are always attacking. Is not this a little strange?

To go on from such a position to declare that everything good in the Church has been borrowed from her enemies, or is but the beginning of apostasy, is only a step : and it is often taken.

But these are operations of war, not the fruit of serene and serious appreciation.

Undoubtedly the historian must note that the Holy See disavows this splendid effort.[1] But after-

----

[1] In particular by the Encyclical *Pascendi*, Sept. 8, 1907, § 154 [see the complete official text in Sabatier's *Les Modernistes*, p. 218]. It is true Pius X finishes with these words : " The adversaries of the Church will undoubtedly abuse it [the Encyclical] to spread abroad the old calumny which represents her as the enemy of science, progress and humanity : To give a hitherto unpublished reply to this accusation—which is, besides, reduced to nothing by the history of the Christian religion with its eternal witnesses— we have conceived the design of supporting with all our power the foundation of a special institution which shall group together the most illustrious representatives of science among Catholics ; whose purpose it will be to favour, with Catholic truth for light and guide, the progress of all that can be described under the names of science and learning. Please God, we shall be able to realise this design with the help of all who truly love the Church of Jesus Christ."

It does not seem that the pontifical scheme, so solemnly announced, is on the road to realisation.

wards it is his duty likewise to note its Catholic
origin and also its Catholic aim.

．　　　　．　　　　．　　　　．　　　　．

We will pass over certain attempts to found new
Churches, in absolute silence. Among these are some
which have lasted more than half a century, which
have buildings of their own and a legal existence—
are even perhaps recognised as establishments of
public usefulness.

Will future scholars, finding in the archives of the
revenue entries of the taxes paid by these, be induced
by such irrefutable documents to assign to them a
posthumous importance?

At the "International Congress of Progressive
Religion" in 1910, we had the spectacle of a man
who looked no fool introducing himself to the best-
known members, taking them aside and holding them
with some such talk as this: "Let me ask the help
of your knowledge. My mind is entirely emanci-
pated. Born in Catholicism, I early detached myself
from it, without effort and indeed with enthusiasm:
I inquired into Protestantism, and gave it my adhesion, becoming the heart and soul of our congregation
at X. Protestantism, however, is not yet what I
require. At first, we had an orthodox pastor, worse
than any priest in his uncompromising attitude.
Then I got another to come who was a 'liberal'—
for I must tell you I had a little money, and was
the only person who interested himself in this parish.
The liberal differs indeed from the orthodox, but
scarcely for the better. He repeats over and over,
'No dogma!' Yet dogmas are necessary if one is
to have a Church! For myself they would be un-

necessary, but we must have a Church—and consequently dogmas; and besides, we must have music. Believe me, sir, I have come here to talk over this with you and others. Instead of wasting time, as we do, in congratulating one another, we ought frankly to tackle the great question of our day—that of founding and organising a new Church in harmony with the needs of the time. With the advance of criticism it should not be difficult.

" You will agree with me, sir, will you not, we must have a religion? We must set our brothers free, by giving them the true religion to replace the superstitions to which they are attached.

" What a splendid thing it would be if only this Congress would speak out clearly! I could understand hesitation if the requisite resources were not assured; but in this parish I do everything. The congregation scarcely contributes a twentieth of the total expenditure; and I could give ten times as much as I do. I am free and without heirs." . . .

I do not know whether these proposals led to anything. It is rare for intentions so generous to find no means of realisation : and in various parts of France buildings may readily be pointed out which still look new, but have already been abandoned because their foundation was solely due to analogous desires and needs.

A religion can neither be borrowed nor bought : it is made and won. And it is precisely because this generation, supposing itself to be irreligious, pursues an ideal it does not succeed in grasping—because it is jealous of its own autonomy, and refuses the helping hands stretched towards it with the charity of a ready-made religion; for this reason, however it may

D

appear to the contrary, it is religious, perhaps more religious than any that preceded it.

It is this that is new, important, and of social significance: this that we must catch in the midst of its work.

That is as much as to say there is no place here for portraits of those who are, or imagine themselves to be, the most efficient collaborators in the religious movement.

.　　　.　　　.　　　.　　　.　　　.

One meets, on the other hand, in the intellectual and moral revolution through which we are passing, with some who have been for days or years interpreters of the general restlessness, and have marched at the head of the new movement. Then comes a moment when suddenly they are tripped up by some trivial accident.

Spectators, always prone to see only what is going on close to them, can scarcely understand that the man who is to-day only a wreck may yesterday have been a living force.

Certain apologists for the past think to triumph by demonstrating that the innovators are neither infallible nor impeccable. They are as much in the wrong as the Jewish Conservatives who absolutely convinced themselves that the movement of Nazareth had failed. Had they not seen Jesus abandoned by his disciples in the supreme hour, Peter himself denying his master when he was being condemned to death?

In social evolution, long successions of woeful apparent checks are as necessary as the squandering of innumerable germs in physical nature; and in art, the rough studies of the masters, and before these the painful and naïve essays of infantine art.

It is one of the glories of the nineteenth century that it understood this, and taught us to turn from certain perfect works to the efforts, awkward as yet, but ennobled and, as it were, illumined by striving, by labour and sincerity.

We would put ourselves at the same point of view, for it is that of reality and life.

．　　．　　．　　．　　．　　．

There are other reasons for introducing but few proper names into these pages. One is that many are co-operating in the religious movement without knowing it. Deceived by current speech, which tends to identify religion with clericalism and anti-religion with anti-clericalism, some profess to entirely ignore religious problems; yet by their restless desire for intellectual progress and social amelioration they become indirect and very effective collaborators in the movement we seek to describe.[1] Among them

---

[1] This fact has impressed some of the most distinguished of the clergy. Here is an example : Every year there are great festivities at Lyons on the return of the Catholic Faculty. All the bishops from the South-east are assembled. The Primate of the Gauls chants the Mass of the Holy Spirit, and one of the bishops preaches a sermon.

Some years ago, when discussions on the Separation [of the Churches and the State] were at their height, the bishop charged with the special sermon was invited to dine with a family of his acquaintance on the evening of the great occasion.

In the drawing-room he was surrounded and complimented. "You cannot imagine," he said, with a modest but mischievous air, "the jealousy I feel when I realise the impossibility for the secular clergy, but especially for bishops, to do as well as the *irregular* clergy. On my way here I saw a morning paper which

are some who, if they were named, would have the right to protest and declare that their activity was without religious orientation.

If we attempted to include every effective collaborator in the religious movement, we should be obliged to make a place for many a forerunner: for men unknown and misunderstood who nevertheless have brought a new stone each year to the building of the future city. Unhappily the angel of vanity has been brushing his wing against some of these, and now they think more of themselves and their renown than of the work to be achieved. They still bring their stone, but if it is large it has been dressed with less care on the side that will not be seen; and instead

---

had just arrived, and contained one of the finest sermons I have read in my life. Will you let me read you part of it?"

And in a fine, measured, restrained voice, in which increasing emotion could be felt, he read several passages.

When he ceased there was a pause as if of uncertainty. Some embarrassment was felt about resuming the conversation.

However, several ladies came up and asked the bishop: "May we, my Lord, have the name of the celebrated preacher?" "Ah —this is feminine curiosity! Well, if I must, I will satisfy it. But let me hope you will find his name without my telling you. Ladies, you are all good Christians, you hear many sermons. I like to think you will guess." And pointing to a group of priests, he added, "I assure you, these gentlemen will be much more embarrassed than you."

There was a moment's silence. The ladies, young and old, looked at one another, not knowing what to answer. To break the silence a voice murmured the name of Father Janvier, and at once a string of others followed. They ran through the names of all the preachers of France, and even of some foreigners.

The bishop, visibly diverted, kept answering "No." At last they besought him: the hostess begged him for the name. "Well, Ladies, the piece I read you was taken from a sermon delivered yesterday in the Palais—Bourbon by Father—Jaurès!"

of bringing it to the anonymous building of knowledge and of faith, they bring it with much ado to the
undertakings of self-interest.

Very different from these are those true saints,
passionately devoted to the ideal—who are so much
the more worthy of admiration because they are outside the Church, without the guidance and com-
panionship of those innumerable witnesses to the
truth whom Hippolyte Flandrin has evoked in the
frieze of St. Vincent-de-Paul.

These are more than saints; for saints witness to
a truth already here, while these announce, and in a
sense create, the truth of to-morrow.

Alas, as yet we see them from afar! The general
public knows nothing of their life, their shy independence, poverty and heroism : their names only
arouse in its memory an image whose outstanding
feature is some nervous twitch or grimace.

In these pages, then, proper names will not be
assigned the place they would receive if we sought
to please some and to irritate others, or to make this
book more interesting with a savour of the picturesque
and topical.

Besides, it is no purpose of ours to pronounce
judgments or to define the part of each in a work
still incomplete, but rather to endeavour to grasp that
work as a whole. *Lampada tradunt!* We shall pay
less attention to the torch-bearers than to the torches.

.   .   .   .   .   .

It will be seen why we have no place for the many
conversions—and by that term we would indicate the
breaking with a Church as well as the breaking with
unbelief—which have of late years been so loudly
forced upon our attention in France,

Even those which represent real crises of conscience
are so much exploited for party profits that acts, in
themselves sincere, lose all their disinterestedness in
consequence of the gross advantages anticipated from
them by the parties who, without being invited, put
themselves forward as their sponsors.

Moreover, no recent conversion has had the effect
on public opinion that was hoped for.

Effects of quite another kind have not perhaps
been remarked, and must here be briefly pointed out.

When the first Christians proclaimed the Gospel,
they drew attention to a source of life at which they
themselves had first slaked their thirst : and when
they faced martyrdom to propagate this "good
tidings," the power in them was irresistible, for it
was pure love.

The situation has changed since then. The greater
and more sincere is the attempt to renew the miracles
of the first centuries, the more obvious is its failure.

This contrast between the results arises thus :
Certain of the apostles of to-day are actuated—perhaps without knowing it—by feelings very different
from those of the first Christians : their activity has
for its basis a personal preoccupation, of the highest
order to be sure, but yet personal.

They feel the need to verify the truth of the Gospel
in the reality of facts. They show themselves so
eager to try experiments only because they hope they
will succeed, and that their success will prove the
truth of their thesis. In other words, doubt has
stolen into their soul : and they work so hard that
they may cast it forth.

This intimate, unacknowledged insecurity among
some who display great missionary zeal, whether or

no it be to the Church's profit, is very keenly felt by the masses of the people.

It is the little rift. And though it is difficult to fix with precision the exact influence it has had in the religious movement, that influence may safely be set down as considerable, and as one of the factors in the situation.

When believers scarcely believe any longer save in order to persuade others to do so; or when they long feverishly that others may believe in the hope that the faith of these may give new warmth to their own—they have come near indeed to believing no longer at all : and the Church, be it great or small, which has many such believers may as well set about weaving its shroud.

Do the old Churches and the sects born yesterday, alike, live so far from the conscience of the people that they cannot see how they shock it by the display of cordiality, in no wise disinterested, with which they too hastily receive and make much of whosoever will join them?

CHAPTER III

CIRCUMSTANCES DETERMINING THE PRESENT RELIGIOUS ORIENTATION

Effect of the war of 1870 on the national consciousness—As individuals the priests had proved themselves good citizens; but on the morrow of disaster the Church could not rise to her opportunity—Attitude of France towards Germany and Protestantism before 1870—The Prussian victory dealt an irreparable blow to the prestige of the Reformation.

THE first question that will occur to the reader's mind will be that of the origin of the present religious orientation. The human mind loves precision, even, perhaps especially, where it is least possible to attain it. It detests saying, "I do not know;" and detests having it said quite as much.

In the voyage of discovery which we are making to-day it would be hard indeed to tell with any accuracy when and where the movement with which we are dealing began. If it were a question of attempts such as Saint-Simonism or Positivism, which had a founder and a programme drawn up in advance, the task would be easy; but the movement we wish to observe is very different: it proceeds from no man, but from a most mysterious labour, like Nature's Springtime. One has to go to the very heart of society and civilisation in order to find its source.

Let it not be said that to speak of the heart of society is to set up an entity outside the simple observation of facts, for the individual is just as much outside it.

It is not here a question of metaphysics, but of reality; and reality is ceaselessly showing us individuals who exist so much the better as they forget themselves in and for society—who receive just so much more from it as they give it more. The individual exists only by and for society.

The glory and power of the Catholic Church lies in this, that being in fact a society by the side of other similar societies, she has passed beyond this idea. Not satisfied to have her place in the sun, nor even to stand first, she wished to be the only one. And in so far as she claimed this title she created a sort of right in her favour. By symbols which are both the most diverse and the most precise, she proclaimed the unity of humanity, even the unity and solidarity of the whole of nature, thus anticipating the most lofty preoccupations of our day by a sort of bold prophecy.[1]

[1] St. Paul speaks, for instance (Romans viii. 19–22), of " the earnest expectation of the creation " waiting " for the revealing of the sons of God," and adds " that the whole creation groaneth and travaileth in pain together." It was in this spirit he uttered the famous saying which has been so often misunderstood, " All things work together for good to them that love God."

Renan scarcely did more than translate this thought into the undenominational style when he said : " When a revolution becomes necessary, nothing hinders, everything serves it."

For St. Francis of Assisi, nature is not merely the realisation, and, as it were, the expansion of a divine thought, it is a vast body having a mysterious unity, life and mission. Man participates in an eminent fashion in this universal mission, and has as his fellow-workers our lower brothers the animals, to whom, in so far as they aid him in realising the divine programme, he owes obedience : " Sancta obedientia facit hominem subditum omnibus hominibus hujus mundi, et non tantum hominibus, sed etiam bestiis et feris

Despite defects in our observation and the ceaseless alteration of the ground examined, we are coming to recognise in history the labour of a collective conscience, which scarcely knows political frontiers, and becomes stronger and more assured day by day—a conscience which at first has neither number nor strength on its side, but which, with a deliberation like that of the growth of an oak, through numberless contradictions and defeats, at last imposes its judgments upon those who least desire to take them into account.

Though human memory embraces a mere nothing of all time, it can follow the history of some of these judgments; can see their birth on the lips of the precursors, their unfolding on those of thinkers and martyrs—see them taking possession of a generation, and becoming so unquestioned that men suppose them to be an integral part of their existence, and can with difficulty imagine that, a few hundred leagues away, there are peoples who have not yet heard them whispered.

And then an intuitional certainty higher than any reasoning tells them that they themselves are in the way of life, that their judgment will triumph because it ought to triumph. That an Oriental monarch on the borders of Europe should cause his subjects to be slaughtered, and suppose that none will hold him to account because of his sovereignty—such a fact seems to us scarcely possible. We are sure the day will come when methods like this will appear as abominable to his country and his successors as at this moment they appear to us.

---

ut possint facere de eo quidquid voluerint quantum fuerit eis datum desuper a Domino,"—*Laudes et virtutibus*, ed. Bœhmer, p. 65.

Whence comes this conviction? What is the basis of this certainty? We should be hard put to it to tell. It is acquired without thinking of it, and once acquired is never lost.

The religious movement acts in an exactly similar way, with the same slowness and reliability. Here and there its stages are marked by the appearance of powerful personalities, in whom a group, nation or civilisation may come to knowledge of itself. We think of the work as definitive; and, so long as we do not mean that it is immutable, we are not wrong: it has found its way into social life and will bear fruit there.

.   .   .   .   .   .

If the creative genius of the religious movement is none other than that obscure personage, as little known as he is powerful, whom we call the Heart of Society, this creative genius has acted under circumstances known to us—circumstances which have been the moulds in which his effort has been realised.

The war of 1870 occasioned a religious crisis in our country, which still continues.

When, decimated on fields of battle, bereft of two of her noblest provinces, shaken again by civil war, impoverished, wounded in her pride, trembling both with wrath and indignation, France could once more behold herself and cast a look about her, she had no heart to ask the charity of a sympathetic tear from other nations or to take up the complaint:

> " O vos omnes qui transitis per viam,
> Attendite et videte
> Si est dolor sicut dolor meus." [1]

---

[1] Lamentations i. 12: " Is it nothing to you, all ye that pass by? Behold and see if there be any sorrow like unto my sorrow." —R.V.

Those who passed by took care to pass at such a distance that they might not hear her words.

Then she had recourse to the churches.

But the priest, who had been admirable in his charity and devotion on the field of battle, found next to nothing efficacious to say to her when she besought him for the spiritual succour it is his mission to dispense. He celebrated moving requiem services in honour of her dead; canonising them, as it were, by giving them a place in the succession of numberless heroes around whose graves the Church intones her age-long lament and burns her incense. But when in the nave, once more silent and cold, the last candles of the catafalque hurriedly extinguished, the living asked, "And now what must we do?" the priest could only commend them to vain devotions, easy and mechanical, wherein the intelligence had as little part as the heart : he commended miraculous medals to them and indulgence-bearing prayers, or the organisation of some resounding pilgrimage to Paray-le-Monial to beseech the Sacred Heart to re-establish the temporal power and to save Rome and France—Rome by France, and France by Rome.

That is all historical, though these are facts which historians scarcely think of recording. Now it was especially in those hours of tumultuous affliction which succeeded the war that the soul of contemporary France was fashioned.

One saw the old cathedrals invaded by deeply-stirred, vibrating crowds, in which the majority was composed of that working element which called itself indifferent, sceptical or hostile. Notorious heretics, members of more or less masonic associations, contended for seats with professed devotees, and were only remarkable for their attention.

Evidently, all such people were led thither by somewhat obscure feelings. The notion that their action might be interpreted as a renunciation of their ideas did not occur to them. They went to church because social disturbance creates among men an irresistible need to draw nearer, to take one another by the hand, to mingle their joy and their tears together. Without exactly realising it, deep down in their hearts they were grateful to Catholicism for its churches always open to all comers, and its tendency to wish to share in the life of City and Fatherland. In truth, for some months in 1871, the vast majority of Frenchmen drew instinctively towards the Church of their birth.

The simple death of Monseigneur Darboy; the heroism of many a parish priest on the Eastern frontier; the devotion with which the rest through all the territory, organised ambulances and relief—all this had affected the country and profoundly modified its feelings in regard to the clergy.

The people of France were returning to their Mother, quite simply and sincerely, to sit down at her table; for it is a mother's part always to have the board laid for her sons, even for the prodigals; above all, for her prodigal sons.

Now the board was not laid. The old mother had no fatted calf to kill, nor even energy to prepare a little substantial food for the famishing. She had only strength left to work herself into a passion and load them with reproaches. She brought against them accusations of false doctrines and false prophets; and her arguments were rarely sound. Not only were the hungry not satisfied, but they were often roused to indignation by so much ignorance and pride.

They went away irritated, incensed, and with bitter regret that ever they had come.

Thus this propitious opportunity for coming anew into touch with national preoccupations became, through the action of the Church, a source of fresh misunderstanding.

Scholars have given no place in their notes to the thousands of preachers, illustrious and obscure, who in 1871 and 1872 went even into the smallest parishes.   In response to the pangs of the nation they seemed to have but one wish—to create vigorous hatreds : hatred of Italy, the ruler of Rome; hatred of the men whom they represented as being responsible for the disasters of the war; [1] hatred of an undenominational society; hatred of the Republican form.

Yet the sources of the present religious situation lie there.   It was then that the masses of the people in the smallest country towns perceived that the Church clearly did not understand : that she was an institution engrossed above all else in herself and her corporate interests; that she was not, after all, the nation praying and seeking for its way.

On every side, and especially abroad, people are amazed at the ease with which the Separation of the Churches and the State has been voted and accom-

---

[1] In 1872, at the Cathedral of Besançon, I heard the thesis propounded that the war was God's reply to Renan's impieties in his *Vie de Jésus*.

In days nearer our own we have seen most of the papers that call themselves Catholic make out the earthquakes which overwhelmed Messina in Dec. 1908, as a manifestation of God's vengeance against certain verses published by a humorous journal. —See *e. g.* the article entitled " *Blasphèmes provocateurs* " in the *Univers* for Jan. 27, 1909.

plished. It is true that a law which, according to those best informed and of the most opposite views— the bishops and M. Dumay, Minister of Worship, may be mentioned—could not possibly be carried into effect, was applied in the midst of complete indifference. One can readily understand why hurried political writers should wish to attribute the phenomena to some masonic password; but really this is to give such passwords too much importance; and during recent years we have seen so many launched by a power more venerable even than that of Freemasonry, with means of transmission and resources which it has not, which even "The Union of Occult Powers" does not possess, and all without effect.

In reality, the calm indifference of France to the carrying out of the new laws is an entirely natural result of the last forty years of her national life. It can only astonish those who are blind to the fact that mighty changes have far-off causes, or are determined not to recognise the part played by infinitely small things.

They accord no importance to the action of the feverish Capuchin who, in a certain village, imagines he has succeeded in reconciling the people with God when, after terrifying them with threats of divine punishment, and gathering them round a cross of white wood, he has got them to cry with him, "Jesus for ever! The Cross for ever!" (*Vive Jésus! Vive la croix!*)

They accord no importance to the action of the monk of more modern style who, in the neighbouring county-town, having been well posted beforehand as to the parish, its priest and people, organised what he called the Crusade of God; and left, a few weeks later, with the amount raised, whereto went the widow's mite in company with the offering of the rich man and the ransom for sin.

Similar facts are repeated in ten, a hundred—nay, in thousands of communes, great and small; and everywhere preachers, full of zeal and evident good faith, think they have mightily furthered the Christianisation and conversion of France.

Against their wish, no doubt, they have split the population into two hostile camps, sown misunderstandings and kindled hatreds. They have not understood what the intellectual and moral flower of France—as well as her peasants and artisans—expected from the Church : a word of civic peace, a call to work, to the raising up of the nation, to an energetic effort for moral civilisation.

Never has nation honoured its clergy by counting so much upon them. The event shows it was mistaken.

Such rebuffs may remain long without apparent result : the invisible ferments which they have caused to germinate accomplish their slow work of dissolution, and before it is observed the crisis is beyond cure.

This incapacity of the Church of Rome to speak to France " after her heart " [1] is one of the circumstances which have most affected the religious orientation of our time.

. . . . . .

Later, we shall have occasion to remark the isolation in which Protestantism vegetates, but we must

---

[1] Isaiah xl. 1 ; of which the French rendering is " *Consolez, consolez mon peuple, dit votre Dieu, Parlez à Jérusalem selon son cœur.*"

indicate forthwith the reason why the notion of seeking from it what had been vainly expected from
Catholicism occurred to next to no one.

Before 1870 Protestantism, without being exactly
popular, had yet inspired the high esteem of a
thoughtful minority. Without really understanding
it, they were grateful to it for its moderation, good
sense, domestic and civic virtues, discreet antipathy
toward all excesses, its spirit of observation, order and
economy, and finally for the welcome it had offered
to science and criticism. It manifested the advantages of a form of religion which kept its own place
and did not meddle in political quarrels.

The prosperity of the Protestant, and the deca-
dence of the Catholic nations, were expressions
beginning to come into such general use that, except
in purely " ultramontane " circles—to use the phrase
of that time—the very quality of Protestant was a
testimonial and recommendation in itself.

If some Protestants were in favour with the
Government, others were the most effective collaborators of the Opposition. Their presence in the ranks
of the Left conferred upon it, in Paris and in the
departments where they were numerous, that respecta-
bility of which the Opposition parties are often
somewhat destitute.

This marked favour had causes over and above the
characteristics of which we have spoken. Among
many of our fellow-countrymen there was undoubtedly a very lively wish to render justice to a minority
against whom the clergy had sometimes employed
poisoned weapons. There were efforts to make
amends, to those who had been persecuted, for the
wrongs inflicted on them by former régimes.

E

All these feelings, which were accorded less to Protestantism as a religion than to the Protestants as an element of society, were further strengthened by the prestige of German virtues in our literature, and of German science in our university circles. It was almost an axiom that in ethics and science the Germans led all the nations, and that the rest could not do better than learn of them in the school of Luther and the Reformation.

More recently France has contrived, for political motives, to become infatuated with Russia and with her literature; but this sentiment has never approached that entertained by her for Germany towards the middle of the nineteenth century. That was an esteem unmixed with any self-interest : it was a deference, a kind of admiration. The men who were recognised by public spirit on this side of the Rhine as its leaders looked upon the German universities and churches as the hearth-fires beside which those scientific and ethical principles, which should lead the world towards new destinies, were being worked out.

It was only natural that something of this complaisance should be reflected upon French Protestantism; and when among the notable representatives of German science there appeared a number of French names, men cursed the blindness of Louis XIV, who, by the Edict of Nantes, had driven beyond our frontiers such valuable factors of civilisation and progress.

The war of 1870 broke out, and brought in a few weeks a vast disillusionment.

No one, indeed, dreamed of reproaching Germany for her victories; but when people saw the horrors of war, and the conqueror intermingling the roar of cannon with mystical effusions; when they learnt that he regarded himself as God's fellow-worker, and when Protestant voices were naïve enough to exclaim that every Prussian soldier carried a Bible in his knapsack, and to add that if we had had a Luther we should have had no Sedan, the hearts of the conquered were wounded, and their conscience shocked. . . . Many experienced a supreme revulsion from religious sentiment, a sort of aversion for it.

Protestantism, having profited by the favourable feeling which Germany had formerly inspired, suffered—and this was inevitable—from the change of view.

Their enemies have often striven to injure the Protestants by representing them as bad citizens, and even as traitors. The indignation felt against such calumnies may readily be understood. But, after having reduced their adversaries to silence by proving to them—and it was easy enough—that they have done their duty in good and evil days, perhaps French Protestants should inquire why ineptitudes so stupid are still repeated in spite of the constant contradiction of facts.

They would perceive readily enough that if sometimes France has not appreciated Protestantism, it is because she, with her history, temperament and needs, has first lacked appreciation from it. Protestantism is always speaking as though the choice of a religion, whether for the individual or for the nation, were a simple act of will. Now a religion does not bestow itself from without: it only imposes itself on a civilised people if it may come to co-ordinate, complete and affirm their latent thoughts—if, starting from their better selves, it may show them a new stage to accomplish.

I am tempted to think that Protestantism, by insisting as it has done on its efficiency in organising the prosperity of the individual, the family and the nation, wounds the French ideal where it is most susceptible and most noble. This religious pragmatism, which values a doctrine according to its material results, has something repugnant about it.

Our people are only astonished—they are not edified—when the individual and commercial prosperity of the United States is held up to them as a sort of ideal towards which they should make their way by the intermediary of Protestanism : or when certain persons who profess the strenuous life are pointed out to them as the masters whose school they should attend. Such advice is altogether beside their religious instinct.

In France, the United States is only thought of as a friend. But friendship does not forbid differences of judgment on fundamental matters; and on this side of the Atlantic we ask ourselves, not without anxiety, whether the ideal of the New World is really superior to that of the Old.

．　　　．　　　．　　　．　　　．　　　．

Thus almost at the same moment the two principal Churches in France were found, for very different reasons, incapable of responding to the moral and religious needs of the country.

CHAPTER IV

GRAVER AND GRAVER MISUNDERSTANDINGS BETWEEN CHURCH AND PEOPLE

The attitude alike of Alsace and of France has transformed the political question of the annexed region into a moral question—Incorrectness of the formula that patriotism has become the religion of France—New idea of patriotism to which the Church did not give birth—The blossoming of certain ideas, sown by her in other days, seems sometimes to make against her—The undenominational school must be reckoned among the factors strongly affecting religious orientation—It has been arraigned as the nursery of crime—Mistake of the apologists of religion who try to turn terror of the hooligan into a motive for the return to faith—By appealing to the unbounded devotion of her sons, the Church, and the Church alone, responds to the most powerful instinct of the human heart.

AFTER 1870, humiliated France slowly raised up her head, but not to curse her conqueror.

The dismemberment of the Fatherland was rapidly transformed into a question of conscience. The same travail has been at work beyond the Vosges, and has mercilessly falsified the forecasts of diplomats and governments little accustomed to take moral causes into their calculations.

After forty years of annexation and a political regime which has brought them enviable material prosperity, Alsace and Lorraine are to-day less Germanised than ever. Endeavours—somewhat brief and intermittent—to win them over by kindness have succeeded no better than a stern method, and in spite of the German inflow on the one side and the ceaseless emigration to France on the other, these two provinces have forgotten nothing.

There is, however, a great difference between the present situation and that of twenty or thirty years ago; for the intimate labour, which on both sides of the Vosges has caused a moral question to spring out of the political, is gaining ground step by step and forcing itself upon the international conscience.

Despite the treaties which hold certain peoples bound to Germany, this conscience clearly feels with what ardour their hearts turn to horizons which are not exactly those of their powerful ally.

When M. Loubet went to Italy, the enthusiastic welcome given him by the populace left far behind the manifestations made to various sovereigns, now correct, now cordial. That a part of their respect was offered to the man himself, kindly, plain and smiling, who kept his part as first citizen of his country without a dream of playing the monarch, is likely enough; but what had prepared the outburst of sympathy at Rome, which so astonished diplomatic circles, was the moral prestige of France. The plaudits went to a people risen again, a people towards whom, more than towards any beside, the other peoples feel in brotherly wise, because they realise that this people has preoccupations beyond its own national interests.

There is a phrase used in Italy, when speaking of France, which has become hackneyed, the "nazione sorella." The two Latin sisters have indeed mingled their blood on the Lombard plains: but it would be a mistake to see in their present friendship only the consequence of that sisterhood-in-arms. It is far more than that. The sisterhood has been confirmed and perhaps remade upon a surer foundation. It is on the way to become a sisterhood of intellectual and moral effort. Something in the festivities that welcomed the President of the Republic went to the people who, knowing how to prepare war, has chosen peace, and in whose consciousness an obscure work is being fulfilled which we must endeavour to characterise.

. . . . . .

It has often been said that after 1870 patriotism became the religion of France : a hasty and not a very happy formula by which to define a profound growth of national feeling. On some of the lips that have repeated it this has taken a sense entirely opposed to the reality. There have been believers and unbelievers who have imagined—some with grief and others with joy—that in the hearts of their fellow-citizens the old religions were about to be replaced by a new worship. Certain manuals of civic morality, hurrying to outrun public opinion, have sought to replace the catechisms of the fallen cults by patriotic texts.

This is a complete misapprehension. It was right to bring together the two ideas of Fatherland and Religion. But the connection set up between them was a mistaken one.

France essayed to put morality and religion into her patriotism : she essayed to find her path *sub specie æternitatis*. Many a time had her cathedral vaults vibrated to the accents of *Te Deums* thanking God for her victories : now she felt that defeat was about to give her more painful but more useful lessons.

She did, then, two apparently contradictory things : she chose peace and at the same time prepared for war. She realised she had no right to follow the advice of the naïve friends who would have induced her to disarm under pretext of giving proof of her tranquillity and good behaviour. She realised that such an attitude would be construed as an acceptance of the *fait accompli*—that she who was so passionate for her honour would have the air of disguising her renunciation under an oratorical tinsel which would deceive no one.

So she made sacrifices—it may be we are not yet at the end of them—and from beyond the Vosges there came in response, with unwavering perseverance, the declaration that there is no tribunal in the world which can validate a forced marriage.

For what are we making these sacrifices? For a very simple matter : to prevent the prescription being established—to be faithful, undoubtedly, to Alsace; but fundamentally, what we desire above all is to be faithful to an idea, to be the knights of this idea, that it may make its definitive entry into the world through us and through our suffering.

It is obvious that certain facts might be alleged against these views. All deep social evolution begins in ignorance of itself. It seems to have sudden stops and turnings back; it may meet with obstacles; but the chief factors in these considerations—the enthusiasm of France for every sacrifice, and her persistent choice of peace—are facts which any one can verify.

Though the question is a delicate and complex one, I hope I have spoken clearly, and shown what it is that the French democracy is seeking, expecting and desiring. It is in nowise a revision of the Treaty of Frankfort wherein it would dictate every article : but an effort on the part of Germany to apprehend that her honour is in no degree involved in the question of Alsace. What the French democracy desires, or rather what the idea which controls and leads it desires, is that the question be studied under the promptings not of German or French interests, but of those of Alsace : that this gallant people, which has given contemporary Europe the spectacle of an idealism that might have been thought incredible, should become at last the arbiter of its own fate. Does some one exclaim "Utopia"? For to-day perhaps—' Utopia : but if to-morrow it is not a reality, it will be the day after.[1] In any event, it is faith; and it is hope besides : the hope of which a volume that Germany knows well—the Bible—has said that "it does not confound." Thus, when the political attitude of France seemed to be so far removed from all the Churches, it became more thoroughly religious than it had been even under her most pious kings. And what indeed is this effort, which tends to cause the light of the ideal to search into questions seemingly the most foreign to it, but the continuation and unfolding of Christian effort? This respect for one's adversaries, this love for one's enemies, which the Church no longer preaches save as a theory and per-

---

[1] In the end, these feelings will be understood. They are, already, by some of the finer spirits in Germany. At Strasbourg, a celebrated [German] Professor of the University has been known to excuse himself, in a voice trembling with emotion, from addressing a meeting in which he was the only representative of the [German] immigrants ; he had understood and admired the dignified reserve in which the Alsatian populace enwraps itself.

haps as an inaccessible ideal, inspires a people who
call themselves unbelievers because they believe more
and better than their Church. They have even made
of it the principle of political action, the keystone of
the vault of one of the buildings they are preparing
for the new "City of God" whereof they cherish
the dream, and in whose construction they seek
employment with all their brother peoples.

Wherefore, we do not seek peace for the sake of
peace : our pacifism is no more inspired by weariness
than by a faint heart. We might have been misunderstood had we not made the preparations we
have made. If, occasionally, the advantages of peace
have been sung as though they presented a goal, those
who have so sung them have neither looked far nor
high enough; they have only seen the intermediate
halting-place without perceiving the goal towards
which the caravan is journeying.

France desires peace with Germany because a war
is an outburst of hatred, and she feels no more hatred
for her neighbours on the east than for others. She
feels her solidarity with them; she has need of them—
for a work that reaches far beyond commercial,
industrial or financial *ententes*.

And they have need of her.

If an evil fate decreed that these sentiments should
not be understood; that, after being represented for
forty years as those who threatened the peace of
Europe, we should be attacked—then indeed we
should spring up with the enthusiasm of citizens
defending not their soil and Fatherland alone, but
cherishing an ideal that will make its entry into
the world through their efforts—through their martyrdom if that must be; and we should find allies—

disarmed, but not the less indomitable—even in the heart and conscience of our foes.

. . . . . .

I said just now that the seeds of these ideas of respect and love for one's adversary came from Christianity. But they have not germinated in the soil of the Church. Not only has she not created all this vast movement of conscience that has made its appearance since 1870—she has persistently ignored it.

In his letter to Queen Wilhelmina of Holland (May 29, 1899), Leo XIII did not conceal his chagrin that his representatives had not been invited to the Hague; but his complaint aroused no echo : for the more vigorously the Roman pontiff protested that he entered into his rôle not merely of lending moral support to every work of pacification, but of effectively co-operating therein—these are the very expressions of the apostolic letter—the more strange did it seem that he had not sooner perceived it, and that the Holy See had allowed little Switzerland to take almost all the initiative and make almost all the effort required to move public opinion.

If one had listened to the Pope's complaint, it was he who, through his legate, would have laid the first stone of a building whereof the Church of Rome had had no conception, and whose execution it had not contributed to render possible. Throughout the world, Catholic organs would not have failed to declare that undenominational efforts could not do without the blessing of the Church.

I am far from undervaluing the eminent services which the Roman pontiff may render to civilisation : but if, after September 20, 1870, the hope of seeing

the Holy See become, as it were, a witness for the
higher justice may have crossed certain minds, that
hope was of brief duration.

Lord of a realm which is not of this world, the
Pope might have given a new and higher spiritual
meaning to the three crowns of his tiara, might have
made himself heard even by infidels and schismatics.

Leo XIII caught a glimpse of this rôle of supreme
arbiter, but it soon became evident that he was preoccupied above all by the advantages which might be
drawn therefrom for the re-establishing of his temporal throne : " *Pro Tribunali sedentes et solum Deum
præ oculis habentes*," says the protocol of the Roman
Congregations. Now the interventions of the pontiff
did not tend to judgments according with intelligence
and justice, and enforcing themselves on all minds by
dint of their lofty independence. Profession was
made of all this, while in reality political combina-
tions were being fashioned. Services were being
rendered to such and such governments, wherefrom
great advantages were counted on in advance. The
negotiations to be found on every page of the decrees
of this Pope made him as unmindful of the complaints
of the Irish as of Prussian Poland, and led him to
force the policy of the Rally (*Ralliement*) on French
Catholics. All this, far from striking the world as
the endeavour of a spiritual power to further the
evolution towards peace and justice, appeared rather
as an attempt to establish a kind of *eminent right*
over and in temporal things. The Holy See still
continued as in Boniface VIII's vision, and dreamed
neither of enlarging nor of spiritualising it.

.   .   .   .

But to return to the question of the pacifist movement: it must be acknowledged that the great Catholic organs in France seem never to concern themselves about it except in blame or ridicule.[1]

We have seen them arrogating to themselves the monopoly of patriotism, seeking in it a means to regain the popularity which more and more escapes them.

But the patriotism they preach is only a systematic, childish, impossible ignorance of what is going on over the frontier: hatred and disdain for the foreigners whom they picture as employed in setting absurd machinations on foot against France. The principal Catholic journals are continually speaking of the foreign gold which is used to encourage actual plots against us, while Protestants, Freemasons and Jews are denounced as agents of this international conspiracy.[2]

I apologise for speaking even thus briefly of such absurdities, which in some circles have grown into a

---

[1] Let us note, however, that in 1907, " the Gratry Society for maintaining peace between nations " was established (composed of Catholics; its general secretary is M. A. Vanderpol, 40 rue Franklin, Lyons). Fifteen bishops have either joined it or given it their support. The members of the Committee are MM. Chénon, Fonsegrive (Yves Le Querdec), R. Jay, the Abbé Gayraud, the Abbé Lemire, Marc Sangnier, P. Gemahling, the Abbé Pichot. What is more, in April 1910, Pius X sent his benediction *cunctis sodalibus coetus* PACIFISTARUM, and with his own hand underlined the last word.—*Appel de la ligue des catholiques français pour la paix au catholiques belges*, Brussels, 1910, p. 16.

[2] It is a serious error in historical method to wish to judge an age-old institution on isolated fragments of its development: to judge the entire Church, for instance, according to its present manifestations. We do not wish to commit this error, and shall not confuse the Church with its hierarchy or even with its Pope.

veritable literature out of which an awakening of French Catholic feeling is anticipated![1] But it was necessary to show the extraordinary retrogression, intellectual, moral and social, which on this matter has taken place in the Church at the very moment when public opinion is making so characteristic an effort to purify the idea of patriotism.[2]

It was necessary to note the preceding facts with some precision, for they have almost determined the

---

[1] Complaint is often made, and with good reason, of the low intellectual and moral level of the greater number of our papers : and what might not be much condemned in purely commercial undertakings whose character no one misunderstands, becomes much more regrettable in papers put forward with the recommendation of Christ's Vicar.

The vulgar and foolish statements published in the *Correspondance romaine* inspire a part of the so-called Catholic Press throughout the world. The inexplicable favour which it has constantly enjoyed in high circles, despite the complaints and protests of many members of the Episcopate, will always remain one of the saddest facts of Pius X's pontificate. One has to have the complete series of this sheet under one's eyes to credit its existence. —See the remarkable study by M. Pernot in his book *La Politique de Pie X* (Preface by Émile Boutroux), Paris, 1910, pp. 254–97.

[2] In this matter Protestantism behaves in an entirely different way. Among the sermons preached on the occasion of the national holiday of July 14 there are many which show that the orator is in perfect harmony with the preoccupations of his fellow-citizens. To satisfy oneself of this it is enough to run through the volumes in which are collected the sermons of the pastors Eugene Bersier, T. Fallot, Leopold and Wilfred Monod, Charles Wagner, J. E. Roberty and J. Viénot. In the same class of ideas may be noted the address given at Strasbourg by M. Th. Gérold, pastor and President of the Consistory of St. Nicholas, on the occasion of the fortieth anniversary of 1870, and published at length in the *Journal d'Alsace-Lorraine* for Sept. 30, 1910. See another address by the same, given at Wissembourg, Oct. 7, 1909 (in the brochure *Le Monument français de Wissembourg*, by E. Hermann, Paris, *Union pour la vérité*, 1909, pp. 52–9).

course of events since 1870. Being in no state to furnish France with the viaticum she needed then, the Churches did not dream that a little of the fault may have been theirs. They poured recriminations on those who took the liberty of saying to them, " Doubtless your bread was excellent in old time, but to-day it is so hard our teeth cannot manage to bite it. It would only break them without doing us any good."

The anger manifested toward such has naturally resulted in again scattering and driving away many of those who had been tempted to look to the Churches.

Thus the instinctive enthusiasm, so strong among the French, for general ideas and generous causes has been forced to express itself outside the Churches, and sometimes under the cross-fire of their gibes. The unfolding and realisation of ideas, which they themselves had painfully sown in the human heart, is achieved entirely without their aid and apparently in opposition to them.

To-day, internationalism and humanitarianism are regarded as the heresies *par excellence* by the official representative of a Church which yet glories in calling itself Catholic.

* * * * * *

In whatever direction our eyes may look in this country, they are met by phenomena analogous to those we have just been observing : in spite of weaknesses, often greatly exaggerated in the accounts given of them, it represents the vigorous effort of a whole people to impregnate its laws and political life with justice and the ideal. It is not resolved merely to proclaim equality and fraternity on its monuments

and coins: it is determined to introduce them into
the humblest reality. Between the priest declaring
that "injustice rules here below," but "justice will
rule in the future life," and the infidel declaring
"justice must rule from this time forward"—which
is the more religious?

Do not let us be imposed upon by words. At no
period of its growth has France been so much preoccupied with the realisation of ideas. And what is
this but the very inspiration of religious genius?

"Imprudence," does some one say?—"the fanaticism of principles which take no account of practic-
ability leads to the worst disappointments." Those
who should speak thus anent these pages would show
they had not understood their purpose. We are not
asking what France can or ought to do, but what
she is doing. If she is imprudent, that does not
prove her irreligious, but rather the contrary. What
indeed is religion but the joyful, valiant affirmation
of truth, beauty and obligation, without taking
counsel of circumstance or obvious self-interest?

.   .   .   .   .   .

There are many other matters as to which the
various Churches have not shared the preoccupations
of the conscience of to-day: thus they have scarcely
co-operated in the attempts that seek to remove
from our codes those laws which, without openly
avowing it, establish certain natural incapacities of
woman, or set up shameful regulations which make
the traffic in "white slaves" a social institution.
With rare exceptions, the Churches have not understood the astonishment felt at their not hurrying to
the aid of the weak and the oppressed.

It would take too long to speak of all that here;

we do not pretend to be setting forth pictures of all their deficiencies, but simply to be pointing out in what conditions religio-social feeling has been driven to manifest itself outside the old institutions and under shapes they do not appear to have foreseen.

For the same reason we shall only recall, by way of reminder, the political attitude which the Church of Rome, and it alone, has taken in the conflicts about the form of government. Theoretically, it has proclaimed its neutrality : practically, above all and before all, it has figured as a political party—a reactionary and retrogressive party.

These facts are too well known to detain us. Besides, even if they have greatly influenced the feelings of France in respect to her clergy, and if, long ago, they separated the clergy from France and afterwards France from her clergy, that is an entirely negative situation; whereas we choose to hold to the positive side of the development, to what is being born rather than to what is dying.

One matter, however, must be noted, touching which a great majority in the country have not only censured the political compromises of the clergy, but have been wounded by them in their conscience. Strictly speaking, they might have excused an involuntary ardour on the part of the representatives of the old parties. But clericalism is an organised, disciplined thing; and when the battalions of the faithful are seen conducted by their priests to the ballot-boxes, one feels oneself among men who retain a still rudimentary conception of certain civic duties. At the doors of the voting-booths this Catholic battalion may very likely encounter another battalion which will say " Yes " where it says " No," with no

F

more criticism or freedom: but this, regrettable
enough on the part of some ephemeral committee,
becomes singularly sad when it issues from the
Church of Christ.

Another element in its political activity which has
seriously injured its moral prestige is—since we must
call things by their name—the lack of frankness in
its methods. One need not be fifty years old to recall
the time when the words " liberty " and " progress "
were only pronounced with wrath and reprobation by
the political candidates whom the Church supported.

They realised at last that if they did not sacrifice
to the gods of the day they would ruin their cause.
Everybody knows the new turn they have now given
to the words " liberal " and " progressive."

Cleverness of this sort may succeed for a moment,
here and there : but it is inevitably found out, and
reflects on the honour of those who have associated
themselves with it. By encouraging it, the clergy
have for their part contributed to the debasing of our
electoral morals; they have behaved as though all
means were good for the attainment of power.

These are among the causes which, working slowly
everywhere, have aggravated the misunderstandings
already existing between France and the Church.
They explain the indifference with which the law
of Separation of the Churches and the State was
received.

* * * * * *

If out of all that precedes we try to disengage
some general impression, we shall doubtless perceive
that it is not the faith, but the incredulity of the
Churches that alienates our young democracy from
them : it is not the elevation of their ideal, but that

in their ideal which is merely mechanical and too easy of realisation.

Democracy does not like dogmas, because they are represented to it not as starting-points, or as milestones on the road, indicating the way past generations have followed, but because they are imposed on it as absolute and final points of attainment. By fixing the canon of their holy books and closing it, the Churches have not merely honoured the past, they have given it a unique character : they have been unable to regard it as begetting the future.

" My Father works continually," said Christ, and announced that his spirit would manifest itself anew and more effectively in time to come; but the Churches that have taken his name have straitened these visions of the future.

.   .   .   .   .   .

These statements, however, would not correspond to reality if we did not immediately add another to indicate the cause for the immense hold upon souls which Catholicism still maintains. That is one of the rays of its crown which has nowise paled.

I would speak of the ardour and boldness with which it appeals to the most mystical and powerful element of human nature : the instinct of devotion.

Just as Christ, passing of old through the country towns of Galilee, cast his glance on an unknown man mending his nets and said to him, " Follow thou me! " so to-day the Church repeats that word : and in a moment transforms and transfigures the most trivial lives.

Among those whom she thus calls, to lead them whither they know not, whither perhaps they would not go, there are few indeed who do not, some day or other, regret their enthusiasm, the naïve imprudence with which they pledged themselves to follow in a way from which they could never more escape, whereon the bridges behind them are broken. And yet they have chosen the better part, since, tearing themselves from egoism, they have tried to rough-hew the social man within them.

Claiming a perfect devotion, an absolute immolation, the Church has rendered homage to the best inclination of the heart; and for this, in spite of many a disillusionment and shipwreck, the heart has been grateful to her.

Therein lies her great superiority over all attempted reforms and new religions : for these generally seem in a hurry to cast away this high influence over the soul : they think to do wonders by announcing that they will only ask reasonable efforts of their adherents—efforts whose bearing can be readily grasped and whose results may be quickly seen.

They do not perceive that in imagining thus to meet man's wishes they are depreciating them, and denying what is strongest in him.

Doubtless the Church is guilty of an enormous waste of human lives. From a common-sense point of view, the thousands on thousands of existences dragged out in convents, or offered for the conversion of heathens for whom Christianity is unassimilable, are a dead loss to civilisation. But common sense is here completely wrong : it does not perceive that even if these have not reached the glittering summits toward which they feel themselves irresistibly drawn, they have at least affirmed them, and have essayed to trace a path in order to reach them. " *Gloria victis!* "

we cry for those who have not succeeded in defending
the soil of their visible Fatherland, which holds the
graves of their ancestors and the cradle of their
offspring.   And humanity, rising with one stroke of
its wings above mere calculation and appearance,
gives the same cry, with even greater joy and wonder,
when it beholds the procession of the saints and
martyrs passing by.

The   madness   of   immolation   is   the   supreme
wisdom.

CHAPTER V

DEFICIENCIES OF ANTI-RELIGION

Free-thought must not be confused with anti-clericalism—Impressions produced in country districts by certain manifestations of the latter—That a profound antipathy towards clericalism is met with among certain peasants who will not identify themselves with anti-clerical organisations—Civil and religious burial—Inability of the anti-clerical mind to understand the Catholicism of our country-districts—Easter—That the Church bestows a sense of discipline, solidarity and harmony—Scant success of the efforts of scientific religion.

In a preceding chapter we pointed out that religion —the instinctive need manifested under infinitely variable, graduated and even contradictory forms— must never be confused with the Churches, the transitory and concrete expressions of that instinct.

These are constantly being menaced and destroyed by the most religious spirits. It must be so by the very force of things, when the Churches seek to eternalise formulas, excellent so long as they corresponded to the needs of any given civilisation, detestable when one claims to impose them upon civilisations very different from those which elaborated them.

With the same care we must avoid the confusing of free-thought—this, also, an instinctive need to judge according to the data of our intelligence and experience—with anti-religion.

70

Religion and free-thought are two twin sisters between whom there are many features of resemblance : if they often quarrel they never leave one another, and mutually check one another. Free-thought quite naturally becomes the ally of religion against Churches which have become decrepit.

Clericalism is a functional trouble not peculiar to religion. All governments carry the germ of this affection within them, since they always tend to regard themselves as the end and not the means. Just as the machinery of a government is perfected and its means of action are intensified, new needs, which it does not understand and sets itself to combat, manifest themselves in society, and it makes brusque, spasmodic and sometimes violent efforts to maintain its power. So in the Church, a group of priests comes to make of its own temporal interests the interests of the Church, to make laws of its prejudices, and to bring about the most serious and difficult crises, which are at times insoluble except by violent means. It will go so far as to ally itself with the most negative elements of society, and will end by losing sight altogether of the principles from which it set out.

· · · · · ·

Nothing is more dangerous than these groups of embittered men, who profess and believe themselves heirs of a long tradition which they do not serve, but by which they profit—men incapable of any constructive work, but very apt to become a leaven of social dissolution, and persuaded that a cataclysm would bring them into power.[1]

[1] If the *Action française*, of which we are specially thinking as we write these lines, is the spoilt child of certain Catholics, it must also be mentioned that among others it has found an irreducible

At the present time we are familiar with this morbid and essentially anti-social condition. But the greatest danger to which it gives rise is not the evil it does directly, but the reaction it provokes. It makes those before whom it displays itself apt to lose their heads. Taken at unawares, they forget that an invincible tact, patience and respect prove, from the ethical as from the scientific point of view, the best methods to employ.

.   .   .   .   .   .

I wish I had been able to avoid the use of these two terms clericalism and anti-clericalism, which lead us into the most sorry and trivial political discussions; but to do so would have been a sort of affectation, a refusal to see reality as it is, since both these tendencies exert a very real influence on the present religious orientation. Strictly speaking, we might have ignored them if it had been our intention to keep to the serene regions of thought; but since we wish to follow the moral and religious elaboration which is going on in the social body, we must, after pointing out the

---

opposition. See, for example, the Abbé Jules Pierre, *Avec Nietzsche à l'assaut du christianisme. Exposé des théories de l'action française suivi de leur réfutation, par les principaux représentants de la tradition catholique*, Limoges, 1901 ;—A Lugan, *L'Action française et l'idée chrétienne*, Paris, 1910 ;—the same, *La Morale de l'action française*, Paris, 1910 ;—L. Laberthonnière, *Positivisme et catholicisme*, Paris, 1911, with the imprimatur of the Archbishop of Paris. The illustrious thinker, seizing the opportunity offered, by a series of articles by the Rev. Father Descoqs, S.J., in *Les Études* (July to Dec. 1909) entitled *À travers l'œuvre de M. Maurras*, shows how the anxiety that religion should triumph terrestrially and temporally, by mixing it with party polemics, only succeeds in robbing it of meaning by profoundly misrepresenting it (p. 8).

deficiencies of the Churches, note also those which assert themselves elsewhere, and affect just as powerfully the ideas public opinion is gradually forming and the resolutions it is getting ready to take.

The hesitations of this public opinion, and the waverings to and fro of its attitude, disconcert both politicians and certain investigators who are always in a hurry for one to answer them either Yes or No. But for all that, they afford proof of the instinctive effort of the masses of the people, even in the remotest country-side—perhaps there especially—to make no false start. They have a feeling that they may neither sell nor give themselves, but must keep all their presence of mind, all the sincerity of which they are capable, in order to find their way. In this fact there lies an element in the life of contemporary France which is almost unnoted and yet of the greatest importance. Our political Press, busy with other tasks, is scarcely aware of this reserve.

As for the foreign Press, it asks often enough "Where is the soul of France?" But when it thinks of looking beyond the outer boulevards of Paris, which is rare, it puts questions so bizarre, and of so exotic or anachronistic a mentality, that it only obtains a vague answer and a discreet smile which convince it of the absolute scepticism of those it has questioned.

If, in our country districts, setting aside the small number of peasants and workmen who belong to a definite clan, we seek to fathom the thoughts of our fellow-citizens, we find that they will try at first to evade any too intimate question; but if we succeed in reassuring them, and showing them we have no desire to attack their convictions, we may often perceive that their apathy is much less real than apparent.

They try to form an opinion, but scarcely succeed in doing so. No longer feeling themselves Catholic in the way their priest wishes, they have yet no serious temptation to enter the ranks of militant anti-clericalism. They willingly repeat Gambetta's saying : " *Le cléricalisme, voilà l'ennemi !* " and yet they rarely give in their names to anti-clerical societies, or if they do, very quickly repent it.[1]

Is there not a contradiction in this? Perhaps quite the reverse. In any case, if the country people, who often take this attitude, generally find it rather difficult to justify, yet it must have a cause, for it is observable in every district : the very man who but now was showing his aversion to the priest as election-organiser, explicitly refuses to join the anti-clerical societies.

In certain university circles something similar takes place for no very mysterious reason. The Frenchman is a born *frondeur;* the mere fact that by manifesting great anti-clerical zeal a man might seem to be currying favour with the Government or administration is enough to provoke a contrary result. There are humble functionaries who make it their business to go ostentatiously to Mass in order to assert their independence, though they are not clericals at all.

With regard to the inhabitants of our country districts, this cause does not count. To what, then, do they owe their lack of sympathy for organised anti-clericalism? If I have rightly interpreted con-

---

[1] Naturally it is no good inquiring among the smaller employees of the State : postmen, roadmen, etc. The *Bonne Presse* has so insistently repeated to them that the Government reserves all its favours for militant anti-religionists that now and then they behave accordingly.

versations I have heard, it arises from the sectarian tendency of anti-clerical efforts.

What our peasant detests in clericalism are its appeals to hatred, and its success in setting the inhabitants of his little commune—even to the school children—at variance: he blames the Church, and withdraws from her just so far—and it is far indeed —as she shows her solidarity with the clerical party.

What he knows of anti-clericalism is often but little, yet, for all that, it is enough to leave an analogous impression upon him. He has laughed heartily at the ease with which the heads of groups and members of committees, sub-committees, etc., are chosen. He does not like the clerical leaders of his world, and combats them vigorously: but he has no more esteem for their adversaries, whom he sees attaining importance in the district papers by means of communications whose source it is not difficult to guess. All this appears to him to be mean, paltry, dangerous, and, above all, scarcely respectable.

There comes a day when a civil burial takes place in the village, and often the impression made upon our peasant is disastrous.

It is true the consolations of religion, even for our countryfolk, are scarcely more than an expression bereft of any definite meaning; but yet, when at the cemetery beside an open grave the voice of the simple officiating priest is raised to recite the ritual words, there are many who, without themselves believing, feel gratitude towards the priest and to the Church that gives their emotion a setting of nobility and grandeur.

The Latin words, dropping upon the coffin already at the bottom of the grave, do not merely envelop in piety the heavily falling earth: they mingle with the breeze in the cypresses and with the scent of the flowers, uniting the sorrow of unknown peasants with all the sorrows that the Church has chanted or will chant to the end of time.

These sensations, which enlarge and sanctify sorrow, are not produced by civil interments. They produce others which are not always happy. The exaggeration of funeral eulogiums; the lack of dignity on the part of the orators; their assurance, like that of pontiffs proclaiming the dogmas of a new Church; their violent attacks upon any who do not think as they; their inordinate desire to make proselytes— these things produce a painful impression. And it is not rare to see simple peasants disputing the right of some militant anti-clericals to call themselves free-thinkers. There are indeed very few communes in France that, towards the middle of the nineteenth century, did not possess free-thinkers whose memory is still green. Strangers to all Churches, the virtues of tolerance and good citizenship permeated their activity and gave real prestige to the word "free-thinker."

These judgments, passed by our rural people on certain efforts, should not be overlooked. If it is only very exceptional for the Catholic or Protestant faith to characterise our country districts, it is just as exceptional for them to lean towards an anti-dogmatic attitude. Many minds, apparently dim, reflect and come to a sort of pragmatic philosophy; they do not know the word for symbol, and yet they find symbols in their priest's sermon and even the ornamentation of their church. What, above all, they find in Catholicism is union, cohesion, tradition, and

an environment which develops their social instinct.
What alienates them definitely from anti-clericalism
is that they suspect it of being a little insincere and
self-interested. If they do not even accuse it of any
strictly material preoccupation, yet they attribute to
it moral and intellectual interests. If God does not
exist, why waste so much time struggling against
Him? It seems to them that anti-clerical propagan-
dists want to slay God in order to annihilate with
Him all the rules of social life.

Such are some of the notions that haunt our
countryfolk without our ever catching their echo. It
is all very confused, without logical bond, and incoherent; a multitude of reflections mingle therewith on
politics, the effrontery of parties—of every party—
on the Press and its falsehoods. But the time is
coming when it will all grow clear and be co-ordinated
—and become a starting-point for the new orientation
of men's minds.

Despite the smile of sceptics, the education of the
masses does progress, slowly but surely; and it may
be remarked that in very humble circles the prestige
of the newspaper is seriously injured; men perceive
that their local paper is often fed by anonymous correspondents who are experts in the art of insinuating
the worst calumnies against their adversaries; they
realise that by means of its police stories, and its com-
plaisant narration of crimes, the Press has become an
instrument of demoralisation.

.   .   .   .   .   .

The political and religious attitude of to-morrow
will arise out of all this that is obscurely at work
among the masses. In this soil, which to an inatten-

tive glance appears inert, a new synthesis is about to germinate.

For the moment, all one can say of the religious crisis—which is much more vital and serious among the country dwellers, who are less impressionable and external than those of the towns—is that clericalism is vanquished and that its defeat has dealt Catholicism a terrible blow; that Protestantism has played no part; and that, finally, anti-clericalism takes to itself a victory which belongs to Free-thought and not to it, and that its effort to organise victory is a pitiful failure.

Not only has anti-clericalism failed to create a higher state of soul than that which existed before, but it may be questioned whether it ever seriously dreamed of so doing.

This may come of its uniting together two very simple ideas without perceiving that they are not interchangeable. First, it sets in relief the faults and crimes of the clergy in order to show how little qualified is so fallible an authority to distribute spiritual sustenance to humanity; and then it demands, in an entirely unexpected fashion, the suppression of spiritual sustenance.

It is led, however, by mere force of circumstances to contradict itself, and to perceive that the disappearance of Religion, even in her most external form—for it only sees her rites and practices—leaves a gap in the life of individuals, families and society. So it is sometimes driven to organise ceremonies and compose a kind of liturgy, of which certainly it is not proud, but which it concedes provisionally to its inferior brethren, somewhat as certain mothers give their children india-rubber teats to suck to elude their impatience.

And when it has done this, it imagines that all the rituals in the world have been drawn up in the same way : that it has repeated what in all ages the priests have done, and that religious effort has had no other purpose than to fashion " comforters " for the people.

Thus it puts itself entirely outside reality : it does not perceive that rites and dogmas, and the Church with its hierarchy and discipline, are the ceaseless work of civilisation seeking itself. The weakness of anti-clericalism springs in part also from its having learnt to look at facts through certain too-simplistic books, which makes it incapable of observing at first hand. When, for instance, it sees its fellow-citizens going to Mass, it supposes that this betokens an adhesion to the Trinity, Infallibility, and a thousand doctrines of which they do not dream. It does not perceive other factors and forces, so much more important as they are delicate and concealed : the perhaps unconscious desire to perform an act of social solidarity, to meet our fellow-men elsewhere than on the field of material interests and distractions, to accept the rendezvous which they offer to us, and we to them, that we may draw together, and more than that—unite and unify.

At the Easter festival, for instance, orthodoxy is specially concerned with the supernatural event of the Resurrection; while anti-clericalism, adopting that view, rises in protest against the absurd affirmation of an impossible miracle. But French religious art, and popular instinct with it, see something quite different. Without pausing to criticise the evidence, they seize on the pictures offered them and delight in what they tell : the victory of the persecuted, poor and abandoned, despite the coalition of ecclesiastical authority and political power; the triumph of truth,

despite the seals and guards. Jesus has vanquished!
And this victory, which is an historic event, is the
prelude, the prefiguring and guarantee of that of all
the weak, all the oppressed, who suffer on behalf of
truth and justice. This is what the Christian people
chant, this is what gives their festival not the aspect
of a commemoration, a recalling of the past, but of
a present life and its efficacy for the future.

Really to understand the Church, it must not
merely be studied in its public and official manifestations, but its true character, the reality of its faith,
must be sought out behind the formulas that are
learnt by heart. Then it will be seen that, for many
of our contemporaries, belief in God is not adherence
to some scholastic thesis, but an act of will whereby
they practically affirm the existence of the good and
its obligatory character: it is a kind of pledge they
take that it shall triumph. Affirming God, man
affirms himself and, so to speak, creates himself, both
exalting and humbling himself.

He exalts himself because in an impulse of life
and love he projects his better self out of himself.
He humbles himself because, by comparison with this
better self, he acknowledges all the distance that
still separates him from the nearest summits.

More than the formula of the other dogmas,
reverent free-thought should likewise discover potent
realities, and should understand why great intellects
and very noble hearts remain attached to ideas which
are almost devoid of meaning to others.

·   ·   ·   ·   ·   ·

Free-thought is sometimes compared with the
schemes of scientific religion which have attained a
certain success in Anglo-Saxon countries.

None of these has taken root in France. Assuredly the efforts which have been made in this direction sprang from a good feeling. There are many excellent people in the world who spend their lives preparing concordats between science and faith; but their pacific and meritorious apostolate has had no appreciable result amongst us. And nothing shows better the natural religious ardour of the French.

If one could picture the advent of a scientific philosophy which would suddenly make all dogmas clear and evident, Catholics would be heart-broken. They would feel they had been detached from their religion, and would seek something else.

Not that religion is for them a cult of the absurd and anti-rational, but that it must exceed the content of present consciousness, of what may be verified by reason or experiment, and must feel out toward the future in order to quicken it and bring it to birth. It is the heart setting forth as the herald of action.

The much-desired marriage of Science and Faith is really the vanguard abandoning its function to fall back upon the main body of the army.

CHAPTER VI

CONTEMPORARY PHILOSOPHY AND RELIGIOUS ORIENTATION

The philosophers have not brought about the present religious orientation—Endeavours of the flower of the nation, among the working classes as much as among intellectuals, to grapple with living social realities—Christianity, in its beginnings, was a popular movement, not occasioned by philosophical views —Though their high value has been recognised in intellectual circles, the efforts of Messrs. Pillon, Renouvier and Secrétan have had no appreciable practical influence—Why the present generation leans to the thought of Bergson, Boutroux and William James—Tendencies of the new philosophy.

WHEN one thinks of studying the religious orientation of a period one's first idea is to seek out its cults and Churches, and then to inquire as to the philosophical currents which might either occasion the dissolution of beliefs or assist at the birth of a new mentality. In other words, one behaves as though religious changes always resulted from the action of philosophic thought upon a religious thought no longer young, which hesitates and searches for its way.

Yet things did not proceed thus in the days of the most important religious revolutions: for instance, Christianity only encountered and came under the influence of philosophy in its third generation. St. Paul was led by the cast of his mind to constitute for himself a theological armour, but that remained for a long time an isolated and individual occurrence : the strength of Christianity lay in its being a movement of the popular conscience, independent of the philosophical speculation of the period.

It is the same to-day. To-day's religious feelings proceed from a very complex and vast secret labour of the popular conscience. Impregnated with Christian principles, it is applying these in directions unforeseen by the Church; and in this it acts not under the influence of surrounding philosophy, but under the urge of an intimate inspiration whose impulses it follows without the slightest hesitation.

For the moment it is at the stage of groping and aspiration; but just as Christianity existed before Christ, even so to-day's religious thought, which has not yet been christened, is already active and assured as to the future precisely because it rises from the humblest circles in society.

We have tried in the preceding pages to indicate some of the directions in which this popular thought has sought to act and realise itself. Farther on, we shall see it concentrating its attention on the agonising problem of religious and moral instruction in schools, in order itself to solve it apart from the claims of Churches, which are too largely interested in the question.

It would be a mistake, then, to look for the origin of the labour that is here being accomplished in the multiplication and inter-crossing of philosophical essays. This fact is the more significant since there has been no ill-will on either side. Highly esteemed philosophers of the most diverse tendencies have offered their good services to their contemporaries, whether to reorganise the former spiritual city or to build a new.[1] On the other side, the desire and even the hope of the public conscience that it might find counsels in perfect harmony with its needs among eminent thinkers has not been realised.

There has been a chance meeting at the cross-roads, a greeting and warm hand-shake, a rendezvous arranged: but on meeting again no mutual understanding is found; the preoccupations of the two parties do not run in the same direction.

Since the eighteenth century and the Encyclopædists, there has been no other philosophy which has really penetrated the French soul; theirs still inspires all our political and social life. But the thought of to-day is ever striving to free itself from their methods—so seductive to the French by reason of their clear and logical appearance—which are, however, too brief and decidedly too simplistic, too merely negative.

Unfortunately, those who write believe in the power and efficacy of books; nor are they perhaps altogether in the wrong: yet books are far from having the importance attributed to them when one is dealing with a naissant religious orientation, impulsive, full of unexpected energies, and entirely different from the intellectual—or, as it is called, theological—movement which comes later, when the new thought, leaving its youth behind, begins to fix itself in rigid formulas.

.   .   .   .   .   .

[1] Think, for instance, of Charles Fourier and the phalanstery, of Saint-Simonism, of Auguste Comte's Positivism, of Secrétan and his *Philosophie de la liberté*, of Renouvier and Neo-Criticism, of the indefatigable efforts of M. Pillon in the *Critique philosophique*, and afterwards in the *Année philosophique*.

For the last forty years the Latin countries have had their eminent philosophers; but, apart from certain men of secondary consequence who have set themselves to serve a definite and precise cause, not one is to be found among those who exercise an influence on thought to-day who has dreamed of fulfilling what seemed in a way the function of their predecessors—to offer their disciples a complete religious system.

Far from directing the present religious movement, our most highly esteemed thinkers seem rather to be spectators and witnesses of it.

Guyau, Bergson, Boutroux and William James have nothing of the attitude of the creators of a religious, non-religious, or anti-religious doctrine. Despite the variety of their views, there is a basic similarity between them; different as these men are, their considerations and efforts take the same direction: they endeavour to grasp religious evolution, to interpret and, one might almost say, to serve it.

They feel the present crisis is taking place outside themselves; they follow and take notes—not external and objective like those of an official report, but subjective and deeply felt. The notion that we can understand or judge from outside of phenomena whereof, willy-nilly, we are the agents, is the basis of that intellectualist philosophy which has inspired both our orthodoxies and our anti-orthodoxies. It is this which has lost the battle. The whole effort of present-day philosophy tends to make us lose sight of the signs for things in order to show us the things themselves, and to set us before the living reality, or rather at the very centre of reality. Hence the unique and overwhelming importance which the religious fact has assumed in the thought of the men I have just named.

"Place yourself," said James in the fine lecture he devoted to Bergson and Intellectualism,[1] "at the centre of a man's philosophic vision and you understand at once all the different things it makes him write or say. But keep outside, use your post-mortem method, try to build the philosophy up out of the single phrases, taking first one and then another and seeking to make them fit, and of course you fail. You crawl over the thing like a myopic ant over a building, tumbling into every microscopic crack or fissure, finding nothing but inconsistencies, and never suspecting that a centre exists. I hope that some of the philosophers in this audience may occasionally have had something different from this intellectualist type of criticism applied to their own works!

"What really *exists* is not things made but things in the making. Once made, they are dead, and an infinite number of alternative conceptual decompositions can be used in defining them. But put yourself *in the making* by a stroke of intuitive sympathy with the thing, and, the whole range of possible decompositions coming at once into your possession, you are no longer troubled with the question which of them is the more absolutely true. Reality *falls* in passing into conceptual analysis: it *mounts* in living its own individual life—it buds and burgeons, changes and creates. Once adopt the movement of

[1] In his book *A Pluralistic Universe*, London, 1909, pp. 263-4. The French translation is entitled *La Philosophie de l'expérience*, translated by E. le Brun and M. Paris, p. 253 *et seq*.

this life in any given instance, and you know what Bergson calls the *devenir réel* by which the thing evolves and grows. Philosophy should seek this kind of living understanding of the movement of reality, not follow science in vainly patching together fragments of its dead results."

This fine page very clearly shows the direction and method—or rather the inspiration of the new philosophy. The enthusiastic reception which has been accorded it by the younger generation shows that in what we call the ruling classes the same crisis is manifested as that to which we have called attention among the working classes. They are not two separate movements, but one and the same movement in different *milieus*. Here, as there, we are induced to fix upon the religious as the most potent and most real fact, that from which all sets forth, and towards which all converges, and to discard as incomplete the intellectualist explanations of it which used to be given.

The simple peasant, seated by the bed on which the dead body of his eldest son is lying, turns from the indiscreet comforter who attempts to prove eternal life in a better world; but he turns with even more decision from him who, making the contrary assertion, would have him declare that he sees clearly in front of him—would have him proclaim that all those who, across the centuries, have sung the victory of life over death were but fools.

He calls in the priest. "Illogical attitude," say Orthodoxy and Atheism together. Perhaps; but an attitude singularly human and true : for the affirmation of the one and the negation of the other were arguments substituted for reality, a kind of decep-

tion drawn as a veil between us and it to intercept
our view.

He calls the priest, because in his mysterious Latin
he will make echo to the great mystery.

.   .   .   .   .   .

Some intellectuals are astounded at the success of
the new ideas.   After being astonished, they smile,
are shocked, and find refutations for them from which
mockery is not absent.

Doubtless none of those whom I named just now
has come bringing his intellectual scheme with him,
as architects come to exhibit their plans for some
monument at an international competition.   They
have not dreamed of judging the past by some ideal
pattern, nor of imposing it upon the future ; but
that is neither an oversight nor an abstention.   It is
simply a homage to the true function of philosophy,
which to-day is rather to observe life and thought
than to create an absolute intellectual system.

In some circles it is loudly repeated that the new
tendencies, incapable of intellectual virility, take
delight in vagaries which may perhaps be good
enough for artists, but will never do for authentic
scholars.   It is even insinuated that such and such
a fashionable teacher is more interested in drawing
a crowd about his chair than in teaching how to
reason and think : that certain contradictions are pre-
meditated and designed to satisfy every one, and
even to increase the intellectual and moral disorder
of the country.

We must be grateful to the representatives of a
certain rationalism for the naïveté with which they
turn these arguments to account, and for the scarcely
veiled regret they manifest for periods when intellec-

tual and social order was maintained by the secular arm.

We will delay no longer over the opposition with which the new thought meets; still less will we rouse up again polemics inspired, as it would seem, by a wounded *amour propre*.

Among those who carry the question higher is M. Rémy de Gourmont, who recently wrote a page in the *Mercure de France*,[1] which is worth citing:

" À-propos of the death of William James, I have been thinking a little lately about philosophers, and have discovered that their influence may be summed up in a few words. I believe that all philosophy which is not purely scientific (negative, that is, to metaphysics) comes at the end of the reckoning to reinforce Christianity under whatever form it dominates the various nations. Most persons who fancy themselves interested in what they call the great problems are moved by self-interested, egotistical anxiety. They think of themselves and of their destiny: they hope to find by rational means a solution agreeable to their desires, which secretly conform to the earliest teachings they received. Now, since all metaphysical movements are very obscure, or at least difficult of access to most minds, when these movements are confronted with religious beliefs the beliefs are found to be of the same order but clearer, having been known in the past. This phenomenon was exhibited at the beginning of the nineteenth century. The deism of J. J. Rousseau, which seemed so remote from Catholicism, made ready the ground for a renovation of Catholicism. Chateaubriand, thoroughly

[1] For Nov. 1, 1910.

impregnated with Rousseau, was the first of this
description. . . . William James, whose religious-
ness is indifferent to religious forms, has, without
knowing it, wrought in the same way for the sects.
M. Bergson's spiral spirituality, with its scientific but
treacherous charm, achieves the same result. The
metaphysical clouds it eloquently stirs dissolve in a
religious rain, and this rain, as it dries, leaves a sort
of manna upon which belief is fed. There are more
priests than intelligent free-thinkers at M. Bergson's
lectures. The manner of postulating free-will in a
Catholic country like France takes on an apologetic
value. The most illustrious of our metaphysicians
must know very well what he is doing."

This last phrase is extremely precious, for it char-
acterises, with real felicity, the antithesis between the
intellectualist philosophy, as it is offered to us, and
the new thought.

By all evidence, neither M. Bergson nor the other
thinkers who inspire the present generation know
what they are doing, at least in the sense in which
M. Rémy de Gourmont seems to use that phrase.
This brief call to order, addressed to the pupil Bergson, not only sums up the whole page but renders it
useless. The page is only there in order to lead up
to and cover it.

No, indeed! the new thought does not know what
it is doing, nor does it even wish to know. It goes,
greeting every one on its way, even the very animals
it meets and the soil it treads, wishing them peace
and labour and freedom. And if the foes of yesterday meet, are reconciled and commune together in
and by it; if, taking with its right the Christian faith

and with its left the antichristian, it draw them to look at one another, and each suddenly to see the other as very different from what he had supposed, it would not think itself absurd or foolish to reunite the Yes and the No, drawing them to a unique affirmation not by effacing either the affirmation or the negation of yesterday, but by surpassing in order to unify them.

"Thus," M. Bergson has said,[1] " to the eyes of a philosophy that attempts to reabsorb intellect in intuition, many difficulties vanish or become light. But such a doctrine does not only facilitate speculation, it gives us also more power to act and to live. For, with it, we feel ourselves no longer isolated in humanity, humanity no longer seems isolated in the nature that it dominates. As the smallest grain of dust is bound up with our entire solar system, drawn along with it in that undivided movement of descent which is materiality itself, so all organised beings, from the humblest to the highest, from the first origins of life to the time in which we are, and in all places as in all times, do but evidence a single impulsion, the inverse of the movement of matter, and in itself indivisible. All the living hold together, and all yield to the same tremendous push. The animal takes its stand on the plant, man bestrides animality, and the whole of humanity, in space and time, is one immense army galloping beside and before and behind each of us in an overwhelming charge able to beat down every resistance and clear the most formidable obstacles, perhaps even death."

[1] *Creative Evolution*, translated by Arthur Mitchell, Ph.D. London, 1911, pp. 285–6.

In this, as in other pages of the illustrious thinker, it would be hard indeed not to see that tendency which we have already so often pointed out in the work of the conscience of to-day, the tendency to assimilate the age-long effort of Catholic thought. The superb oratorical flights of Lacordaire are to be found again in Bergson, with, perhaps, even finer language. We would say that they are there secularised, if the word had not rather too narrow a meaning. We will simply say they are there triumphant, no longer as a kind of future vision, but as a statement of the supreme scientific reality.

This philosophy, which does not make its appearance armed against error, nor resolve itself into a vigorous hatred of evil, naturally looks very dangerous to the partisans of all the old systems.

" If the speech of metaphysicians," says M. le Dantec,[1] " like that of creative artists, is addressed to a restricted public composed solely of their personal ' resonators,' it possesses yet another property which for a certain public renders it superior (but, in my opinion, inferior) to the eminently impersonal language of mathematicians. This remarkable property is that those who perceive it, those who vibrate in harmony with the metaphysician or the artist, are not ordinarily in accord upon what they understand : they are agreeably affected, and this is their only common ground; but that does not prevent their keeping their first attitude as to other matters, and notably towards religious and social questions. A Catholic and an anarchist who at the same time hear the Symphony in C minor, feel at the same time emotions probably

[1] In an article in *La Grande revue*, July 10, 1910, entitled *Réflexions d'un philistin sur la Metaphysique*.

different, and remain the one an anarchist, the other a Catholic, as before.   I imagine they do not fancy that in his work Beethoven expressed precisely their religious or social belief; while, when they commune together in Bergson or in James, each of them recognises the expression of his own thought in the work of these subtle artists; and both draw from the reading of metaphysical productions new reasons for their being—the one more an anarchist, the other more a Catholic than in the past."

At the bottom of M. le Dantec's criticism there is the finest statement that could be made in honour of the new philosophy—that it is in no wise a negative doctrine.   That in itself is much, but there is more : it is like the whiff of mountain air which gives new hope to the traveller.   "But he is ill," cries a contradictory voice, "and in giving new strength to him you do but give it to his disease."   That is quite possible, but above all we do give the strength to him, and furnish him with the sole really efficacious means of fighting against the disease germs, and gradually eliminating them.

From each contact with the new philosophy, the anti-modern Catholic and anti-social anarchist come forth fortified in their whole being, and also and especially fortified in the reasons that each of them may have for attachment to the ideas he professes. We, indeed, cannot perceive those reasons, but they are there.   And if we do not perceive them, it is often enough because we do not choose to look at them : because we are afraid of seeing them—because, for the sake of peace and quiet, and that we may not have to make changes in our doctrinal ego, we require not to see them.

The new philosophy brings the Catholic, as much
as the anarchist, into the presence of those reasons—
generally very noble and pure—for which he made
his choice of a path; and by bringing his faith back
to its source gives it the opportunity of purifying
itself, of seeing and correcting its errors.

We spoke at the beginning of this book of the
desire for international reconciliation which is so
powerfully manifested in our country : hands, and
hearts too, are seeking one another. The same
movement is manifested in the more restricted circle
of national life.

One must be blind not to see that it is because the
new philosophy vibrates with sympathetic enthusiasm
to this movement of affirmation, love and unity,
that it is attaining such a hold on the coming
generation.

.   .   .   .   .   .

Its success is made the more striking by the failure
of a philosophy which a few years ago seemed
to be on the eve of silencing every other in our
country.

It was a time when many excellent people who had
read nothing of Nietzsche asserted that his thought,
which had scarcely yet arrived, was already triumphant : that France, vanquished materially, accepted
the conqueror's philosophy; that this, indeed, was the
system suited to a civilisation in which successful self-seeking (*arrivisme*) proves itself not only
a conqueror, but an honoured and respected
one.

The pessimists seemed to be so much less in the
wrong as Nietzsche's pages were an inexhaustible

arsenal: every violence, infallibility, passion, or madness could go to him for literary halo and intellectual justification.

Is there, then, something analogous in him to what we have just noted in Bergson? The similarity is there, but it is entirely superficial. The latter, by fortifying his readers and giving them tone, prepares them for a life which is association, understanding and love: the former makes his disciples powerful not because they are strong, but because they are formidable, which is quite another matter.

We need hardly say it is not our business to make an exact and scientific analysis of the celebrated German philosopher's [1] thought, but solely to state the idea conceived by the French public of him and of his teaching—for it is this idea, I was going to say this legend, true or false, which has been at work on this side the Rhine—and to ascertain what influence he has exercised not merely on the thought, but, above all, on the social life of our country. This influence has been as superficial as it was ephemeral.

A recent investigation shows that the younger generation almost completely ignores him. [2] M. Jean Viollis, who organised the inquiry, sums it up as follows:

" The best service that the Nietzschians can

[1] This task has been well fulfilled by H. Lichtenberger: *La Philosophie de Nietzsche*, 3rd ed., Paris, 1899: *Friedrich Nietzsche, Aphorismes et fragments choisis*, Paris, 1899.

[2] " Nietzsche et la jeunesse d'aujourd'hui."—*Grand Revue*, Jan. 10 and 25, 1911.

render Nietzsche is to leave him in peace. It is not
to their advantage or to his, that his thought should
be too closely pressed. Even as a denier, Nietzsche
lacks original force. Others have pressed harder
upon the track of our prejudices and false truths:
less flourish, more deadly shafts.

"Certain minds, more resonant than reasonable,
require crashes and flashes to awaken in them certain
vibrations. To them Nietzsche brings, with his prophetic uproar, some true glimpses which a less
barbarous vision might readily find elsewhere. He
will remain a philosopher for those who are not. For
others he will appear to be the greatest poet of
romanticism. Rich in words, poor in ideas. . . . He
equals the verbal sumptuousness of Hugo, and his
feebleness of thought. What gives him splendid
advantage is that he did truly suffer deeply. His
calls and cries come from the depths of his flesh.
He suffered vehemently, sincerely."

After the noisy welcome afforded him, to what can
we attribute the abrupt eclipse of Nietzsche's influence? Evidently to the fact that, while flattering
certain perhaps superficial and exaggerated tendencies
at the moment when his books appeared, he did not
answer to the need which present-day France manifests in every quarter and direction—to see the living
reality; the need to follow that, to live in and for
that, to avoid the proud and deceptive teachings
which make the individual regard himself as solitary
and isolated, with no debt due to the past, nor
responsibility toward the future.

His teaching conspires with certain exaggerated
egotistical passions; it does not answer to the real, the

better, the deeper needs which our country feels for an intenser and more devoted common life.[1]

[1] It is, perhaps, due to similar lack of contact with the most widespread social preoccupations that a philosophical essay of quite another kind, that of Sully Prudhomme, remained, about the same time, almost without an echo.

CHAPTER VII

THE PHILOSOPHICO-RELIGIOUS VIEWS OF J. M. GUYAU AND ÉMILE BOUTROUX

Guyau : his *Irreligion of the Future*—Growing importance of this work—Guyau's ideas as to a new conception of the love of God, of prayer and of doubt, and as to what is eternal in the world's religions—Boutroux goes yet further in the direction of realism, the comprehension of living truth and the love of institutions—Without asserting the absolute perfection of the Churches, he sees their endeavour towards the ideal, and manifests towards all a disinterested and effective sympathy very new among philosophers—His definition of religion—The philosophy of contingency : historical significance of its success—Boutroux's teaching as to the postulates implied by all self-conscious life ; as to the results of religious evolution ; as to rites and the religious future.

It will certainly be understood that we have no intention of giving here a sort of summary of contemporary philosophical doctrines : we are simply trying to find out how and why some of them are in harmony with the intellectual tendencies, moral desires and religious aspirations of our time. It may happen that as we proceed we shall bring together names whose holders would be surprised at the relationship we seem to be pointing out. Yet they will be willing to forgive us. It is life, and no mere writer's fancy, that brings them together.

When the *diligence* sticks fast, the general and perhaps even the bishop get down from the box seats, the middle-class folk from the inside, and the labourers off the top, all trying to help with the same goodwill. Sharing in a common effort, they think no more of that which ordinarily separates them. It is somewhat thus to-day in the religious orientation. Reality draws together ways of thinking which ignored one another and were, in appearance at least, opposed to one another.

It cannot be too often repeated : the originality and power of the effort we are studying lie in the fact that it is not an intellectual movement, the result of the enthusiasm—greater or less—with which some school of thought may have adopted the system of some teacher to explain the great metaphysical enigmas, but proceeds from an impulse of life springing from the humblest social circles.

And this is why other peoples are so deeply interested in the spiritual crisis through which our country is going. *Hodie mihi cras tibi :* " It is my turn to-day, it will be thine to-morrow," say the old sepulchral inscriptions. And the life that moves forward says the same.

It is the glory of France that she has been brought, a little earlier than her sisters, to search new horizons and make experiments which will be of use to the rest.

The impotence of the intellectualist systems has occasioned the blossoming of pragmatism in philosophy; just as, in the Churches, the failure of scholastic and rationalistic tendencies occasioned a new apologetic, based now on history, now on experience, and sometimes upon both.[1] The thinker in

[1] In the celebrated work, for example, of Auguste Sabatier, Dean of the Paris Faculty of Protestant Theology: *Esquisse*

whom the new tendencies first duly sought to realise themselves is, if I am not mistaken, J. M. Guyau. His fine book—with an inaccurate and unfortunate title: *The Irreligion of the Future*—having scarcely achieved any *succès d'estime* among the advanced or *succès de scandale* among the conservative, is perhaps more read to-day than it was twenty years ago.

Why did he choose a title which made one antici-pate some anti-religious prophecy [1] for a work which

---

d'une philosophie de la religion d'après la psychologie et l'histoire, Paris, 1901; L. Laberthonnière: *Essais de philosophie religieuse*, Paris, 1903, with a letter from the Very Rev. Father Nouvelle, General Superior of the Oratory; the same: *Le Réalisme chrétien et l'idéalisme grec*, Paris, 1901 [Encounter between Christianity and Greek Philosophy—Greek Philosophy—Christianity—Op-position of Christianity and Greek Philosophy—Whither the con-flict of reason and faith is leading—Two attitudes—Of the part of history in religious belief: its insufficiency and its necessity—How immutability and mobility are reconciled in Christianity]; Edouard Le Roy: *Dogme et critique*, Paris, 1907; V. Maurice Blondel: *Histoire et dogme* (*La Quinzaine* for Jan. 15, Feb. 1 and 15, 1904).

[1] The first edition is that of 1887 (Paris, 8vo, xxviii, 480 pp.). We quote from this. [There is a readable but sometimes mis-leading English translation: *The Non-Religion of the Future*, London, 1897.—TRANSLATOR.]

" The dominant idea developed by Guyau and followed in its principal consequences, is that of *life*, as the common principle of art, morality and religion. According to him—and this is the generative conception of his whole system—life, rightly understood, involves, in its very intensity, a principle of natural *expansion*, fecundity and generosity. From this he draws the inference that normal life naturally reconciles, in itself, the individual and the social points of view, whose more or less apparent opposition is the reef which threatens utilitarian theories of art, morals and religion."—Alfred Fouillée, *Pages choisies de J. M. Guyau*, Paris, 1895, p. vii of the Introduction. It is a pity that the writer has not indicated the source of each extract.

did not prophesy, and, far from being anti-religious, is impregnated with the broadest historical and social understanding, and shows the peerless place religion holds, and will probably continue to hold, in the annals of civilisation? I imagine it sprang from a scrupulousness as honourable as it was exaggerated. J. M. Guyau, conscious of all the faith, ardour and life in his work, and seeing the wholly new basis it offered to an apology for religion, was a little embarrassed: he wished to avoid all ambiguity and to proclaim—from the very title—on which side of the barricade he was fighting.

But he confesses in his preface that his irreligion retains what is purest in the religious sentiment, "On the one hand, admiration of the universe and of the infinite powers therein displayed; on the other, the search after an ideal not merely individual but social and even cosmic, which surpasses present reality. . . ." And he concluded: "Irreligion, as we understand it, may be considered as a higher stage of religion and of civilisation itself."

With a wonderful sense of life, which continued Renan without repeating him, Guyau saw the innumerable interpretations of religious feeling and contemplated the unique beauty of this evolution, wherein many of his contemporaries chose only to perceive vulgarities, superstitions, errors and falsehoods. Thus having, as a matter of form, declared war upon the Churches self-styled immutable, he showed them with an undissimulated delight that they were more evolutive, and consequently more alive, than they supposed.

This professed teacher of irreligion proclaims a future in which "there will be less faith but more

free speculation; less contemplation but more reasoning, more hardy induction, more active impulse of
thought ": in which "religious dogma will be ex-
tinct, but the best elements of religious life will be
propagated, will be augmented in intensity and exten-
sion.   For he alone is religious in the philosophical
sense of the word who searches for, who thinks about,
who loves the truth." [1]

With fine honesty, he does not hesitate to point out
to the Churches certain counterfeits of religion against
which he sets them on their guard.   What a confession of impotence, for example, to accept the services
of certain sceptics who would carefully preserve
religion as though it were a delicate knick-knack on
a whatnot—or to ally themselves with people who
would not have it disappear because its steeples,
scattered over the hills, go so well into the landscape;
or because the teaching it dispenses to the people is
a pledge of social preservation and of submission to
the powers that be!

Finally, recalling a phrase of Renan's in a letter to
Saint-Beuve : "No, indeed.   I did not want to detach
an unripe soul from the old trunk," he added.   "No
more than M. Renan are we of those who think they
have done all when they have shaken the trees and
flung the whole bruised crop on to the ground; but
if one must not shake down the green fruit at random,
one may seek to ripen it upon the branch."

.   .   .   .   .   .

In spite of all these strong and serene declarations,
in spite of its wonderful style, M. Guyau's book did

[1] For all the preceding quotations, see *Irréligion de l'avenir*,
Introduction, pp. xiii–xxiv, and cp. Eng. trans., pp. 1–14.

not win the success it would have had to-day. Scientists found it too poetical; anti-religionists were disconcerted by so much piety and mysticism; the most liberal representatives of the Churches scarcely looked beyond the title.[1]

How could a pure anti-clerical argue with one who said: "At bottom it is not such a bad thing that fifty-five thousand people in France should be, or appear to be, concerned with other cares than their material ones. Doubtless, one never fulfils the task given one, and the ideal disinterestedness of the priest is rarely a reality: yet it is good that some men here below should labour at a task beyond their strength; so many others work at tasks beneath them."[2]

A little farther, among the pages devoted to the progress yet to be realised, we read: "The second thing necessary is that the priest, who is one of the people's educators, should himself receive a higher education than he does to-day. Far from seeking to diminish the pay of priests—a very slender economy —the State might, at need, augment it, and exact diplomas, analogous to those of school-masters, in

[1] The Rev. M. Grotz, pastor at Nîmes, one of the most distinguished and attractive figures of liberal Protestantism, made a round of lectures against this book.

True, Guyau recalls some of the cruellest pages of Herr von Hartmann against the liberal Protestants who, persisting in the determination to remain in the old Churches, are as much in their place there " as a sparrow in a swallow's nest."

Again, they resemble, always according to Herr von Hartmann, " a man whose house is riven in many places and going to ruin, who perceives this and does all that in him lies still further to shatter it, but continues nevertheless tranquilly to sleep in it and even to call in the passers-by and offer them food and shelter."—*Ibid.*, p. 144 *et seq.*; Eng. trans., pp. 182–3.

[2] *Loc. cit.*, p. 229; cp. Eng. trans., p. 275.

scientific and extended historical knowledge, and in knowledge of religious history. Already some country priests study botany and mineralogy, and others music : in the ranks of the clergy there is a considerable amount of live force, sterilised by the want of an adequate primary education; by want of initiative and habits of freedom. Instead of seeking to separate Church and State by a surgical operation which is not a cure at all, free-thinkers should take their stand on the Concordat, and profit by the fact that the State has the income of the priesthood in its hands, to act upon this great torpid body and endeavour to rouse it up. In sociology, as in mechanics, one need not always try to break the forces which obstruct the forward march; one must be able to turn them to account. Whatever exists is, in some measure, useful; by the mere fact that the education given by the clergy still subsists, it may be asserted that it still plays a part in social equilibrium, if only a passive one, and one of counterpoise. . . . We must not seek the priest's ruin, but the transforming of his mind, by giving it other theoretical and practical occupations than the mechanical one—for instance—of his breviary. Between the literal religion which alone the majority of the French clergy still teach, and that absence of positive religion which we take to be the national and human ideal, there are innumerable steps which can only gradually be climbed by a slow elevation of the mind, an almost insensible enlargement of the intellectual horizon." [1]

The great political value of these views will escape no reflecting mind. Their importance was the greater

---

[1] *Loc. cit.*, p. 229 *et seq.* ; cp. Eng. trans., pp. 275–6.

that at about the same period, for reasons naturally very different, a section of the French episcopate was making vigorous efforts to raise the intellectual level of the parish clergy.

Persuaded that faith has nothing to fear from science, various prelates were reorganising their seminaries, and at no distant day in several dioceses the bachelor's degree would be required of all candidates for the priesthood. Among those dioceses in which the renewal of the course of studies was in 1905 complete and especially brilliant, I will only mention two; I choose them because they were directed by two bishops of a widely different turn of mind—that of Mgr. Lacroix (The Tarentaise) and that of Mgr. Turinaz (Nancy).

To-day, Guyau is being read again; and the younger generation will soon recognise in his book one of the finest works of the last quarter of the nineteenth century. And he is read, loved and admired far from us. I shall never forget the tone of enthusiasm with which a young teacher of book-keeping in an Italian country town, who had been cured by Guyau of anti-religious fanaticism, read me the passage which had set him free : " When you fill yourself with indignation against some absurd old prejudice, remember it has been the travelling companion of humanity for perhaps ten thousand years, that men have leaned upon it when the roads were bad, that it has been the occasion of many a joy, and has lived, so to speak, on the life of man; is there not something fraternal for us in every thought of man ? " [1]

[1] *Loc. cit.*, p. xxvii ; cp, Eng, trans., p. 19.

It is indeed especially because he taught reconciliation with the past; and because, going further than toleration, he preached respect, understanding and love for one's adversaries; because he set up this disposition of soul as the crown of all scientific work, that the name of Guyau waxes each day, and that the last lines of his Introduction may be applied to his own ideas :

"Sometimes, during long night marches, the soldiers in the ranks fall asleep, without, however, pausing; they march on in their dreams, and only awake when they reach their destination to offer battle. Thus advance the ideas of the human mind; they are sometimes so benumbed that they seem motionless, their strength and life are only felt by the way they have made : at last the day breaks and they appear; they are recognised and are victorious." [1]

We will not leave him, then, without calling attention to some of these ideas, which seem to be entirely triumphant in thought, even if they are not as yet in fact.

"If the love of the personal God, mystically conceived, tends to be effaced in modern societies, it is not thus with the love of the God-ideal conceived as a practical type of *action*. The ideal does not indeed oppose the world, but simply surpasses it : it is at bottom identical with our thought itself which, while springing out of nature, goes before it, foreseeing and preparing perpetual progress. The real and ideal are reconciled in *life*; for life, as a whole, both is and

[1] *Ibid.*, p. xxviii ; cp. Eng trans., pp. 19–20.

becomes. Whoever says life, says *evolution;* now evolution is Jacob's ladder, supported at once upon earth and heaven : at its base we feel ourselves brutes, at its summit we divine ourselves to be gods. Thus religious feeling is not opposed to scientific and philosophic feeling; it completes them, or rather it springs from the same source. We have said that religion is a science which is beginning; a science which is still unconscious and vague : in the same way, science is a religion which returns to reality, taking again its normal direction, finding itself again, so to speak. Science says to men : 'Enter into one another.' Religion says to men : 'Unite with one another' : these two precepts are but one.

"Finally, a substitution tends to take place in our affections. We shall love God in man; the future in the present; the ideal in the real. The man of evolution is indeed the man-God of Christianity. And then this love for the ideal, reconciled with that for humanity, instead of being a vain contemplation and ecstasy, will become a spring of action. We shall love God so much the more as we shall make Him, so to speak. If there is at the bottom of man's heart some persistent mystical instinct, it will be employed as an important factor in evolution itself : in love with our ideas, the more we adore them the more we shall realise them. Religion being transformed into the purest thing in the world, love of the ideal, becomes, at the same time, the most real and, in appearance, the most humble of all things— labour." [1]

"We have to find gods of flesh and bone, living

[1] *Loc. cit.,* p. 169 *et seq. ;* cp. Eng. trans., pp. 210–11.

and breathing among us—not poetic creations, like
those of Homer, but visible realities. We have to
behold heaven in human souls, providence in science,
goodness at the very basis of life. We must not
project our ideas and subjective pictures outside this
world, and love them with a barren love; but love
with an active love all the creatures of this world
in so far as they are capable of conceiving and realising the same ideas as we. Just as the love of our
country tends to disappear in so far as it is the love
of an abstraction, and resolves itself into a general
sympathy for all our fellow-citizens, so the love of
God will spread over the whole earth and will be
distributed among all beings. To know living things
is to love them : thus science, in so far as it studies
life, becomes one, we believe, with the constructive
feeling of the most lofty religions, with love." [1]

"Fundamentally, doubt is not so much opposed
as might be imagined to the loftiest religious feeling :
it is an evolution of this very feeling. Doubt, indeed,
is only the consciousness that our thought is not the
absolute, and cannot grasp it, either directly or in-
directly. From this point of view, doubt is the most
religious attitude of the human mind. Atheism itself
is often less irreligious than the affirmation of the
imperfect and contradictory God of the various
religions." [2]

"What alone is eternal in religions is the tendency
that brought them forth, the desire to explain, to

---

[1] *Loc. cit.*, p. 315 ; cp. Eng. trans., pp. 366–7.
[2] *Ibid.*, p. 329 ; cp. Eng. trans., p. 381,

draw conclusions, to unite together everything within and about us; the weariless activity of the mind that cannot stand still before the brute fact; that projects itself into everything; at first perplexed and incoherent, as it was formerly, then clear, co-ordinated and harmonious as science is to-day. What, then, is worthy of respect in religions is precisely that spirit of scientific and metaphysical investigation which to-day is tending to overthrow them one after another." [1]

" Hence the belief in the divine will no longer be a passive adoration, but an act. And in the same way, the belief in providence will be no longer a justification of the actual world and its ills in the name of the divine intention, but a striving to introduce into it, by human intervention, more of justice and goodness." [2]

" The cure for all the sufferings of the modern brain lies in the enlargement of the heart." [3]

It is hard to understand how so many pages, which ought, when they were read by the Churches—little or great—to have awakened in their hearts memories of ancient days, to have recalled the enthusiasms and flights of their youth, only called up instead the long, sad stare of indifference, lack of comprehension, or impotent wrath.

On Guyau's grave—in the cemetery at Mentone,

[1] *Ibid.*, p. 331 ; cp. Eng. trans., p. 383.
[2] *Loc. cit.*, p. 394 ; cp. Eng. trans., pp. 448-9.
[3] *Ibid.*, p. 410.

between the blue sea and the heights of which he sang
so often—a pious hand has copied these words, taken
from his last book : " What has once truly lived will
live again; what seems to die is only preparing to be
born again.   To conceive and choose the best, to
attempt the splendid enterprise of the ideal, this is
to invite, this is to persuade the generations that
come after us.   Our highest aspirations, which seem
to be the most vain, are as waves that, being able to
reach us, will flow beyond our reach, will perhaps, as
they meet and swell together, shake the world.   I
am very sure that my better part will survive me.
Not one, perhaps, of my dreams will be lost : others
will recover them and dream them after me, until
one day they are achieved.   By dint of dying waves
the sea succeeds in fashioning its shore and outlining
the vast bed wherein it stirs."

These words were not the spiritual testament of
Guyau only—they were that which the declining
nineteenth century bequeathed to the century following it, by way, as it were, of preface and programme.

M. Émile Boutroux also is in love with realism,
living truth and reconciliation.   He delights to show
that the oppositions which usually, in abstract reasoning, appear absolute and final, resolve into concrete
relations when confronted with reality.   But if the
old philosophical desire to understand and explain
the universe expands for him, as for other representatives of contemporary thought, and takes on new
vigour as it becomes a kind of communion with actual
realities, it may nevertheless be said that this tendency
goes far further with him than even with Guyau.
Guyau, having already attained the power of

seeing in all the innumerable variety of religious institutions the external and transitory manifestation of that eternal sentiment which leads humanity with each renewal of its thought to make for itself a farther ideal, would, doubtless, had he lived, have succeeded in regarding all these institutions with equal sincerity and equal admiration. Nevertheless one does feel in him something of impatience, and even here and there of anger, against those " positive religions," as he calls them, which are so slow to evolve. It is true that, rightly taken, this impatience and these velleities of irritation were but the echoes of a great love.

With M. Boutroux the serenity is complete, but the intensity of admiration has altered its direction. While with Guyau it went most freely and fully toward religious essays in the distance, whether of time or space, with M. Boutroux it follows the opposite course : it asserts itself and increases the more as we draw nearer to our own time and to religious essays now in full swing. It is not merely a high deference, somewhat resembling the respect manifested by an ambassador on speaking to the sovereign of a great foreign power : it is a sincere and cordial sympathy.

That is a new event in the history of French thought. Doubtless philosophers have been seen before offering their aid to religion, but that was usually for reasons not purely scientific. The great significance of M. Boutroux's attitude toward the Churches arises from its having in it nothing forced or affected; it is the natural result of the situation created by circumstances and the triumph of the new ideas.

At the very moment when superficial observers supposed that France had become anti-religious, the natural evolution of ideas leads the most undenominational philosophy not indeed to conclude an alliance more or less political, utilitarian or sentimental with religious feeling, but to meet and co-operate with it for experimental and scientific purposes.

M. Boutroux's attitude, and that of intellectual and religious circles in regard to M. Boutroux, could not have been foreseen by any of those who, forty years ago, were studying the philosophical and religious future of our country. It was not within the logic of the systems; but it is in that of life, which is better.

Émile Boutroux has faced reality not that he might make it submit to him, but that he might submit to it. He sees it interpenetrated by potential ideality, and does for it what he did for Pascal.[1] "Pascal, before writing, knelt down and prayed the Infinite Being to subject all that was in him, so that this power might accord with this lowness. By humiliation he offered himself to inspiration. It seems as though he who would understand so rare and high a genius in its very essence must follow a similar method; and while employing according to his power the scholarship, analysis and criticism which are our natural tools, must seek in docile abandonment to the influence of Pascal himself, the inspiring grace which alone can direct our efforts and render them effective."

.   .   .   .   .   .

But from 1874 onwards, whence did there come

[1] *Pascal*, Paris, 1900, p. 5.

to this philosopher, who was then still young,[1] the final assurance with which, in the very title of his doctor's thesis, he defined the fundamental point of the system he has since only extended and developed? Obviously, from the happiness with which, while speaking in his own name, he felt himself the interpreter of the most widespread preoccupations of the thought of the time.

Take, indeed, the effort of contemporary thought in Boutroux, Bergson, James, Eucken, Flournoy, Oliver Lodge, Poincaré, Le Roy, Blondel, Fonsegrive, Laberthonnière, Tyrrell and Guyau: on every hand it will reveal itself as an appeal to life, to experience, to the will, against abstract reason: and it was at the very moment when it might be supposed that a dogma, styling itself scientific and looked upon as absolute, was at last about to reign in France that its relativity was proclaimed.

Now at the same moment, at the other pole of the intellectual world, the Church had just proclaimed not only the absoluteness of its dogma, but, by defining the infallibility of the Roman pontiff, had brought a keystone to its construction which seemed to complete and finish it.   But there, too, by a movement entirely similar to the one we have just described in undenominational thought, life was again avenged. This was so unforeseen as to astonish even those who were its instruments when they perceived its power and fulness.

In that is the grandeur and beauty of the present hour.   Certainly many are disconcerted who still

---

[1] He was born in 1845. His French Thesis was entitled *De la contingence des lois de la nature*.   New edition, 1896.

I

belong to the preceding generation, and have had
neither the time nor the power of attention necessary
if one would understand the thought of to-day. They
still see religion hurling itself against science, and
science against religion, in the name of their common
claim to absoluteness. They do not perceive that
if the two hostile armies still exist they no longer
succeed in obtaining recruits.

.   .   .   .   .   .

There can be no question here of examining M.
Boutroux's system to the bottom, or studying in
detail the incomparable plasticity with which he
expounds the principal religious doctrines of to-day.
We only desire to indicate the bearing of his thought
and the direction of his effort, and to show how they
coincide with the most characteristic tendencies of
our generation. The philosophy of contingency has
already deeply penetrated into contemporary thought
and has become a factor in the social movement.

"To rise to the creative principle of life is not a
necessity. We can live by mere instinct, or by routine
or by imitation : we can live, perhaps, by the abstract
intellect or by knowledge. Religion offers man a
richer and deeper life than purely spontaneous or even
intellectual life : she constitutes, so to speak, a synthesis—or rather a close and spiritual union—of
instinct and intellect, in which each of the two,
merged with the other, and thereby even, transfigured
and exalted, possesses a fulness and a creative power
which separate action could not yield."

These words are taken from the conclusion of

Science and Religion, pages in which the writer's thought is summarised with accomplished clarity.[1] Until he has read and meditated on them, no one ought to let himself speak, I will not say of the philosophical thought of our country at the present moment, but of its thought at all. They make one see how superficial and false are the judgments which the Press is still propagating, and according to which France has attained to a system of brutal negations, to absolute scepticism or to materialism, and to a war against idealism in all its forms. If full account be taken of the fact that all the eminent French thinkers I have enumerated in the course of these pages, save perhaps two, have occupied, or do now occupy, chairs supported by the State, it will be seen how erroneous is the notion that our public teaching is subject to a kind of official and quasi-obligatory atheism.

There is no country in Europe where, in the teaching given by the State, idealism is so well represented as it is in France; and by that I do not mean to speak of the number of teachers who mechanically repeat religious formulas, but of those who make a vigorous and scientific effort to continue the idealist tradition, by renewing and completing it, and giving ideas a hold upon facts which they have never had.

This statement is of great value for the history of the present religious movement. The general French mentality has been profoundly changed. The undenominational movement is only one side of a very deep and complex change which can only seem anti-

---

[1] *Science et religion dans la philosophie contemporaine*, Paris, 1908, p. 371 ; Eng. trans. by J. Nield, London, 1909, p. 378. See also the lecture on *Morale et religion* of May 3, 1910, published in the *Revue des Deux Mondes* for the following Sept. 1.

religious to a hurried and superficial observer. Not only would it be impossible to imagine a philosophy like that of M. Boutroux coming to flower fifty years ago, but supposing it had been possible, he could not have acted as he has; or, had he done so, he would have had too great a part of public opinion against him. When the State protected the Church, opinion could not have understood an independent scholar not only offering a new general apologetic to the Churches, but even a justification of their dogmas, discipline and rites.

The universal respect accorded to such men as Messrs. Boutroux, Bergson and Le Roy shows what an important development ‾has taken place in the general opinion of the country.

Here are some quotations, extensive enough to show with accuracy M. Boutroux's attitude towards religion and the Churches : [1]

" Morality claims that one thing is better than another; that there are within us lower activities and higher activities; that we are able, at will, to exercise the latter or the former; that we ought to trust the instigations of a faculty (ill-defined and irreducible, moreover, to the purely scientific faculties) which she calls Reason; and that, through following her advice and obeying her commands, we shall transform our natural personality into an ideal personality. Of what value are all these phrases if science is the sole judge?

[1] They are taken from the conclusion of *Science et religion*, Eng. trans., p. 367 *et seq.* The same ideas recur with something yet more attained, from the literary point of view at least, in the article on *Morale et religion*, *Revue des Deux Mondes*, Sept. 1, 1910.

" But even science herself, considered not in the theorems that schoolboys learn by heart, but in the soul of the scientist, presupposes an activity irreducible to scientific activity. Why should we cultivate science? Why should we set ourselves tasks that become daily more arduous? Must we maintain that science is necessary for living, when we regard life as good and real? Are we quite certain that science will obtain for us a life more agreeable, more tranquil, more consonant with our natural liking for comfort and for least effort? Will it not rather be a life higher, nobler, more difficult; rich in struggles, in new feelings and ambitions; specially devoted to science, *i.e.* to disinterested research, to the pure knowledge of truth? What are the intense and superior joys of initiation in research, still more those of discovery, if not the triumph of a mind which succeeds in penetrating apparently inexplicable secrets, and which enjoys the victorious labour, after the manner of an artist? How can science be duly estimated save through the free decision of a mind which, dominating the scientific mind itself, rises towards an æsthetic and moral ideal?

" Faith, representation of an ideal, and enthusiasm —these are the three conditions of human action. But are they not precisely the three moments in the development of the religious spirit? Do not these three words express accurately the form that will, intellect and feeling take under religious influence?

" Human life, therefore, on the side of its ideal ambitions, partakes naturally of religion. As, undoubtedly, on the side of its correspondence with Nature, it partakes of science—seeing that it depends

on science for the means of attaining its ends—we
are apparently justified in regarding life as the connecting link between science and religion.[1]

"Either by evolution, or by the action of the
media which she has traversed, religion—at one time
so overburdened with rites, with dogmas and with
institutions—has, more and more, disengaged from
this material envelope the spirit which is her essence.
Christianity, in particular, the last of the great religious creations which the story of humanity shows,
has, so to speak, neither dogmas nor rites as it is
taught by Christ.   It calls on man to worship God
in spirit and in truth.   This spiritual character has
dominated all the forms which it has assumed.   And
even to-day, after the attempts to imprison it, either
in political forms or in texts, it continues, amongst
the most cultivated peoples, an irreducible affirmation
of the reality and of the inviolability of spirit.

"Let religion display herself thus in the world,
according to her own nature, as an altogether spiritual
activity, aspiring to transform men and things from
within, and not from without, by persuasion, by
example, by love, by prayer, by fellowship of souls,
and not by compulsion or by statecraft : and it is
certain that she has nothing to fear from the progress
of science, from morality, or from institutions.

"Freed from the yoke of an immutable and dumb
letter, or from an authority which is not purely moral
and spiritual, and brought back to herself, she becomes, once more, entirely living and flexible; capable of reconciliation with the whole of existence;

[1] *Loc. cit.*, pp. 361–4 ; Eng. trans., pp. 367–70.

everywhere at home, since, in all that is, she discerns
an aspect Godward (*une face qui regarde Dieu*).
What may appear to be at variance with modern
ideas or institutions is such and such external form,
such and such dogmatic expression of religion—the
trace of the life and the science of bygone generations; it is not the religious spirit, as we see it cir-
culating through the great religions. For this spirit
is nothing else than faith in duty, the search after
well-being and universal love, those secret channels
of every high and beneficent activity." [1]

Truly these are the conclusions of an apologetic
weighty after a different fashion from that which is
offered to those who drink in the Lenten addresses
at Notre Dame. And it is a layman who offers it to
the Church and to the Churches not because he desires
to please them, but because he has been quite naturally brought to these conclusions by his own studies,
his philosophy and science.

Such a fact, when it does not stand alone, and
appears so natural to contemporaries that its novelty
is scarcely mentioned, reveals a profound development in present-day thought.

If M. Boutroux's attitude in the presence of the
Churches is quite out of line with what was anticipated no long time ago, the attitude of the Churches
with regard to him is just as unexpected.

Catholics—I naturally speak only of those whose
thought is active—were the better prepared to hear
and understand the eminent thinker, since there had
developed among them during the last twenty years

---

[1] *Loc. cit.*, p. 376 *et seq.* ; Eng. trans., pp. 383-4.

a philosophy ready to meet these views part-way; but it will be easier to explain this matter in ten years' time. There would be no advantage in these pages serving as evidence against simple priests whose only crime is that of choosing to think for themselves.

As to Protestants, one recalls the singularly cold reception given even by the most broad-minded to M. Guyau. It would seem probable, then, that a philosopher who came forward without circumlocution under the banner of contingency would be no better regarded. But not only is M. Boutroux not anathematised, the most orthodox circles arrange conferences at which he is invited to set forth his teaching.[1]

---

[1] The article *Morale et religion*, of which we spoke above, and which has material value as the summing-up of M. Boutroux's thought, is no other than an address given on May 3, 1910, under the auspices of the editors of *Foi et vie*. Now the manager of this paper is the Rev. Pastor B. Couve, and its editor the Rev. Pastor Paul Doumergue. The address was published in this review Sept. 16, 1910. On March 4, 1909, M. Boutroux had taken the chair for M. Henri Bois, Professor of the Protestant Theological Faculty of Montauban, and had introduced the subject *Truth and Life*, with some remarks. These are published in *Foi et vie* for Dec. 1, 1909.

CHAPTER VIII

RELIGIOUS ORIENTATION IN ART AND LITERATURE

The most superficial facts are constantly soliciting our attention
—Segantini, Böcklin, Courbet, "The Burial at Ornans "—
Eugène Carrière : his "First Veil " ; his biography, by M.
Gabriel Séailles ; his ideas as to art and its union with life—
Scanty religious influence of Russian and Scandinavian literature
in France—Causes of this—Sully Prudhomme ; Maeterlinck ;
Charles Péguy.

ONE of the most regrettable results arising from the
excessive influence of newspapers upon public opinion
is that we become accustomed to live upon fugitive
and scrappy impressions. Many of our contemporaries imagine themselves well documented on what
is occurring when, day by day, they have collected
in their files quantities of scrupulously indexed notes
upon every event; but even if we admit that the Press
is always accurately informed, the most complete of
such collections would be but a kind of cinemato-
graph, in which only fragments of the real world
would be found.

The newspaper is always interposing between us
and reality, and succeeds—though this has not been
sufficiently recognised—in imposing itself as a vision
of reality not only on those who do not know, but
even upon those who may and should be its actual
witnesses.[1]

---

[1] It is enough to study some sensational trial to perceive that
frequently the witnesses, whose first and authentic deposition has

This constant soliciting of our attention by the daily event makes us lose sight of wholes; it accustoms us to the grouping of facts together in an external, materialistic way, and brings us, little by little, to regard history as the chronological juxtaposition of all the events of the day.

That is a serious mistake; and its next result is to veil from us the life of our time, that we may only see its mere external gestures or even its affectations.

Preceding chapters have shown that French thought has never been more saturated with that active idealism which does not consist in repeating formulas accepted on trust and learnt by heart, but in choosing to sow reality with the ideal. Is not this ceaseless labour which never attains its goal, which is strengthened and exalted even by its defeats, near neighbour to that constant, persistent seeking which Christianity indicates to its believers as the sum of their duty? "Seek and ye shall find! Blessed are they that do hunger and thirst! Blessed are they that feel themselves poor!"

We may find the same spirit triumphant also in contemporary literature and art.

It is true we no longer write beauty and ideal with a capital letter. Is this because, without perceiving it, we have lost the ideas to which these words correspond? On the contrary, one star has gone out in heaven, but thousands of others have been lighted on earth. Each of us has his star; it calls him and he creates it.

---

been travestied by hasty reporters, and by submitting to these travesties and repeating them with docility like a suggested lesson, without any self-interested intention.

Each of us beholds a statue to be carved, a page to be written, which resembles that of no one else; and just because it is unique and is duplicated by no one else, it will harmoniously take its place beside the others. Thus the act which is *par excellence* individual, becomes *par excellence* the social act.

We may see this in the literary and artistic world if we know how to look and will take time to do so. By the side of a multitude of imitations and repetitions, we may contemplate sincere work in which the artist seeks himself; pursues, as in a dream, the unfolding of himself—not of the egotistic self, but of an ego distant as the eternal hills, the supreme affirmation of life and love.

How great would be that historian who revealed to us this striving of so many a contemporary artist often unknown to the public!

Every spring we are told that the number of religious pictures is diminishing. Whereupon it is as regularly concluded that religion is disappearing, and no one so much as dreams that for long enough religion has been scarcely more than a label on most so-called religious pictures. There was often no trace of religious faith where the artist had undertaken to display it—the modern rooms of the Vatican gallery provide eloquent proof of this—and often there is real evidence of faith in those canvases wherein the artist has allowed his hand to direct his brush without clearly realising what he was doing. Is there anything more religious than the work of Segantini [1] or of Böcklin? How loyal and splendid the effort of these very different men to incarnate

---

[1] At Milan.

the soul of reality! "The Isle of the Dead and of Silence," [1] by the second of them, breathes the eternal song and stirs in our subconsciousness a whole world of feelings which have been deposited there by the ages.

Before such efforts one feels the truth of Christ's word to Pascal, "Thou wouldst not search for me so well if thou hadst not already found me." The ideal sought is found already, even by this, that it is sought—found, but never attained.

Courbet's "Burial at Ornans," [2] also proceeds from a fundamentally religious inspiration. Before this canvas, which to many contemporaries appeared ugly, brutal and vulgar, we are now seized by intense emotion.

For its realism does not stop at the surface: it involves the entire reality, and thus attains to an idealisation which is not merely a kind of superficial varnish, as in so-called religious paintings, but an intimate flame that, shining outwards from within, vivifies and gives life to the whole.

For him who will pause long before it, this sheet is no mere burial at Ornans; better than any other document it enables one to realise what a large part of the French clergy was like about 1850, and the sort of hold Catholicism then had upon the souls of the people. The funeral ceremony brings out upon each of these faces no conventional expression, but a true, sincere and profoundly individual impression, to whose mutual harmony the painter has thrilled. Such as it is he has let it remain; but to render it with this perfection he must have mastered it, he must

[1] At Bâle and Berlin.   [2] At the Louvre.

have outdistanced and understood it both with his intellect and heart.

The most general impression resulting from a quiet and meditative visit to the Luxembourg is of a sincerity which does not dream of repeating those insipid motives that claim a religious title—a sincerity which is no better satisfied by a mechanical and materialistic noting of reality.

Of several of our artists, we may say what M. Gabriel Séailles has written of Eugène Carrière: "For him, painting is neither an amusement nor a profession: it is his language, his mode of research and expression; the way nature has imposed on him of setting out on the discovery of himself and of the world. This discovery fascinates him: he pursues it with joy and enthusiasm. He casts on all about him a frank regard. He works naïvely, simply, ever strenuously, ever progressing. With slow step and sure, guided by an instinct which he only obeys with the application of reflexion to it, he mounts toward the beauty that answers to his deep and passionate soul. His life is a circle, always widening from the same centre. Art, as much as science, is a point of view about the universe. Questioning nature, attentive to its answers, in this perpetual converse, as by immediate experience, he proves that one and the same thought is realised in the forms of sense, and is self-conscious in the mind of man. He is in communion with his fellows and with the whole of nature, and finds invincible strength in the feeling of this solidarity. His love of beauty fulfils itself in heroism." [1]

.   .   .   .   .   .

[1] Gabriel Séailles: *Eugène Carrière : essai de biographie psychologique*, Paris, 1911, p. vi.

What the present generation thinks and desires may be learnt better from the biography we have just quoted than in long volumes. In it one may watch the artistic consciousness attaining to the vision both of its ideal and social function, to the idea of its collaboration in the mysterious labour of humanity. But Carrière is not a unique example in the world of art. Biondi in his " Saturnalia," Ségoffin in " Man and Destitution," like Millet and Puvis de Chavannes, Rodin and Bartholomé, have passed through similar experiences. Gabriel Séailles, noble thinker that he is, has truly done the work of the historian of philosophy in the highest sense of the term by showing the significance of such an uneventful existence.

" The First Veil " is one of the most religious works art has produced. Before pausing a moment to take it as a type of the religious movement in contemporary art, it may be well to draw near to its creator, guided by his biographer. We may then see in what degree his views coincide with those set forth in the preceding pages.

" Eugène Carrière is a veritable artist : his nature goes beyond, or at least goes before his reflection. He has not begun by imprisoning himself in formulas; he has respected his ignorance of himself; he has sought the revelation of himself in life, in the endeavour toward complete living without the sacrifice of any part. . . .

" Man must consent to life : to be an artist is to live in the awe and agitation caused by unknown forces made manifest only by work when the hour is come. For Carrière, art is not a profession which feeds and enriches its man, or by whose means one may win pleasure; his art is so mingled with his life as not to be distinguished from it: it is the language of his sorrows and joys, his thought at all times, his morality, his religion; the intimate action, the positive experience which has revealed to him all he knows. Carrière is not one of those artists who halve themselves, and put into their work the sentiments they do not utilise in their lives; his work is an acquiescence in his nature; his reflection does not change his emotions, it is born of them, it deepens them; his tenacious will is only the clear consciousness of his true destiny; his genius is indistinguishable from his moral life and is its essential form; his work as an artist is his work as a man; he is making himself at the same time as it, and by means of it. . . ." [1]

" I understand "—Carrière wrote one day, returning to the past and speaking of the time when, after his first successes, came severe criticism—" I understand that if the public was not ready, no more was I, and that the strong and simple things choose to be strongly said; that this takes long and long, and is never achieved: I know now that life is a succession of efforts [2] continued, later on, by others. This idea gives me courage, since it leaves everything at work and in action; for only the thought of coming to an end is sad." [3]

" It is not art for art's sake that is to be feared,"

---

[1] *Loc. cit.*, p. 3.

[2] " The conquest of one's self," he once said, " is not achieved without trouble, as you know. It is a ceaseless effort, in which fatigue, and even despair has its part; one must be always beginning over again and ceaselessly renewing one's hope and fortifying one's desire."—*Écrits et lettres choisies d'E. Carrière*, Paris, 1907, p. 215.

[3] *Ibid.*, p. 30.

Carrière said again to M. Séailles, "but the profession for the profession's sake. Detached from the feeling that creates it, the process is nothing; plagiarists are robbers robbed. Art is something inward and personal; one works to give one's best. Vision depends on sight; sight depends on the spirit. A process is barren, a vision is fruitful. Doubtless, the artist's vision has a unity which depends on his temperament, but, just as it depends on the man's nature, and is its sincere expression, so it is not settled and fixed, it obeys the progression of life, it makes each work an occasion for deepening its own thought by discovering some new aspect of it. . . ." [1]

"Everything is a confidence which responds to my avowals, and my work is one of faith and admiration. . . ." [2] "May our faith of living for a higher life keep its activity, and decay find us weary in body but unquenched in mind and heart." [3]

Could a more religious confession be formulated? Hence M. Bidou [4] could say of him that in his mind "a technical idea of painting germinated and bore the unexpected blossom of a metaphysic and an ethic. Looking at life as a painter, he found himself a philosopher."

He even found himself something more, and in his "First Veil" this artist free-thinker has left us a sheer masterpiece of religious inspiration.

Perhaps there is no picture in which the incomparable power of religious symbolism has been observed with more marvellous sincerity: its value and

[1] *Écrits et lettres choisies d'E. Carrière*, Paris, 1907, p. 33.
[2] *Loc. cit.*, p. 41.   [3] *Ibid.*, p. 162.
[4] Quoted by M. Séailles, p. 142.

necessity for arousing certain emotions and expressing them discreetly enough for them—mysterious as
they are, subtle, beneficent and sorrowful—to be able
to speak, in their turn, to every heart without violat-
ing its secret, and to fuse all these various emotions
into a single whole wherein men may commune
together.

The confidence of the little communicant, moved
and wondering, yet, at the same time, serious and
composed, before the thoughts she feels stirring in
her heart—the appeal to life and to mystery—was
none other than the attitude of the painter himself
toward religious feeling. He looked upon it with
perplexity, but right in the face, and wrought this
work, wherein, after the manner and in the language
of the artist, he declares that certain facts in individual life can only find expression through the aid
of religious tradition.

With a noble, deliberate, caressing, almost respectful gesture, a mother is about to place the first communion veil on her daughter's head.

She drops her eyes, for the child appears to her
aureoled in mystery and poetry. She would fain
find words in which to utter her maternal pride,
admiration and joy, but she cannot; for she has felt
reviving in her heart the memory of wounds yet
unhealed, the indistinct but none the less invasive
and terrible murmur of sorrows she must not awake.
Dumb before this rush of visions of the past and of
anxieties for the future, she desires to prolong the
moment. There is a great silence. The young girl,
suddenly grown up, and guessing her mother's
trouble without being able wholly to understand it,
gazes at her long, to assure her of her affection, her

K

courage, and her devotion both to her mother and to the ideal.

Younger brothers and sisters stand there too, arrested before that white apparition; pensive, as they see mother and sister so different from their usual selves. The youngest joins his hands together, in an ecstasy.

A little behind them the grandparents, who have just entered, pause on the threshold, daring neither to advance nor speak.

Thus the emotion brooding over the scene, while single in its source, is infinitely diversified in each person. And it is religion which in this simple room has suddenly harmonised this symphony of feelings, and given them the opportunity and means of revealing themselves. Even before setting out for the church where she will be united to her God, the young girl is already quite prepared and, as it were, transformed by those obscure but powerful feelings to which free course was given by the domestic hearth. She has felt on her brow the benediction of the past, and has given her brave adhesion to that past; as for the future—"You tremble for me," she whispers to her mother; "I love you, I will be worthy of you."

The consecration thus given by religion to realities it did not create, but in whose unfolding it singularly assists, has never been seized with greater truth or more delicate reserve.[1]

Of this work of Carrière's, it may be said that it is a "proof before letters" of pragmatism.

[1] This picture is in the gallery at Toulon. *L'Union pour la vérité*, 21 rue Visconti, Paris, has had a fine reproduction made of it in photogravure, which is on sale at its offices.

In the noble description, worthy of this master-piece, which M. Séailles has devoted to it, he has characterised, with a deep feeling for the most finely shaded psychological realities, the attitude of the grandparents who have just entered : " The grand-father, not quite at ease in his best coat, a free-thinker who knows how to take things, with his hand in his beard, marvels to feel himself affected; tranquil and grave as she goes back through her memory, the grandmother vaguely feels the resemblance of festivals to days of mourning." [1]

A kind of radiance emanates from the group formed by the mother and her child. The grand-father, still vigorous, is somewhat annoyed at his emotion, for it is in contradiction to the ideas he holds, or rather sets himself to hold. Before this girl his logic finds itself wanting. But since he is an honest man who will not lie to himself, he is already reflecting and probing his emotion.

This free-thinker seems, indeed, to be at precisely the same point as a considerable number of our contemporaries who, out of scrupulous sincerity, have suppressed fixed rites from their lives as forms wherein many a superstition lodged, and who one day ask themselves whether, when they thought only to lop off a superfluous growth, they have not brought down a main branch and robbed their life of an essential element.

Not being able to believe the dogma their priest preaches, they have brought up their children outside all religion, and the time comes when they are abruptly obliged to make a kind of self-examination.

[1] Gabriel Séailles : *loc. cit.*, p. 61.

Have they not been mistaken as to what sincerity requires? How could they have acted so as not to warp their children's minds and yet, at the same time, not to rob their moral life of the support religion offers?

"The veil is nothing," says the reasoning reason, "let it be suppressed." But to suppress it is to snatch away from this family a red-letter day in its life: a day which is both a point of attainment and of new departure. Outwardly nothing has been changed between the eve and the morrow of this day; inwardly all is changed. The young girl feels herself bathed in the ineffable emotion of the maternal kiss set this day on her brow, and beholds an unknown horizon appearing in her life.

Thus, in its own way, Carrière's picture puts the question whether the old religious song, that only accompanied the inner, individual music, must be renounced on the pretext that, now and again, it led to dissonance. In avoiding certain malformations and mistakes, do we not fall into a worse mistake—that of depriving ourselves of an instrument which, while it may wound and even kill if wrongfully used, we have not yet succeeded in doing without?

Many very free spirits are setting themselves a multitude of questions analogous to those indicated in Carrière's work. At the moment when the struggle for material existence is becoming more and more difficult, they are seized by anxiety, seeing a kind of impoverishment in the ideal inheritance which the past has bestowed on our individual, family and social life.

On the pretext that symbols, dogmas and rites are but a provisional and imperfect language, must we renounce their service and reduce to silence that in our spiritual life which is the strongest and most eager for expression?

. . . . . .

These preoccupations most frequently remain as personal reflections; but gradually they manifest themselves in literature, as we have seen them manifest themselves in art.

If a critic should disregard all the works which only arise out of an unwholesome need to flatter the taste of the day, to earn money and achieve notoriety, he would undoubtedly find more than he might have supposed in which the new religious orientation markedly appears. There has been no other cause for the success of the Russian novel among us, the kind of enthusiasm with which Ibsen, Björnson, Ellen Key, Jörgensen, Sienkiewicz and, pell-mell with these, every foreigner and even exotic has been read in France. French religious feeling, not finding in its own country the food it needed, went forth to seek it over the frontier. It soon came back. And it did well. One may say so without being in the least in favour of intellectual frontiers. Religious feelings are not articles of importation. Every man and every society must make his own by personal effort——an effort for which no substitute can be found. Even Tolstoy, for all his vast genius and the enthusiasm with which we have followed him, will be found to have had but little influence on the spiritual evolution of France.

We have been able, then, to admire wholeheartedly, without comparing or judging them, those who were doing spiritual battle afar. We could not

follow them, but the salute we gave them was as
cordial as it was disinterested.

We cannot here pretend to survey the whole
literary output of to-day in order to show the involuntary and, as yet, unobserved return towards a
very novel religious sentiment which differs from the
old especially in being really deeper, more invasive,
more potent.   It is not confined to special publications which one would have to seek in the neighbour-
hood of St. Sulpice : it penetrates everywhere.   Who
can describe the attraction exercised by the cathedral
over Huysmans and Zola? [1]

The persistent effort of Sully Prudhomme to
attain to faith was unsuccessful, but his very failure
had considerable religious value. [2]   The striving had
been sincere, gallant and singularly important; it was
like one of those rough drafts that life rejects, but
which are the very condition of a new fact—the
prelude to a masterpiece.

The younger poets and writers approach religious
preoccupations by another route than his : by that
upon which in the preceding pages we have met
philosophers and artists—the way of experience and
reality.   As a result of this method certain works
are being hailed both by the authorised representa-

[1] The religious movement manifests itself even in archæology
and the history of art.   In this domain it has inspired works of
high scientific worth by showing how religious art may be understood from within, I mean by going back to the ideas and feelings
to which it gives expression.

The very remarkable and novel work of M. Mâle, *L'Art religieux
du XIIIe siècle en France*, links itself to the tendencies which have
given us a fresh idea of history.

[2] See all his later works, especially *La Vraie religion selon Pascal*,
Paris, 1905.

tives of the Churches and by those of Free-thought.
Quite recently the Rev. Pastor Bertrand [1] asked:

" Why should not we, also, pronounce the name of
M. Maurice Maeterlinck, whose works bear the im-
press of so potent a personality and interpret so
intense an inner—let us say a religious—life? No
doubt many believers find his temple actually too
much buried under literary preoccupations and philosophic doubts, but how can we deny that the principal
feelings excited in us by religion are aroused by contact with his work? Where shall we find more
solemn calm than in his study of *Silence;* more
stupefaction in the face of the world and of life than
in his pages on *The Daily Tragedy?* Where find
more weighty seriousness than in his meditations on
the problem of suffering and of the relation between
Wisdom and Destiny: more reliance than in his
Invisible Goodness: more anguish than in his *Deep
Life?* There is no one in our time who has leaned
with more mystical ardour over what Carlyle called
' the great inner sea of beauty.' Here, indeed, is
the true religious free-thought, earnestly seeking
what new ideal it may present to the world in the
place of the Christian. There is nothing more revolutionary than M. Maeterlinck's attempt; nothing
more pious, nothing more fervent than his soul. By
ways that are not our ways he seeks the eternal principle of things and of life, and finds without difficulty
the means of exceeding and dominating existence."

Among those in whom, at this confused time, we
may trace the evolution now being accomplished in

[1] *Problèmes de la libre pensée*, p. 203.

the religious feeling of a great number of our fellow-citizens I will only name Charles Péguy, founder of the *Cahiers de la Quinzaine.*

His *Mystery of Joan of Arc's Charity* has been hailed with equal delight by Free-thinkers, by the most orthodox of Catholics, and by the broadest-minded of Protestants. The beauty of this work is wholly wrought out of sincerity and simplicity; it lies in the frankness with which the author lets us see the tremendous function the sacred liturgy may fulfil in a human life.

In this age, devoted to speed, Péguy can give ten or twenty pages to prepare for the unfolding of a feeling. He repeats the same words and phrases with an insistence which is at first exasperating, but soon imposes itself on your mind and takes your heart. It is the same again and yet different—this litany with its motionless air is a procession advancing slowly but with a purpose of its own; when you have read a third of it you cannot stop.

Now this unrepentant Dreyfusist has attained to a wonderful expansion of the Catholic sense. The whole Catholic faith is in him, and the whole Catholic vision.

It is a lived and conquered, a living and a conquering Catholicism. There are Paternoster and Ave, Eucharist and Angelus, thirst for unity, sense of the cross and of sacrifice, of liturgy and of tradition. And, above all, there is the feeling that the humble work of the toiler is blessed by the Church.

All this surrounds, bathes and penetrates you with so much the more force that the author never abdicates his free judgment.

" All the weakness, and perhaps one ought to

say the growing weakness of the Church in the modern world, comes, not as is supposed from Science having raised up self-styled invincible systems against Religion; not from Science having discovered, having found arguments against Religion, supposed victorious reasons; but from this— that what remains of the socially Christian world is profoundly wanting to-day in charity. It is not reasons at all that lack—it is charity. All the reasons, all the systems, all the pseudo-scientific arguments would be nothing, would have but little weight, if there were but one ounce of charity." [1]

[1] Charles Péguy : *Notre jeunesse,* p. 136.

CHAPTER IX

CHARACTERISTICS AND DIRECTION OF THE PRESENT RELIGIOUS MOVEMENT

To-day Man has above all else the sense of life, and understands alike his powers and the limits of his liberty—History tends to invade the whole intellectual domain and even to supersede metaphysics; but contemporary thought does not oppose a materialistic conception of history to the dogmatic under the pretext of reality; it realises the life in history, and from that point the guiding principle is found—To whom does the child belong?—Neither to the Church, the State, nor its parents—Historic feeling in the toast proposed by a village mayor—Features of an undenominational ethics and religion that issue from the new conception of history—Incurable weakness of some religious reforms.

HAVING endeavoured to grasp the action of the new preoccupations on the political, philosophic, artistic and literary life of our country, we may take one more step towards defining the character of this orientation and attempting to see it as a whole.

The religious movement of to-day, manifesting itself particularly outside the Churches and in matters which at first do not seem to be directly related to religion, has not always been recognised. The bad reception it has had from the Churches has even caused it to be taken for an anti-religious effort.

Perhaps we might describe it as a tendency—often unconscious and entirely unsystematic—begotten of circumstance, to focus attention upon realities; not to view them across the abstract reasonings of an absolute doctrine, whether mystical or rationalistic, but to follow them in their development: a tendency to seek in their past *life* the explanation of their present value; and finally, to hope that we may find, in this contingent and relative view, practical indications for individual conduct, for politics, whether national or international, and for the solution of social questions.

If this is indeed the direction and, as it were, the leitmotiv of the mentality of to-day, we may say that here is an eminently religious effort: it puts forward, indeed, as the unquestioned and unquestionable basis of all activity, affirmations which are the most characteristic fruit of religious evolution; affirmations which imply man's freedom, the beauty and value of life, the possibility of man's collaborating in the indefinite perfecting not only of his individual life, but of the whole of nature—affirmations which further imply that good action is action by whose means man realises his better self, and demands of this self which is within him—within him and yet more than he—a programme, method, inspiration and duty. This is not an abstract and absolute duty inscribed in some code; it is his own duty, and his alone; it imposes itself on him, sovereign and imperious, because nothing can make any one else capable of fulfilling it in his stead.

And just as each individual has his personal incommunicable duty, requiring him to pilot his own life across the shoals he alone knows, so, in the same way, communities constitute moral individuals, and also have their special duties—a particular mission which is that of no other society.

The little being who comes into the world is no incarnate abstraction. Potent and free as he may one day become, he cannot but remain the heir of a past whose duration cannot be conceived, whose every convulsion, revolution, stress, sigh and vibration has left some trace in him.

He may rebel, he cannot cancel this. He may change his name, his nationality, his Church. But no more than a negro can become white, can he cease to be the creation of such race, nationality and Church.

Are individuals, then, and groups of individuals, slaves pure and simple? No. If we acknowledge the power of the past, we must as fully acknowledge that life never repeats itself, that absolute determinism is as foreign to it as absolute liberty; it is alive. Speaking thus, we know we are using an expression we cannot define. Is that a reason for not using it? Life is a mystery. We do not know its secret; but we well know that its advance may go with more or less vigour and rapidity in a direction other than that of pure logic, a direction we call progress, and which without hesitation we describe as good and higher than that of rational logic. And in this progress, whose origin and end he does not grasp, his sight embracing but a brief moment of it, the man of to-day realises, with an intensity which the thought never possessed before, that he may partially intervene. He does not know the foundations, he will never see the building's crown. What matter! He is happy in being called to carry a stone to it.

The present tendencies imply catholicity of endeavour, the feeling of solidarity across time and space. And this feeling, which experience only confirms, transforms itself into understanding of the past that it may blossom in love for the present and preparation for the future.

No doubt it will be said that all this is metaphysical. Very likely; but what matters to us, since we wish simply to observe what is passing, is that the various affirmations we have just observed are constantly regarded by our contemporaries either as the immediate data of consciousness, or as proceeding out of the most concrete reality considered apart from any philosophic or religious systematisation.

. . . . . .

These experimental data are big with consequences which arise out of them not by logical reasoning, but by vital development, like that by which the oak is seen issuing from the acorn : here are the germs of an intellectual, moral and religious evolution already in vigorous manifestation on every hand.

History tends to invade the whole intellectual domain, taking the place of metaphysics without even condescending to struggle for it, and also superseding a merely actual and narrow view of reality. Having sought the absolute everywhere for centuries, it seems as though our mind had become unable to think of it; yet far from finding ourselves impoverished, we feel disembarrassed of tendencies which isolated us, nourishing us upon pride and illusion. We turn away from deceptive images to consider the humble reality which created obligations for us at once precise, numerous, efficacious, individualised and mutual.

While history tends to invade every intellectual

domain, our conception of it has been completely transformed. The only characteristic it retains to remind us of what we formerly understood by history is that its face is turned towards the past. Its spirit is renewed, and it seeks to fashion for itself methods in harmony with this new spirit.

Many savants have opposed, and not without reason, the evidence of facts to what may be called the dogmatic idea of history [1]—that of grouping all facts about a dogma, as Bossuet did in his *Discourse on Universal History;* but they have been wrong in allowing themselves to be dominated, without perceiving it, by a materialistic view of these same facts. Erudition has too often delighted in a kind of idolatry of detail, and in methods so mechanical and external that they have led to results their authors themselves would not have desired had not fear of being thrown back into the old track constrained them.

If the grandiose constructions of dogmatic history do not correspond to reality, they have the advantage of being readily grasped. What is more, if they are a mere symbol, at least they let this be seen, and deceive no reader as to their nature. The exaggeration of historic scholarship, on the contrary, is often worse than error; it easily becomes deception. It

[1] It is needless to recall here the primordial part played by reasons of conventional propriety in the works of ecclesiastical historians. We know *nothing,* historically, about the father and mother of Jesus; but thanks to motives of convenance, large volumes have been written entitled *History of the Holy Virgin, History of St. Joseph,* armed with every possible approbation, in whose course the authors seem to have had not the slightest hesitation as to the legitimacy of their method. In this sort of work, which we often owe to eminent persons, purely theological contemplations may be seen taking the place of history.

proceeds from a juridical and judaistic conception of truth. It tends to persuade both author and reader that, once one has collected all the documents upon any question, and has classified and analysed them without *parti pris*, one has an adequate picture of the facts. Now erudition, pushed to its extreme limits, ends in the most deceptive of impasses; it resembles certain of our modern libraries, where the law ordains that everything printed in the country should be preserved, and which become unusable because having everything is much the same as having nothing.

Present-day thought does not set these two conceptions of history in opposition to one another; still less does it dream of establishing a kind of *modus vivendi* between them by using now one and now the other : it assimilates what is best in them, founds it upon a new idea, and, where scholarship only amassed material, and dogmatic history made a display of unverifiable systems, it sets itself to study the life and the evolution of societies.

The mere introduction of the idea of life transforms history,[1] socialises it in every direction; changes it into a philosophy, an ethic, a religion, the basis *par excellence* for individual and political education.

We can only take full possession of ourselves and of our latent energies on condition of working by the side of our fellows. The peasant boy, when he has not been spoilt by some extraneous suggestion, is in a hurry to work by the side of his father and brothers;

[1] There has been no other cause for the revolution which in the last few years has been wrought in geographical science. Instead of the crabbed nomenclatures known to our young days, geography is now the most living of sciences, and one of those in which memory plays only a secondary part.

sometimes one sees him secretly trying to carry heavy burdens, and to do all those tasks for which he has been told he is yet too young. But he does not succeed in doing them; for to set the individual in perfect muscular activity requires union, cadence and harmony with other men. In the same way our mental energies, if they are to attain their fulness, need to feel their relation to those of the past and their solidarity with them.

Not long ago, a certain morality sought to forbid this knowledge of the past; it would have hidden from the child the uncertainties and difficulties through which our actual morality has been formulated. The purpose was excellent: to have parents respected, to have them regarded as infallible, and to give the child the impression Moses must have produced upon the Israelites when, descending from Sinai, he placed the two tables of the Eternal Law in the Ark of the Tabernacle. But unfortunately the means was not so good as the end. Children, even quite little ones, were not always the dupes of pious parables, and while they made a show of belief began to mistrust the whole of the education given them. Some even wondered if society were not tacitly agreed to deceive children.

To-day, this method seems to have been abandoned. The theory of parental infallibility beat itself against too many lamentable contradictions.

The depth of the evolution, which in this respect is being wrought in our customs, was revealed in the course of the very interesting discussions that took place a few years ago on scholastic matters. Entirely new ideas sprang up in answer to the question "To whom does the child belong?" We have not time to

discuss the subject at length, but must indicate it in
a word; for the solution manifestly adopted by public
opinion was neither that ordained by the Church nor,
again, that which is inscribed in our civil law. It
was inspired by the moral and religious orientation
we are endeavouring to outline.

Conservative polemics have not dared to hark back
to the old orthodox idea, pure and simple, though in
theory it still exists, that the child belongs to God;
that is to say, in practice, to the Church, or rather to
its head, the Pope, and to his delegate, the priest.
Without confessing their change of front, they said :
"The child belongs to its parents." This was to
return to the old secular and pagan notion; but only
in appearance, for those who reclaimed for the parents
all rights over their children added mentally : in order
to direct these children conformably to the teaching
of God (of the Church).

Strange that this point of view, which should, if
taken as it was carefully set forth, have flattered the
amour propre of parents, left them instead completely
indifferent! In this respect the great effort made by
all the elements of the various Conservative parties,
and attempted, moreover, in complete harmony, was
without success. This fact, which passed unobserved,
is nevertheless a sign of the profound changes going
on in the thought and habits of society.

A similar check has been sustained by a small
number of theorists, who opposed their claims to the
Conservatives, saying : "The child belongs to the
social group."

The response made to both theories by the refusal
of public feeling even to take them into consideration
has not been clearly formulated in any record, but it

L

is formulating itself all the time in facts. In opposition to the old pagan idea—which still inspires many of our laws in that which touches the family—we now admit that the child is not made for its parents, but that it is the parents who are made for the child. The child is a living stone brought to the building of the future. Our tears when a child dies are not all selfish tears, and the transports of procreative love are not a shameful concupiscence of the flesh. The day will come when men will recognise the beauty, the incomparable grandeur, of the communion of bodies; when they will no longer be able to separate it from ineffable communion with the mystery of the worlds. We do not turn our backs on truth, on life and revelation. We come thence and, more truly still, we go thither : we are of truth, of life, of revelation; we even make them, in so far as we enrich the still too restricted domain humanity has created by its labour, tears and love.

Seeing the mistakes of the past, the mistakes of our parents, we lose our pride. We learn to suffer the mistakes of the men around us; we divine that we ourselves are not exempt, and thus become more modest, patient and strong.

The old philosophy taught that it is not worth while to spend one's life in the pursuit of a perfection which is not absolute with the certainty that one will not attain it. That was to traduce human nature, which is much less enraptured with the absolute than some schools of philosophy would have us believe. The labourer is not sure he will harvest the corn he sows. There is something infinitely sweet in planting trees under whose shade we shall not rest. These trees will not be immortal; perhaps next winter's north wind will wither them up. Take heart! Let us plant them, for all that: it is not our concern that they thrive, but that they be planted. Moreover, they will thrive after some fashion; their poor boughs, blackened by frost, shall yet be, for those who come after us, a witness of our faith.

Let us, then, plant trees, sow ideas, shape institutions, as did those who went before us. Far from being hindered by the notion that our strivings will inevitably fall short, let us sustain ourselves with the assurance that they prepare for others, and yet others *ad infinitum;* and that our labour has entered as a harmonious note into the eternal symphony.

. . . . . .

The silence that is generally preserved before those who debate theoretically as to whom the child belongs is worth noting.

It is a mark not, as has been sometimes said, of scepticism in the public or of disinclination to discuss serious matters, but simply of a tendency to see things as they are and to decline to indulge in mere words.

Our people are tired of verbal polemics which do not enlighten the mind and give rise to misunderstandings. They perceive that life draws together and unites.

Last year, on the national holiday, a village mayor in the Cévennes, proposing his toast to the Republic, spoke somewhat after this fashion : " I recall our old teacher, forty years ago, telling us that political life resembled the ascent of a man who is trying to climb towards the summits of the Alps which glisten yonder, higher, always higher. Ours is one of the most advanced communes in the department. I am proud of it, as you are. But let us continue our advance. Who knows if there are not some higher than we, whom we cannot see? It is, however, of those behind we ought, above all, to think. Do not let us throw stones at them, do not let us abuse them. That would be to waste our time. Besides, we should be making them believe a lie; for, at bottom, we love them well. Without them we should not have advanced so quickly. We are proud of our legs, but it is largely emulation which has pushed us forward. And besides, while criticising them and laughing at them sometimes, we feel ourselves their brothers. Where they are now, there were we a few years back. Sooner perhaps than may be thought they will be where we are to-day. You know it is for them as much as for ourselves we are working. We are an advance guard. All credit to us! But we cannot triumph alone; and we would not if we could!

" I conclude as I began, by reminding you of the fine things our worthy old schoolmaster used to tell us of the Republic, one and indivisible; I did not understand them forty years ago, but it seems to me that now I am beginning to; and I raise my glass to those who shall follow us, who will be better servants than we to our Country and Republic."

These simple words, uttered with perfect naturalness in the village market-place, are not exceptional; they indicate the attainment by some of our rural populations to a political and even local conception which exceeds that of " stagnant ponds."

The desire to understand the past is no longer unusual; and even in the mountains, people begin to reverence all its vestiges, of whatever nature, with a kind of pious love toward those who left them.

In such *milieux*, there is in this neither snobbishness nor mercenary preoccupation, but a feeling of historic solidarity and of a love for the local soil that, after seeming a long while as though about to disappear, is manifesting itself anew with unexpected intensity.

No doubt each generation is the daughter of the preceding, but in old days the feeling of filiation only existed among the highest ranks of the social hierarchy, while to-day it is becoming general and changing its content: modelling itself on scientific tendencies, and instead of showing us the ideal far behind, revealing it now before us, won hour by hour not by a monotonously repetitive toil, but by an effort which is ceaseless creation and perpetual progress.

The Church spoke to us of tradition and its value in religious teaching; life discovers to us the power of tradition in every domain, and while showing us what we are, suggests what we should and may become.

Realising our solidarity with the past, we are brought to see that evolution may be fulfilled by very various ways; that it may be achieved in a direction we call good, and that we can help it to set forth, persist, and more rapidly and surely advance therein.

From this we may derive all the features of an entirely undenominational morality which owes too much to its seniors to make war upon them, and feels itself neither poor nor insecure.

Realising the endeavour which runs through history, and indeed constitutes it, we unite ourselves to it with all our might; we offer ourselves to it, and

feel that in this sacrifice we are acting as the citizens
of a city both present and eternal.

Is not this a new faith—a Religion that does not
come, cross-bow on shoulder, to decapitate statues
or defile sanctuaries, but will frequent these as one
who loves them more and better than those who
naïvely imagined themselves their owners? She will
not drive them away, but will make their holy places
yet more precious to them by telling them their
history: no dead history, no catalogue of the names
of problematical architects, lists of unknown bishops,
enumerations of questionable relics, fragments of
charters, bulls and edicts, but the living history
wherein the cathedral is seen springing from the
ground, in a whole city's superb ardour of faith, the
religious affirmation of God's commonalty trembling
with ineffable love for her who said:

> " Fecit potentiam in brachio suo,
>   dispersit superbos mente cordis sui ;
> Deposuit potentes de sede,
>   et exaltavit humiles ;
> Esurientes implevit bonis
>   et divites dimisit inanes." [1]

Thus the originality and power of the present
religious orientation is seen to be due to its proceeding from life and reality, and to its essentially
social and even solidary character.

[1] Luke i. 51–53.—R.V. :

" He hath shewed strength with his arm ;
He hath scattered the proud in the imagination of their heart.
He hath put down princes from *their* thrones,
And hath exalted them of low degree.
The hungry he hath filled with good things ;
And the rich he hath sent empty away."

CHAPTER X

The unity of France is not chiefly political—How it expresses
itself in the movement we are studying—Moderate enthusiasm
of our country for industrial and commercial success—Our
present religious orientation not of foreign origin—France
unable to enter into intimate relation with the German mentality, whether political or theological—Renan the precursor of
present tendencies—Dr. Harnack—Manifesto of a broad-
minded German pastor who proclaims the piety that may
exist among Atheists—Why " unconscious Christianity " would
have no success in France.

BEGOTTEN, not created; such, when we seek its
sources, is the clearly marked quality of the orientation we are engaged upon. It is born on the soil of
France, and results from the toil, the thought and
spiritual activity of our whole country seeking out
its way.

Considered aright, our national unity was never
so strongly affirmed, for it infinitely exceeds a terri-
torial unity cemented upon battle-fields; it exceeds
the unity of customs, civilisation and politics, which
already in the Middle Ages had set our knights
dreaming of *la douce France;* it is again becoming
that unity of ideal striving which it was in the
thirteenth century and at some moments in the
Revolution. In every age nations have been seen

to rise up as one man before the enemy, finding in
the common danger a cohesion they had not known
before. The union of France at the present moment
is of quite another character : her children press close
to one another not for defence or attack, but for
understanding, for labour, in the desire to realise
something already present in them all, which is,
nevertheless, still to come.

I have already endeavoured to indicate the feelings
we cherish in respect to Germany. As to the friendship we feel for our other neighbours, it is no vain
word, but corresponds to a profound reality. Our
diplomacy, by concluding " *ententes cordiales*," has
only followed opinion which goes beyond what official
relations stipulate.

One has but to open one's eyes to see that the
movement carrying us toward other nations is
as a rule entirely disinterested. Eminent publicists
who flash in our eyes the commercial successes we
might attain here or there by methodical activity
remain, as a rule, amazed at our indifference to the
world of which they talk. That is because much
more than utilitarian interest is needed to set a whole
people repeating that dictum of the poet-philoso-
pher : " *Homo sum: humani nihil a me alienum
puto*," and saying it over with the fulness of feeling
that Terence himself put into it.

Family unity is not created by community of
material interest. The necessity for a common
struggle, good sense, custom and instinct itself would
not suffice. All these are needed, but something
more : the common search for an ideal, and the
common worship of that ideal. Now it is just this
that our country is at this moment essaying, through

ESSENTIALLY FRENCH 153

inevitable mistakes and innumerable misunderstandings.

Even the form of government influences this state of mind. Under the old regime, national unity was realised after a fashion in the king's person. To serve the king was to serve France. The disappearance of royalty, far from striking a fatal blow at unity, on the contrary fortified it. Every citizen was led to realise what united him to the national community.

And it is because this spiritual unity is completely realised that we reach a stage from which this unity can envisage new problems—international relations, for example—and examine without political preoccupations peace, war, commercial interests, etc.

People are sometimes amazed at the extreme indulgence of the juries at assizes in cases of anti-militarism. Instead of being shocked and giving fantastical interpretations of these acquittals, it would be better to try to understand them. It would soon be seen that the plain citizens composing the juries have not chosen to apply to the accused laws which no longer correspond to our condition. They do not wish to endorse certain anti-militarist follies, but no more do they wish to mistake the excellent feelings whereof these follies are but the hasty, ill-considered consequence. Constantly in contact with social preoccupations in the most varied circles, these men recognise that among many of our contemporaries —Conservative just as much as Radical—there is an unhealthy exaltation, a kind of religious intoxication. Their clemency is no endorsement: it signifies that prison is by far too primitive a cure for certain aberrations whose origin is a generous one; it also signifies that these aberrations are bound up with crises of conscience, with very profound views of faith which are eminently worthy of respect. They refuse to judge in cases which look to them like trials for heresy.

.   .   .   .   .   .

In the spiritual situation of France there is, then, at the moment, something extraordinary and incommunicable. The glance we are now casting over its life is especially directed to those gropings, so difficult to characterise; those often disordered velleities; those accesses of mysticism in non-mystical individuals, followed by discomfort, sudden faintness and fits of depression—all those traits which cause our country to be at times so misjudged, even by her best friends.

This feverish state was never so characteristic as to-day; and if behind the words we try to grasp the realities, we shall see that this sickness proceeds from a spiritual crisis. For there are several ways of being religious: one consists in belonging to a Church, obeying it, making moral and material sacrifices for it; while another consists not in giving religion its share, but in desiring to quicken with it the whole of our activity.

Between the man who devotes his life to the increase of his wealth, but gives a generous tithe to his Church, making himself the good providence of the parish priest—between him and the unbeliever who ignores priest and Church, but cultivates his mind and makes no least effort to enrich himself, how are we to decide which is the more religious?

The economists who despair over the miscarriage of their efforts to persuade France that she must needs launch into great commercial enterprises and create industries, seem never to have dreamed of one of the reasons why they so often agitate themselves in vain : that there is a commercial and industrial prosperity of which we have no desire. There are certain forms of material success which are not worth the trouble of winning, even when they are respectable. And how often they are not! Doubtless poverty is not synonymous with virtue, but there is a disdain of money which really is the beginning of wisdom, faith and freedom.

The poverty of the Latin lands is much talked of. Those who alarm themselves about it would, however, do well to inquire if it be not for nations what it has so often been for individuals—the mark of election.

However that may be, one of the essential characteristics of the religious orientation of France to-day is that it cannot be isolated from the political and intellectual life of the nation. It would be quite otherwise if it were one of those foreign importations which have abounded in our country. If it were a matter, for instance, of studying such a movement as Spiritualism, an almost daily outline of its progress could be made; the part played by its founders could be marked out, and that of its recruits; its crises, conquests, miscarriages and all the rest could be indicated. All that would, on the whole, be easy. A somewhat expert patience would be sufficient for the task, because there is no point of contact between French thought and the new doctrines. Their history consists of a succession of episodes. In the religious movement it is, on the contrary, a matter of often invisible currents which create an unexpected atmosphere in our spiritual life.

Scientific views, or a metaphysical system, may be borrowed from a neighbouring nation; but a nation cannot be asked to respond to preoccupations other than its own, or to point out the right way on paths it has not travelled. By a curious coincidence, it is at the very moment when France has become more than ever eager to understand other nations, to maintain fruitful relations with them—at this very moment that she must solve problems in which her sisters can be of no assistance to her.

We have seen above how, after having exhibited her enthusiasm with manifest goodwill for every foreign literature and philosophy, France has at last been compelled to fall back upon herself.

She could not go to Germany to seek example and inspiration; that nation had, naturally, the mentality of a conquering people, widely different from that of a conquered people, especially when the conquered was not hypnotised by the longing for vengeance.[1]

---

[1] Bismarck's influence has been no more potent in France than Nietzsche's. His Will to Power (*Wille zur Macht*) has remained as foreign to us as the imperialistic spirit that succeeded him. The idea of brutal revenge has never, even at our moment of greatest suffering, been more with us than a kind of physical return shock. To-day that is all past : it was replaced, first, by an intuitive feeling of the profound labour which is achieved in civilisation, and soon this vague sentiment became transformed into a more conscious choosing of that which it followed. The physical suffering of former days has become ethical and more intense. Those who suffer for the sake of Germany, seeing this great and noble nation assume an attitude other than that of her better self, become more and more numerous.

In speaking thus, I am thinking of certain manifestations which unfortunately made more stir in Europe than the severe criticism they evoked from representative men in Germany itself. In reply to the blustering declarations of Dr. Stengel, of Munich, Professor

By the side of this political mentality our eastern neighbours had another also, that of theologians in general and exegetists in particular; but in this direction again we had not been prepared to profit by the lessons they were so much disposed to give us and which we were so eager to receive.[1]

Köhler, Dean of the Law Faculty at Berlin, wrote in the *Zeitschrift für Völkerrecht und Bundesstattenrecht*, of which he was (1910) the editor, an article entitled *The Pacifist Movement and International Law*, which one would like to quote entire : " When a Dutchman or a Belgian," he there said, " undertakes to justify war, it has no political importance and may simply be neglected. But when Germans, at a time of extreme political tension, make similar manifestations, they may greatly prejudice our cause. Declarations of this kind contribute more than anything else to support the suspicion which, as I am personally convinced, other peoples entertain with regard to us. As though our love of peace were not sincere, as though we had no other aim than to attack and crush other nations under the superiority of our arms ! Arguments such as ' We are hemmed in by foes,' are corrected by ' We are surrounded by civilised peoples of whom none desire war, and we desire it even less.' This is why it is in the highest degree impolitic to assign as the ideal of our activity the affirmation of the national will against the tendency of nations to associate together juridically. The foreigner would be justified by this in pointing to Germany as a State which refuses to adapt herself to the community of nations, and would feel an increase of that antipathy from which we suffer. The dictum *Oderint dum metuant* is a false political principle. With such maxims have the distrust and suspicion been sown, and that anti-German nervousness excited which we have observed—myself in England, and Professor Manes even in the Australian Colonies."

[1] I cannot resist the pleasure of laying before my readers' eyes a page in which Dr. H. Weinel summarises the tendencies of the Protestant scientific élite of his country (*Hibbert Journal*, July 1909, pp. 730–2) : " What unites us all is not so much our method as a strong and common determination to apply our studies to the service of life, to rescue Christianity from its state of isolation in regard to the modern world, and to put our fellow-countrymen

The admirable exegetical effort of Germany only carries its full value in the country of its birth. There it has developed with wonderful fecundity, because it was necessary there. Germany, a Protestant country, had given the Bible an importance which it never had in Latin lands. In these it has never been placed outside history, nor regarded as the sole authority in matters of faith.

The eagerness with which its theologians have devoted themselves to exegesis is not the outcome of a passion for erudition; at the last analysis, it springs from the need to free themselves from the

once more in possession of its best elements, its eternal content, which amid the vast technical and intellectual development of the last centuries it had almost lost. We are all agreed in an unconditional and unreserved recognition, that the ultimate foundations of our modern theory of the universe are to be sought in Nature and History. We have seriously embraced the conviction that the notion of miracle cannot be introduced any more into science or into history. We have all admitted into our work the great scientific idea of evolution, and we confront the results of science with entire impartiality, accepting them all without prejudice. We have abandoned not only the old proofs of the existence of God, but also the attempt to build any purely metaphysical foundation for religion ; seeking the basis of our faith in God, with Kant and Schleiermacher, in quite other provinces of life. We believe that God meets us in the persons of those great men who are the active agents in evolution, the creators of ideals and the prophets of the unknown Deity."

I would like to quote it all, but what has just been read is enough to indicate at least the direction of present-day German thought. Unhappily these views are those of a minority even among the few.

Those who read the rest of the article will see that there is a kind of melancholy brooding over the whole of this profession of faith.

The French movement we are studying is less conscious of itself, but it is not the affair of the few, it is of the people—it is, above all, of the people.

yoke of a book, and to set it back again amid the current of the evolution of human thought as an historic record.

In France only the very small Protestant minority finds itself in a similar intellectual religious condition. This, then, was interested in the exegetical literature, while other French circles of thought, just as naturally, continued to ignore it.

To see in our exegetical indifference a kind of scepticism or indolence would, therefore, be exaggerated. It arose simply from the fact that we have not had to tear out of our hearts and minds the narrow standpoint of the Reformation, which has made of the Bible the definitive and absolute Revelation.

Neither the enthusiasm nor the fury which in Germany greeted Dr. A. Drews' book, *The Christ Myth*,[1] would be understood among us, for the good reason that Liberal-Protestant theology is as foreign to our thought as Lutheran or Calvinist dogmatics.[2]

---

[1] Arthur Drews : *Die Christusmythe*, Leipzig, 1909.

[2] Those who would get an exact idea of the present orientation of thought in Germany have a guide of the first order in the very remarkable work of M. Henri Lichtenberger, *L'Allemagne moderne, son évolution*, Paris, 1907. [An English translation has recently appeared.—TRANS.] For what concerns exclusively religious thought two studies from a different point of view must be mentioned : one, M. G. G. Lapeyre's *Mouvement religieux dans les pays de langue allemande*, in the *Revue du clergé français* for Jan. 1 and Feb. 1, 1911 ; the other by Dr. Weinel, Professor of Theology in the University of Jena, *Religious Life and Thought in Germany To-day*, in the *Hibbert Journal* for July 1909.

In *Noris, Jahrbuch für protestantische Kultur*, which has appeared annually since 1908, at Nuremberg, under the management of Dr. Hans Pöhlmann, will be found a kind of well-documented self-examination of the spiritual life of Protestant Germany.

It is no good!—the labours that appear most objective will always answer, at the end of the reckoning, to some subjective preoccupation. Our admiration for the monuments upon which German exegesis very rightly prides itself is mingled with a vague wonder. Our neighbours, moreover, have no more comprehension of Renan's work; and it is perfectly natural, since he was not inspired in the slightest degree by the ecclesiastical preoccupations—whether conscious or no—which have directed the scientific activity of theologians beyond the Rhine. He is treated as a literary man, even indeed as an amateur, without realisation of the fact that the theological disinterestedness with which he is so much reproached is a pledge of the serenity and independence of his outlook.

Renan's work, even from the scientific point of view, was substantial enough for it still to make a very good figure to-day, after so many thousands of books devoted to the same questions. Where the great writer is entirely happy is in his inspiration, in the vision he had of the incomparable value for our civilisation of the Christian current of thought : and in his persuasion that, in the interests of science as much as of religion, the history of religious feeling must be incorporated in general history and treated by the same methods.

By the tact and pious love which he brought to his labours, he was perhaps the most efficient herald of the present movement. The various orthodoxies only felt hatred and fury towards him : they could comprehend nothing either of the man or of the success which his work met with. With disconcerting persistence they were to be seen seeking in Renan the spiritual son of Voltaire, and admitting the disdain of certain jealous scholars as a definitive judgment when they wished to judge his works from the scientific point of view.

.   .   .   .   .   .

I have felt obliged to recall these facts to show how difficult it is for one people to understand the worth and significance of works which, while very important for its neighbours, do not answer to its own needs.

The noble figure of Dr. Harnack inspires the most respectful sympathy and sincere admiration among all the élite of France. Yet these feelings do not resolve themselves into a community of sentiment and effort because—except, naturally, in Protestant circles—the vast majority of our fellow-citizens have eliminated [1] the very idea of dogma, and so find themselves far to the radical Left, if one may so speak, of the celebrated theologian. At the same time, they find themselves far to his Right also, because many things which Dr. Harnack's thought does not assimilate, and which, remaining foreign to his intellect, remain also outside his vision, have for us, on the contrary, a high pragmatical and sentimental value.

In other words, minds that, in Germany and France, would seem made to understand one another have really quite a different orientation. While German theologians cultivate the field of exegesis with wonderful perseverance, and with the evident purpose of setting up traditional dogma once again, or of attaining a new one, the French mind of to-day

[1] They eliminate it the more decisively as the number of dogmas proposed to them is reduced.

M

finds the great reality in history, and seeks to understand it that it may live in harmony therewith.

The distance that separates this attitude of soul
from the Church of Rome is far less than that which
separates it from every Protestant theology : indeed,
Catholicism, in demanding adhesion to the Church,
speaks of a concrete institution, visible and living,
whose plastic and evolutive energy every one may
ascertain. Protestant theologians, on the contrary,
bind their pupils to postulates which have no basis
in history (Biblical revelation, divine paternity, sin,
redemption, etc.), momentary results of individual
positions without contact with the average conscience.

Neither French Catholicism nor French Protestantism could dream of seeking fruitful lessons across the
Rhine. If the former had allowed itself to be at
last persuaded by Pius X to form a sort of French
Centre,[1] the abundant unpopularity which clericalism

---

[1] A few moments after reading the dispatch brought him by
Cardinal Merry del Val, in which the recall of the French Republic's
ambassador to the Holy See was announced, Pius X accorded
a long audience to one of our fellow-countrymen, and, with a
familiarity which since then he has lost, declared that France
was being led to her ruin by a minority of sectaries, that there
only remained one means of salvation, to wit, the formation of
a party of upright men, after the fashion of the German Centre,
which should conform to the instructions of " Our Holy Emperor
William."

Evidently the Sovereign Pontiff was led to these views by the
conception he had formed of authority ; and he, who had taken
his seat in the Chair of St. Peter with the firm purpose of being
a " pious pope," did not even perceive that he was giving an
essentially political orientation to Catholicism.

To interpret the preceding words in a narrow and brutal sense,
as if Pius X, forgetful of his rôle as supreme shepherd of all the
sheep, had not the same love for all, would be a foolish mistake.
But it is not less true that, by seeing a kind of model and ideal in

already enjoyed would have grown as much more formidable as the attempt might for the moment have achieved a measure of success.

As to German Protestantism, if the crisis through which it is passing is all to its honour, showing it a-thirst for truth and for sincerity, and eager to go through with its thought, none the less it is above all things a logical and negative evolution, similar to that of French Protestantism. This, far indeed from finding help beyond the Rhine, only sees there the ravages of an epidemic analogous to that which decimates itself.

"The situation of Christianity in Germany [1] seems disquieting to-day. Despite the labour and devotion put forth on every side, it is evident that the masses of the people are not being made religious or Christian. Even the most recent German theology—which abandons every vulnerable position of the old

---

the organisation of the German Centre, the present Head of the Church linked its fate with an essentially political notion.

If a French Centre came to be constituted, and if, by its discipline, it became the arbiter of the country's political life, there would be such an outburst of public opinion against this confounding of religion and politics that the old Catholic and idealist leaven which remains in the hearts of most of our fellow-citizens would suddenly manifest its presence and power, and would discover, in its indignation, creative forces we do not suspect. But it is probable that on this point Pius X will entirely fail.

An effort made a few years ago, to create a "party of God," broke itself against the almost unanimous passive resistance of the representative Catholic elements. To-day there is no vestige of it except a weekly paper almost without subscribers : Count Xavier de Cathelineau's *L'Entente catholique* (Offices, 152 rue Montmartre, Paris, II).

[1] Dr. Friedrich Reinhard in the *Christliche Welt* for Aug. 18, 1910, the most widely-read religious paper in Germany.

believers—even the modern way of conceiving the cure of souls, which avoids any humiliating alms-giving and all ecclesiastical procedure—has not succeeded, as was everywhere anticipated.

" There is something worse. The youngest German theologians seem to be almost devoid of large directing ideas or of clear plans which would show their trust in the future. Theology as a whole goes on spiritlessly in the old paths. Sometimes some one really wants to adopt some new philosophic dress, but in the end it is always recognised as an old one, which was worn and cast aside a century ago. What is more, sometimes the best men are mistaken in primary matters. The picture of Jesus wavers with less certainty than ever in history, despite the brilliant refutations directed against Arthur Drews. They are but few who, on such insecure ground, find courage to go forward with confidence to meet the future.

" In this situation, many lose the taste for theology and the Church, quietly leave the Christian camp, and enter into relations with all kinds of people who hold aloof from Christianity, and who, eager for action, set forth to conquer. They are to be seen at work in the *Dürerbund* or in the *Mutterschutz*. They are to be seen around Drews and the Monists. They are to be seen going among the workmen, among the young men, and talking to them of Goethe and Kant, of the Descent of Man, of marriage and alcohol ; but no longer of God, scarcely even of Jesus or of Luther. Is not this the beginning of the end ? Was not Pius X right when he saw the torrent which formerly rushed out of a lake, well banked-up by the Church, going to waste with us in the sandy desert of atheism ? And are not the groups of the

Evangelical Church which remain attached to the old tradition right when they say of the partisans of progress, 'It is your fault! Why did you abandon the pure Gospel'?

"And indeed it is undeniable that German Liberal Christianity has, during these last years, developed strongly in the direction of atheism; that, in the very heart of our Christianity, there has been a perceptible neglect of God and of divine things: there has been less preaching on these subjects; and perhaps also, less entering into secret communion with Him; more absorption instead, in other forms of Christian or non-Christian activity. Think alone of those great examples of the modern German Christian spirit—Frenssen, Naumann, Johannes Müller; with striking accord they have all three withdrawn further each year from the specifically Christian manner of thinking and living.

"All this alarms and disturbs many. But we have courage to see in these circumstances which seem so grave, a very happy turn of events, the promise of a great new era."

The writer proceeds with fine enthusiasm to show the reasons for his confidence. He then makes statements very similar to those which may be made in France: to wit, that atheism is often only a higher form of religion, that in the midst of the noisy de-Christianisation of our time there is a great *urge of unconscious Christianity*.

All this is most interesting, and seems the less extraordinary to us that religious irreligion is so common in France. But what interests us just now is the situation of Protestantism in Germany.

Although the religion of the majority, and in a
great number of the Confederated States the State
Religion, it is very nearly in the same position as
is Protestantism in France : it reminds one of a sort
of Babel, of indescribable confusion, in which every
one distracts his mind by shouting; in which tiny
groups declare themselves certain of victory at the
very moment when they show themselves most alien
to the powerful currents of the new age.

We will not, then, inquire whether there is not
something naïve in the eagerness with which Dr.
Reinhard prepares to baptise with Christian and
Protestant names all the good that is being done
by unbelievers.

> " . . . Vous leur fîtes, Seigneur,
>   En les croquant, beaucoup d'honneur." [1]

He has obviously the best intentions in the world;
and in Protestant circles in our country there may
be individuals ready to take a similar attitude : but
if you observe it well, this attitude will scarcely be
found to resemble that of French democracy to-day,
making towards a new ideal.

The tendency to exalt national sentiments to the
profit of a Church; the exaggerated generosity
addressed to those whom one desires to win over;
the entire contempt for institutions which, though
doubtless very imperfect, have yet done what they
might; and finally, the ecclesiastical bent of mind
which only regards history as a means of establishing
certain theological dogmas—these turn an interesting
manifesto into the testament of a social group anxious

---

[1] " . . . Lord, you do them great honour, crunching them."

not to die, rather than the inspired word of an apostolate interpreting the irresistible feelings of its contemporaries. Were those pages read in Paris, in undenominational circles, some of them would be loudly applauded; but the whole would probably seem to be a clever—though perhaps an unconsciously clever—effort to recapture control over men's minds.

At the present moment our people is athirst for idealism, justice, union, progress and disinterestedness: it longs to put them not into speech, but into action: it loves not the abstract man, but the men whom it meets in the street, or about whom it thinks without dwelling on all the divergences which separate them from it. Even for the criminal it is coming to have stores of compassion, and in this respect goes so far as to compromise its own security. It loves, without knowing why: which is still the best—perhaps the only—way of loving.

In the page we were just now reading the sentiment is not precisely this. The miscreant is loved, but with self-complaisance; what is more, there is an ulterior purpose in this love: he is loved for the sake of a metaphysical entity one would fain create, and of which one speaks with a kind of mystical exaltation: "Whatever the *Church* may decide, one thing is certain—the *School*, which is already full of the new movement, will soon be entirely conquered by that movement. Then we shall have attained what the best among us have long desired, and what the teachers also come more and more to regard as their highest and noblest purpose: our youth will be put in possession of the German spiritual patrimony *in its unity*, a patrimony which, in fact, is already everywhere in existence among us. . . . Then, from these schools, will issue the *new* German Empire, truly one, which is yet to found. These schools alone can create the great *single German culture*, after which we are all longing as parched fields long for water under a burning sun."

The undenominational religious movement in France also gives rise to many dreams and prophecies. But none of them would be found analogous in its import, *mutatis mutandis*, to Dr. Reinhard's hopes.

.   .   .   .   .

It is the custom abroad, and even among ourselves, to regard the French as essentially intellectual : by sheer repetition we have almost come to believe this. The mistake—for mistake it is—is doubtless due to the influence exercised abroad by some of our eighteenth-century philosophers. Perhaps it is the consequence also of a rather simplistic reasoning : France to-day is the daughter of the Revolution; and that was the work of eighteenth-century philosophy. The conclusion is plain. . . . But we really honour the Encyclopædists too much when we regard them as the fathers of the Revolution. We are the result of a strangely longer tradition; and if we have not always supposed so, we are coming to perceive it more and more. The effort to rediscover our true tradition is the special characteristic of our present thought; it is the direct opposite of an intellectualism which isolates itself from facts.

.   .   .   .   .

We hope our insistence in showing that a new religious feeling, influenced by the thought-currents of neighbouring lands, is about to blossom in our country may not be misunderstood. We have been

at pains to indicate, also, that it is no more a consequence of triumphant philosophic and scientific
currents nearer at hand.

It would indeed be a gross mistake to isolate the
French thought of to-day, as though it had no contact
with such men as Newman, James, Walt Whitman,
Tyrrell, Sir Oliver Lodge, Fogazzaro, Flournoy,
Tröltsch and Eucken, and was not in continual
spiritual commerce with them. The choice of the
Nobel Prize Committee in 1908, when it awarded
that high distinction to the venerable head of the
School of Jena,[1] was applauded in France with veritable delight. The various publications of the eminent
idealist have legitimately provoked long discussion
amongst us, for he, too, speaks the language of the
new thought, always bringing us, as prime element,
to a statement of fact, to the independent life of the
spirit, which exceeds human consciousness though it
first manifests itself in the conscious man. As M.
Boutroux puts it,[2] "Eucken's merit is to have
effectually, it would seem, determined the way by
which the spirit may realise itself in its originality,
not in spite of its union with material realities, but
thanks to that very union."

If we were writing a history of philosophical ideas
in France at the present moment, we should have to
devote a chapter to each of the eminent men we have

[1] One of Dr. R. Eucken's most important works has been recently translated into French by MM. Buriot and Luquet, with
a preface by M. Boutroux : *Les Grands courants de la pensée
contemporaines*, Paris, 1911.

The most important of his other works, from our point of view,
are the *Wahrheitsgehalt der Religion* and the *Hauptprobleme der
Religionsphilosophie*, 1907.

[2] In the preface mentioned in the preceding note.

named, and to many another besides; but it is well understood that our ambition is not so lofty: without pausing, as we are fain to do, in the *templa serena* where a chosen few prepare to-morrow's thought, we must everywhere push open the doors of peasant, factory-hand, skilled worker, poet, artist and even priest—of all those who make up the actual social mass, in our endeavour to see if they have an ideal, and if so, what it may be.

CHAPTER XI

ITS MANIFESTATIONS IN CATHOLICISM

Two Catholicisms co-exist in the Church—Her great strength
lies in having created the sentiments of unity and tradition—
Students from Catholic institutions at the lectures of State
professors—Rome's prohibition—Modernism—Administration
of the Church in the hands of a Committee of Public Safety
—Success of the new tendencies—The diocese of Milan accused
of being a nursery of Modernism, just as is the University of
Fribourg (Switzerland)—A page from Father Sertillanges—
Note on *Le Sillon*.

AT the present moment there are two Catholicisms
in France.

Such an assertion will call forth equal protests from
the Catholics who love to call themselves "intransi-
gents" and "integralists," and from militant anti-
clericals.

These bitter foes agree to maintain that there is,
and can be, but one sole Catholicism, which is, above
all, a discipline to be obeyed, and which regards the
Sovereign Pontiff as a kind of incarnation of God.

Fortunately, it is not the purpose of these pages
to meddle in dogmatics, nor even in politics. But if
it is premature to think of performing the work of
a historian upon events occurring under one's eyes,
we would at least try to observe them accurately and
without preconceived notions.

Now, when one considers the Church of Rome, it is

obvious that, if there are not two Churches—any
more than there are two Frances—there are two
Catholicisms: one coming, the other departing. And
it is precisely because there are two Catholicisms—
one already aged, and the other quite young—that
the Church continues alive for all the defeats she has
suffered, and that no prophet has dared to stand up
and predict her ruin.

The two tendencies live side by side, one proceeding out of the other. They may be considered
separately, but the vital bond which unites them
must never be forgotten—a bond altogether similar
to that which unites together the generations of
man.

The Church's great power lies in having understood this bond, and in having by incessant labour
made her children conscious of it. Her symbolism
and liturgy join the ages together in a mysterious
harmony; her discipline aims at calling all the inhabitants of the earth to communicate in the same Host,
and in a single effort.

Let us not be deceived: Tradition is the elder
sister of Evolution. It is, at the very least, its pre-
figuration, as theological language would phrase it;
and it is not to be wondered that many young
Catholics have seen the coincidence of these two ideas.
Refusal to rise to this complete view involves a risk
of seriously misunderstanding the events unfolding
themselves before our eyes, but especially those which
are now preparing.

It is customary in certain circles to imagine you
are writing history when you prepare a list of the
errors of the Church of Rome, and to wonder that a
terrified people does not at once turn with indignation

from the pretended mother who has taught so many errors to her children.

Let us admit that these lists may be made with scrupulous care for historical truth. Their end is rarely achieved, because public good sense vaguely suspects that if they tell the exact truth, yet by isolating it they give it an inexact bearing. The errors of the Middle Ages are no more those of the Church than of the lay society of that period. We have no right to take our inheritance from the past, and, sorting out all its errors, to debit the Church with these, while we credit lay society with all its truths. We are the legitimate sons of those who were mistaken.

Per contra, there is one fact which the Church has made the centre of its teaching, thus preparing our minds and hearts for modern ideas: the fact of the solidarity in time and space of all beings.

Hence, at a time when absolute metaphysics is becoming foreign to the conscience and thought of our generation, some Catholics have found, in the new intellectual orientation, not the reversal of their moral and religious life, but a means of further deepening it, of living it out with greater intensity, greater enthusiasm, and also with greater clairvoyance and intellectual security.

If it is true, as we have shown above, that the essential tendency of the modern spirit is to consider reality in order to try and seize it in all its complexity, dynamism and vitality; if this incessant gaze of science and of present-day thought at phenomena is an act of attention—that natural prayer, as Malebranche said—of work—*i. e.* of participation in a work which outreaches the observer's grasp, and in which he is glad to feel himself a collaborator; if little by little our humblest and most individual action changes into a social act, the consequence of an age-long labour, into which it has found its way; if our present undenominational thought is really this, it must inevitably meet another thought——the Catholic——which, by different paths, is finding its way toward the same goal.

Some ten years ago, certain teachers in our universities did not know what to think when they saw their lectures being followed, with an eagerness rare among students, by groups of young priests. Some members of our universities felt, as it were, confused and embarrassed by the vigour with which these unexpected——and sometimes undesired——auditors welcomed theories which were devoid of any flavour of orthodoxy. The priests were never offended, went on taking notes, and often followed the professor after the lecture to ask for information. They gave evidence of such faith in him, were so open in heart and mind, that in some lectures he would feel himself, as it were, supported by the active sympathy which had grown up between him and the group of his ecclesiastical auditors. Sometimes there was opposition, but it was offered with so much sincerity, and let it be so clearly seen that it concealed no ill-will, nor even any poor-mindedness, but betokened such a desire for unity in a higher truth, that it awakened a cordial response, even among men who are the interpreters of organised free-thought. Here and there orthodox anticlericals began to find this swarming of cassocks at the Sorbonne disturbing.

Pius X, too, was disturbed, and the students of the various Catholic institutes were ordered not to show themselves any more on the premises of the State universities.[1] They obeyed.

There is one bridge less in France, and it was not the undenominational world that blew it up.

But we must see things as they are. If this bridge suddenly disappeared, on an order from Rome, yet it was the Catholic youth who had built it. It is they who renewed under our eyes the ardour and hard-working light-heartedness of St. Bénézet and the *Frères Pontifes*—Bridge-building Brothers—who united the two banks of the Rhône. A cyclone— which the stained glass of Avignon symbolises under the features of an ugly little devil, all black and hairy —might destroy it in a night, but the state of mind which made bridges possible and necessary did not disappear. "The next day," say the good Avignon windows, " St. Bénézet was anew at his post, and the angels of heaven came to bring him stones and to mix his mortar."

We must not overlook this if we would obtain a just idea of what is going on—above all, of what is preparing around us.

There are two Catholicisms : one that builds bridges, another that destroys them. It may perhaps be said that the Pope, who has the sovereign author- ity, being on the side of those who destroy, we

[1] By a circular letter to the Bishops of France in October 1908. By a similar measure Pius X forbade first the Italian, and then the German Catholics to organise interdenominational societies. (See Letter of Pius X to Count Medolago Albani, Nov. 22, 1909, and the *communiqué* in the *Osservatore Romano* for April 23 in the same year.) These documents are only the prelude to general measures, whose details cannot here be enumerated. They are so much the more significant as they run counter to the evident desires of Catholics in the countries concerned.

cannot consider any effort as Catholic which is not inspired and dictated by him.

Are those who speak thus sure that they are disinterested? Are they certain they are not delighted to find a specious reason for escaping the trouble of rectifying their opinions?

A consideration of what occurred during the last years of the nineteenth century leads us to assert that the university incident I have just recalled was not an isolated one, but belonged to a whole body of circumstances which had prepared it—to a profound evolution in the Catholic religious world.

Neither the orders from Rome, nor the desires of certain polemics, can efface the reality. And the reality is this: that the youngest elements of the religious world have for several years been drawn with irresistible eagerness toward the undenominational world, neither to give themselves up to the foe nor to bring him vanquished to the foot of the altar. A new spirit has come to change the attitude in which so many generations had become set.[1]

[1] To obtain an idea of the ensemble, the fulness, force, decision, delicacy, intellectual worth and religious feeling of the new movement, one should read, especially, *Demain*, published at Lyons under the courageous editorship of M. Pierre Jay, from Oct. 27, 1905, to July 26, 1907. It was one of the victims of Pius X's syllabus, dated Wednesday, July 3, 1907. And also *Il Rinnovamenta, rivista critica di idee e di fatti*, founded at Milan under the editorship of Messrs. Aiace Alfieri, Alessandro Casati, and Tomasso Gallarati Scotti, in January 1907—last issue in December 1909. Among the works which constitute a kind of inquiry as to the attitude of the calm, thoughtful and foreseeing among the orthodox must be cited L. Birot, Honorary Vicar-General of Albi, *Le Mouvement religeux*, Paris, 1910, and Dr. Marcel Rifaux, *Les Conditions du retour au catholicisme. Enquête philosophique et religeuse*, Paris, 1907.

These young priests felt themselves strong because there was neither any fear nor any hatred in the bottom of their hearts.

This movement had enjoyed a piece of good fortune rare in these days; it had been able to develop for a long while without attracting the notice of the Press. Unobserved, it could spread and realise itself in every direction. The situation changed when the papers began to call attention to it: from every corner of the horizon ran inquisitive, unemployed, and indeed even uprooted ecclesiastics. Some came to look on, others hoped to glide into the ranks of the young enthusiastic phalanx and succeed in making themselves an important position in it.

The tendency of these young people was so novel that the most varied and opposed circles misunderstood their intentions. Pius X attributed to them a unity, a cohesion and a sort of plan of campaign, and went so far as to imagine them a formidable army which had installed itself in the very heart of the Church to destroy it. Many free-thinkers regarded the movement, without satisfaction, as the periodical renewal of that effort whereby the Church, after having set herself as long as she can athwart all progress, ends, as a last resource, by accepting it. The Protestants were contemptuous: did they not know that any good there might be in the new movement was their own work? Here and there some might propose a friendly bearing; but, once they perceived that the movement would certainly not find its goal in the Churches of the Reformation, they resumed the attitude more natural to them.

The new tendencies required a new name. Pius X charged himself with the solemn baptism, and

N

called them " Modernism." [1]   The name was neither
better nor worse than another.   It is true the Pope
hastened to furnish a description of the new-born,
which was singularly unfaithful to it.   Its intentions,
activity and mentality were all depicted in colours
scarcely corresponding to the reality; but if it was a
bad portrait, there was at least no mistake about the
persons who represented the new movement, so we
were able to correct the mistakes and accept the
name.

To-day, it can scarcely be used without rendering
oneself liable to confusion; some anticlericals and
some Protestants promptly imitated Pius X, and,
without troubling themselves too much about facts
or their observation, they characterised every revolt,
however pitiful, against the hierarchy or against
dogma, as Modernism.

In this way they prepared two results of equal advantage to themselves : on the one hand, they persuaded both themselves and public opinion that the
vast movement which had declared itself in Catholicism and which is transforming it to its foundations,
would culminate either in a mere negation or in some
Protestant groups; and thus, to speak the dialect of
Canaan,[2] they enrich themselves by "spoiling the
Egyptians"; on the other hand, they escape the
necessity of ascertaining all the life revealed by this
intellectual springtime, this new blossoming of moral
energy in the Church they detest.

[1] In the Encyclical *Pascendi dominici gregis* of Sept. 8, 1907,
Yet this appellation was not invented by Pius X, but, as it seems,
by the Jesuit Fathers of the *Civiltà Cattolica*, from whom it was
borrowed by the Pope.   The official French text is reproduced
in extenso in *Les Modernistes*, by Paul Sabatier, 1909, pp. 149–219.

[2] See p. 192, note.

To disinterested witnesses, Modernism is a movement which manifested itself in the Catholic Church at the close of the nineteenth century, noiselessly, without shock, without direction or unity. According to country, circumstance, degree of culture, it has taken on various forms : here philosophical, there historical, farther on strictly exegetical, elsewhere social or political; but in these very different fields it has been quite specially a movement of the clergy, and has been inspired by one dominant idea : that of the incomparable value of religion in general and of Catholicism in particular, as a synthesis of life and progress. To the Modernist, the Church was, of all spiritual societies, that which best realised itself, its own life and its destinies; for him it is the future, because of the marvellous plasticity with which it goes on realising itself. Having assimilated modern thought, the Modernists believed that they discovered in it the features of a new apologetic, which, after giving splendid scope to their personal faith, added thereto the hope that it would find an answer to the uncertainty, the agonised questionings of the modern conscience. Hence, in history and in their intimate experiences, the Church appeared to them not as a society which had reached its goal, but as a society on the march.

With a generous impulse they drew towards all their fellow-citizens, always ready to receive as they were always ready to give. And to the timorous, who bade them beware, they answered, " All truth is orthodox."

Thus Modernism in nowise represented an epidemic of disillusion or discouragement, still less a conspiracy of mutineers to organise a gigantic movement of desertion.

The condemnation pronounced by Pius X only struck at a phantom. If, to soften the chagrin of the sovereign pontiff, some insignificant papers announced, on the day after the Encyclical *Pascendi*, that Modernism was dead, they have had since then many an occasion to recognise their mistake.

The Pope, subjected to the logic which in 1793 caused the fall of a greater and greater number of the heads of suspected persons, was driven each day to strengthen the anti-modernist organisation and to pronounce new condemnations.

If one were to draw up a list of the ecclesiastics who at the end of Leo XIII's pontificate seemed to be the men on whom the Church must count for the future, one would find hardly one in ten of these who has not since that time been struck at, in some way or other, by the Supreme Authority.

And this effort, which was certainly very grievous to the heart of Pius X, but which he regarded as an imprescriptible obligation, has remained without result.

Must we cite a definite case? After the Encyclical *Pascendi*, the seminary of Perugia, one of the most flourishing in Italy, found itself, despite all prescribed precautions, invaded by the new spirit. Its professors were abruptly changed. Then, in the spring of 1910, the Archbishop himself, Mgr. Mattei-Gentili, accused of being insufficiently energetic in repression, was asked to resign. Finally, the germination of the new ideas not having been thwarted, the Holy See, in November 1910, took an unheard-of decision : it suppressed this seminary, which Leo XIII had regarded as "the most precious jewel in his tiara."

As I write these lines it is Milan, the great metropolis of Northern Italy, that is being denounced as a centre of Modernism.   Cardinal Ferrari has protested in a letter to his diocese.[1]   The Pope has made no response to the Cardinal, whose manifesto must, however, have reached the shores of the Tiber;[2] but he has congratulated the vigilant sentinels who opened the fire of revelations, and has sent them an order, whose imperial clarity our readers will admire : " Spare neither powder nor cartridges! "[3]

Such facts show how the most improbable things may yet be true.   The administration of the Church is in the hands of a kind of Committee of Public Safety, by whom individuals, without responsibility or mandate, are substituted for the episcopate, make it tremble, and lord it over the Catholic world.[4]

We cannot think of going into all this in detail, nor of showing how the reform of the Roman Con-

[1] Inserted in the *Rivista diocesana Milanese* of Jan. 1911, pp. 5–24.

[2] The whole episcopate of Lombardy has, since then, joined its protest to that of its metropolitan by a collective letter published in the *Corriere della Sera* for March 2, 1911.

[3] *Riscossa* (published at Braganza, province of Vicenza), Feb. 4, 1911.   Adding impertinence to its threats this same paper, a week later, gave as a title for its first article the proverb

" Milan può far, Milan può dir
Ma non può far dell' acqua vin.

" Milan (*i. e.* the Cardinal-Archbishop) acted vainly, Milan spoke in vain, he cannot turn water into wine."

[4] I have thought it right to choose events which occurred in Italy, although in France there have been many as grave, because it may be supposed that Pius X would only know of the latter through the information of agents and officers of surveillance, ill-affected towards our country.   Perugia and Milan, on the contrary, are two Archbishoprics known directly to the former Patriarch of Venice.

gregations—*i. e.* of the various Ministries of the
Holy See—has resulted in placing all the strings of
the management of the Church in the hands of the
single Cardinal Merry del Val. Monsignor Montagnini, the author of certain papers whose publication recently moved public opinion [1] in so lively a
fashion, and Monsignor Benigni, director of a famous
paper in whose success no one would believe had they
not the proofs under their eyes—both work on the
Board.[2]

But these facts, though they are big with consequences both near and distant, do not enter into the
compass of our study. They are ecclesiastical, not
religious facts. We had, however, to allude to them,
for they represent the reaction from a panic in
religious life. Absolute as the authority of the
sovereign pontiff may be in theory, in reality it is
bounded, corrected, dammed up at every moment,
by traditions, customs and influences. The abrupt
substitution of a group of audacious place-seekers
(*arrivistes*) for an administration as complex, leisurely
and prudent as that of the Holy See had been

[1] See *Les Fiches pontificales de Mgr. Montagnini, ex-auditeur
de l'ancienne nonciature à Paris.—Depêches, réponses et notes historiques,* Paris, 1908.
I had an opportunity of stating all this at somewhat greater
length when this regime was only beginning; and in noting the
rôle given by Pius X from the first days of his pontificate to certain
journals specially employed in delation, I noted the slope down
which authority would be hurried. (See *Les Modernistes,* pp. xxii,
n. 1; 10, n. 1; 41; 58, n. 1; 221; 224; 225.)

[2] Concerning *La Correspondance de Rome* (the new title for
La Corrispondenza Romana), there is a study rich in precise and
well-verified facts in M. Maurice Pernot's remarkable volume
La Politique de Pie X, Paris, 1910 (with preface by M. Émile
Boutroux), pp. 254–97.

hitherto, was only possible as a consequence of the confusion and alarm with which authority had been seized on perceiving that Catholicism was about to be transformed, and that the new thought had crept in everywhere.

We will not do this authority the wrong of supposing it would not have employed other means than terrorisation and violence if such had been at its disposal. Silence is not imposed upon a child by threatening to fling it into the street and leave it there to die of hunger : still less is silence thus imposed upon a people spread over the whole world.

The more Pius X perseveres in the struggle to the death on which he has set forth, the more we see him driven to take measures which can only hasten the transformation of the Church. In Rome it has been clearly seen that every scientific institution is destined sooner or later to become a bulwark for the new tendencies; and it is openly confessed that the international scientific centres, founded with a view to their being impregnable fortresses of orthodoxy, have to-day become centres of Modernism.

If Modernism is as strong as they say at the Catholic University of Fribourg, for instance,[1] this simply arises from its teachers toiling and striving to respond to the preoccupations of their students; and if an army of Vatican gardeners does not arrive in spring to root out every plant from the *Cour St. Damase*, no one in the world—not even the persistent Pius X—will be able to cut off all the buds which,

---

[1] See *La Libre parole* of Jan. 29, 1911; *La Croix* for Feb. 5; *L'Entente catholique* of Jan. 1, 1911; and especially *La Critique du libéralisme* of the Abbé Emmanuel Barbier (formerly of the Company of Jesus), Vol. V. p. 486 *et seq.*, Jan. 15, 1911, 601, I.

little by little, have announced the rising of the new
sap at every point in Christendom.

Modernism is present everywhere; nothing has
been able to stay its course. Already its adversaries
have been compelled to form the hierarchy into a
sort of body of police [1] which must watch with
perpetual fear lest there be weakness, complaisance,
infidelity—nay, even betrayal. The best-informed
police organisation has never been anything but a
very precarious safeguard for political regimes which
had no other means of government. It has had no
better success in the Church, and only compromises
the honour of those who have recourse to it for a
spiritual task.

Once on this path, the force of things leads to precautions both useless and puerile. What are we to
think when we see Pius X forbidding the seminarists
—those who will to-morrow be directors of conscience—to read any periodicals, even the best? [2]

Be it as it may, one would have a very false notion
of present-day Catholicism if one only beheld it in
the official, officious documents of the Holy See.

---

[1] By the Bull *Pascendi*, Pius X originated *conseils de vigilance*
(§ 149–51), but these do not see everything, and the *censeurs
d'office* are not infallible. Even those of Rome have, it would
seem, shown culpable indulgence for gross errors. (See *Armonie
della Fede*, for March 25, 1909.) *Quis custodiet custodes ?*

[2] We must quote the text : "*Ne juvenes aliis quæstionibus con-
sectandis tempus terant et a studio præcipuo distrahantur omnino
vetamus diaria quævis aut commentaria, quantumvis optima, ab
iisdem legi, onerata moderatorum conscientia qui ne id accidat religiose
non caverint.*"—Motu proprio, *Sacrorum Antistitum*, Sept. 1, 1910.
Acta apostolica sedis, Vol. II, p. 668. See also the reply to the
Hungarian episcopate, which had asked for elucidations as to this
passage.—*Ibid.*, p. 855.

There is perhaps no *milieu* wherein religious evolution has been so potently at work.

Father Sertillanges, the Dominican, and Professor in the Catholic Institute of Paris, concludes a recent work on the prince of scholasticism by a page which is worth quoting :

" In the brief space of a life so prodigiously full—scarcely thirty years—St. Thomas lived out his system, in certain parts, at the least, under more than one recognisable form.   The St. Thomas of the Sentences is not he of the *Summa Theologiæ*.   One proceeds from the other, but they are not identical. If he had lived seven centuries, can it be supposed that, with that miraculous fecundity of spirit, the *Aquinate* would have been ceaselessly repeated?   He who took so much from Aristotle, from Plato, from Averroes and Avicenna, from Albert the Great, from every one—for thought is always a universal collaboration—can it be supposed that he would have passed by a Descartes, a Leibnitz, a Kant, a Spinoza, and twenty others, without taking anything from them ?

" To suppose it would be to offer him a deadly insult.   It may be good for the grasping and effeminate political exile to return to a changed land, having for his part ' forgotten nothing and learnt nothing.'   But is it not rather our ideal to be Thomists such as St. Thomas himself would be to-day ?

" When he had nearly brought his *Summa Theologiæ* to its conclusion, he talked, they say, of burning it; after six centuries would he subscribe, without change or addition, to a single one of its articles ?

One could wager on a certainty that he would begin them over again. They would be both the same and yet other, for the scope would be different, the nutrition and, in consequence, the nutritive capacity, renewed." [1]

Let us make no mistake about it : if a political party has installed itself so securely in the Church that it persuades itself and often makes others believe that it is the only true Catholicism, to accord credence to these self-interested pretensions would be the grossest historical error concerning our civilisation which we could commit.

Not only does there exist a Catholicism cured of all clericalism, but this Catholicism, which was not born yesterday, has behind it an infinitely longer tradition than has clericalism, and has manifested itself in every direction by a fruitfulness whose power we cannot yet estimate. Let us recognise the splendour of light in which we are living! French Catholicism has a *Pléiade* of philosophers of the very first rank : Maurice Blondel, Laberthonnière, Edouard Le Roy and Fonsegrive, are men who need fear no comparison, and to every one of them a chapter ought to be devoted.

The scientific work of M. Loisy, severe as it is in appearance, is so bathed in reality that the dry bones of Erudition disappear, and the reader has no more than the beneficent sensation of reascending through the centuries to study a thought whereof he is the heir.

The innumerable works of Canon Ulysse Chevalier

[1] *Saint Thomas d'Aquin*, Paris, 1910, 2 Vols., 8vo. The passage quoted is in Vol. II, p. 330.

—like those of Monsignor Duchesne and of many others whom I must not cite—are works in which the Catholic spirit, far indeed from beating a retreat, or even from only accepting scientific methods as a last resource, extends them in new directions, tests them, makes them pliable, vivifies them.

All those whom I have just named share in science, in philosophy and in history, more fully with our generation than if they had not been Catholics, because from their childhood their thought has been directed not only towards the idea of fraternity, but towards that of a universal cosmic society, whose name the Church stammers, whose secret science is searching for, whose realisation democracy pursues.[1]

---

[1] In the heart of French Catholicism there is an Association of which for several years much has been said, *Le Sillon* (the Furrow). I have said nothing of the noble efforts of Marc Sangnier and his collaborators, because, though they offer a splendid affirmation of faith and virility, they remain aside from the new movement.

Doubtless the *Sillon*, which aims at realising democracy in France, and requires its members to saturate their whole life with the ideal, and to be the frank and glad servants of the faith of the Church, has found in the spirit of the new age a sort of pre-established harmony and prevenient grace; but, in choosing his ground in the political and economic field, the founder of the *Sillon* and his official fellow-workers (in some provincial sections the spirit blows where it listeth) have appeared timid and fearful, anxious not to compromise their cause with the efforts of philosophers, exegetists or historians. No doubt this prudence was instinctive, and an application of the principle of the division of labour; but the *Sillon's* lack of contact with the intellectual Catholic movement has been serious for both currents of thought.

By the Bull *Notre charge apostolique* (the official text is in French), of Aug. 25, 1910, the *Sillon*, which counted about 500 sections, was dissolved and invited to reorganise itself under the direction of the bishops. Pius X seized this opportunity to set forth at length the political and social views which he regards as alone orthodox.

To give an idea of this document we will quote a few lines : " This [*Le Sillon*] which formerly aroused such hopes, this limpid and impetuous stream, has been captured in its course by the modern foes of the Church, and henceforward is no more than a wretched affluent of the great movement of apostacy, organised in every land, for the establishment of a universal Church which shall have neither dogmas nor hierarchy, nor rule for the mind, nor bridle for the passions, and which, under pretext of liberty, will bring again upon the world, if it should triumph, the legal reign of ruse and force, and the oppression of the weak, of those who suffer and who toil."—*Acta A. Sedis*, Vol. II, p. 628.

This condemnation was the outcome of an anti-democratic Press campaign. It is enough to read, among many others, a brochure by M. Albert Monniot, of the journal *La Libre parole*, entitled *Le Sillon devant l'episcopat*, Paris, Dec. 1909, to see by what means mere journalists succeed to-day in giving rise to the more serious decisions of the Holy See.

To know the *Sillon* one must first of all read the pamphlet of M. Marc Sangnier, *Le Sillon, esprit et méthodes*, Paris, 1905, written at the moment of the institution's full prosperity, when Rome lavished upon it her most precious encouragements.

Marc Sangnier's attitude, since the Pope's letter, has been defined by him in a series of addresses given in Paris during the spring of 1911. They were analysed at length in *La Democratie* for April 30, and May 7, 14, 21 and 28, 1911.

A precise conception of the kind of association officially approved by the Holy See may be obtained by studying, *e. g. L'Association catholique de la jeunesse française* (The Catholic Association of French Youth), founded in 1886, by M. Robert de Roquefeuil and his friends, advised and guided at the beginning by the Count Albert de Mun, to co-ordinate the living forces of Catholic youth, with the idea of inaugurating a Christian Social Order.

This, in the Conservative direction, is what the *Sillon* was in the democratic. *L'Association catholique de la jeunesse française* has two periodicals in Paris : *Les Annales de la jeunesse catholique* and *La Vie nouvelle*, completed by a series of regional district supplements (Offices at 76 rue des Saints-Pères, Paris).

A women's organisation, which shows exactly what political orientation the Holy See favours in France, is the *Ligue patriotique des femmes françaises* (Patriotic League of French Women), 368 rue St. Honoré, Paris—presided over by the Baroness Reille ; 325,000 members, 2000 correspondents and 582 committees.

CHAPTER XII

ITS MANIFESTATIONS IN PROTESTANTISM

Or rather its absence of manifestations—Unity of the Protestant character amid its ecclesiastical divisions—Individualism—The separation of the Churches and the State has permitted new schisms in the Reformed Church—Why the furthest evolved among Catholics prove so rigid in regard to Protestantism—Its situation stated by Pastors Lafon and Morize—Are Protestants so much misunderstood as they suppose ?—Pastor Wagner and the Abbé Lemire—Dean Auguste Sabatier—What it is in Protestantism that wounds the feelings of France—Is Protestant freedom complete ?—Pastor W. Monod—How far has he grasped the religious character which atheism may possess ?

If above we have had to assert the existence of two Catholicisms in our land, living together side by side in the same Church, we must now assert the existence here of one sole Protestantism, divided into a multitude of sects.

This has a paradoxical air, but it is the most precise reality.[1]

---

[1] " Alike but divided : such to-day are French Protestants. Or one may say : separated and yet brothers. We live in a monstrous paradox. There are everywhere barriers and excisemen to examine merchandise and even to search the passer-by. Yet all pass by, and all merchandise therewith. And all opposites are fellows.

" Likewise, before this unfathomable mystery of irrational and unintelligible divisions, the observer puts questions destined to remain unanswered, ' wherefores ' which resound in a void of universal silence. In ecclesiastical matters, French Protestants can only escape the madness lying in wait for the brain of him who

The Separation of the Churches and the State, which might, and as many sons of the Reformation hoped, would occasion a union of hearts and fusion of wills, or lead at least to a corporal approximation, has had an absolutely opposite effect. On the morrow of the crisis, the Reformed Church of France did not even choose to remember the unity it might have kept by adopting a common financial administration, but profited by the opportunity to form itself into three fragments.[1]

---

tries to comprehend the incomprehensible, by seeking refuge in an absolute agnosticism, or perhaps by seeking shelter in some theory of necessary though impenetrable mystery."—Pastor Louis Lafon, editor of *La Vie nouvelle*. Beginning of leading article in the issue for Nov. 12, 1910.

[1] Before 1905 there were two Protestant Churches united to the State, which appointed and paid their pastors and maintained their places of worship : the Reformed Church of France (Calvinist) and the Church of the Augsburg Confession (Lutherans).

Beside these two Churches there was a multitude of groups, from clearly constituted associations like the Free Churches or the Methodist Churches, to more or less amorphous and ephemeral institutions, mostly bearing the name of the " evangelists " who founded them. These groups naturally remain what they were before the Separation, and we shall here only speak of the three branches sprung from the single Reformed Church of France ; one has called itself, " National Union of Evangelical Reformed Churches " (orthodox traditional tendency) ; another " United Reformed Churches " (liberal) ; the third, " Reformed Churches," more usually designated under the name of " Union of Jarnac," desired to act as a bond between the two preceding and secure their union, but was compelled to constitute itself separately. In order to obtain some idea of the activity of French Protestants, their numbers, geographical distribution, and theological schools, their organs and literary production, etc., one may consult *L'Agenda-annuaire protestant*, which has appeared since 1880 ; now under the management of the Rev. Pastor A. Gambier, of Dijon.

Rare indeed are the doctors in Israel (if indeed there are any) who could point out the reasons for which this rupture occurred in spite of all the arguments of expediency, sentiment and good sense which should have prevented it. It took place, and the subdivision goes forward, inevitable, implacable, in the heart of each of the three sections.

How can we, then, speak of Protestant unity in face of such facts? Because the force which urges Protestants to subdivision is one. It is stronger than any choice—than any reason; it is the same in all these men who seem so different, and it creates in them all an identical mentality.

Obedience produces the unity of Rome; spiritual pride brings forth Protestant unity and engenders its incurable divisions. This pride is unconscious; it even imagines itself to be full of humility because it relates everything to God.

At the moment when science and philosophy, meeting with the old French religious spirit, speak above all of unity, solidarity, tradition, evolution and social effort; when the thought that appears the most novel and individual is compelled to recognise that it is not its own, but the result of myriads on myriads of anterior thoughts—the Protestant, the most intelligent equally with the most ignorant, seems only able to give himself up to his individual task. He isolates himself from the past and the present, and " searches the Scriptures " in the persuasion that the sense of the Bible is obvious. Quite naturally, in the vast collection he succeeds in finding passages in harmony with his preoccupations, and confirming his most extraordinary notions.

Hence some particular point becomes his conquest;

and sometimes the most naïve, the most destitute of
instruction, becoming an itinerant preacher, will call
this his " message." [1]

Just as St. Paul, he speaks of his " gospel," and
believes he has received from God the charge of
proclaiming it and, in consequence, of defending it
against error.   Thus the very men who claim most
loudly for themselves the liberty of interpreting in
their own fashion such and such a text or book of the
Bible refuse to accord this right to others.

Protestant freedom is thus very far from being
what it calls itself.   In Catholicism there is but one
authority, and for that reason it generally succeeds
in its pretensions.   In Protestantism, the liberty of

---

[1] This is a hallowed expression. It belongs to the dialect of
Canaan.   This term designates a style, impregnated with Biblical
phrases, which prevails with special virulence in " awakened "
circles. It varies from sect to sect, and like all things human
changes with time.   Its name comes to it from its abuse of images
borrowed from Canaan. Perhaps the most popular song of
French Protestantism begins with the words :

> " En marche ! en marche ! allons en Chanaan
>   Volons vers la terre promise."

> (" Forward, forward ! let us go to Canaan,
>   Let us fly unto the Promised Land.")

Another—

> " De Chanaan, quand verrons-nous
>   Le céleste rivage ?
> Vers le Jourdain, entendez-vous ?
>   Christ nous appelle tous."

> (" When, oh when, shall we behold
>   Canaan's heavenly shore ?
> Hark ! towards the River of Jordan
>   Christ is calling us all.")

each one is ceaselessly limited [1] by the authority of all the others—of each of the others. As all these various authorities are most usually in disagreement, it follows that in general you remain free, but not out of respect for your freedom, only because each one of these infallibilities finds it impossible to constrain you.[2]

---

[1] It is very rare for any one to take the trouble to give an exact account of doctrinal authority in the Church of Rome. People always argue as though it created, or was supposed to create, Absolute Truth. It is true that by dint of so speaking about it they have partially made it believe this.

Really, the authority, whether it be the Pope alone or the General Council, states the truth, defines it, is its witness and interpreter : but no more. The infallibility of the Roman pontiff does not imply that he can make black white, or white black; but that he cannot be mistaken when he says that such a thing is white, and such another thing black. The famous maxim of St. Vincent de Lérins should be remembered : "*In ipsa item catholica Ecclesia magnopere curandum est ut id teneamus quod ubique, quod semper, quod ab omnibus creditum est. Hoc est etenim vere proprieque catholicum, quod ipsa vis nominis ratioque declarat, quæ omnia fere universaliter comprehendit.*"—Quoted by Father Lépicier, *De stabilitate et progressu dogmatis*, Rome, 1908, p. 171.

[2] We must recognise that eminent Protestants are very far from sharing our way of looking at this matter. "The only thing that we may not admit," says Charles Wagner (*Libre-pensée et protestantisme libéral*, p. 114), speaking of Liberal Protestantism, "is the government of minds, for it is impossible without constant usurpations. So it happens that some among us are almost orthodox while others are of an amazing heterodoxy. But as no one claims authority, all listen while they discuss together, and complete one another." Farther on (p. 138) : "Free believers mutually appreciate and accept one another in the diversity of manifestations given to their faith, while their mutual sympathy teaches them the art of transposing the speech of their brothers, so that they may understand and assimilate it." I felt I ought to quote these words, for the attitude of Liberal, as well as of other Protestants, produces a considerably different impression upon me.

O

This jealous individualism separates Protestants from their fellow-citizens more than the Alps and the Pyrenees separate France from neighbouring lands. It leads them to confound the strong personal convictions acquired by their intellectual labour with the truth—a word which on their lips has nearly all its scholastic and absolute sense—and communicates to them that doctrinal intransigence, in infinitely varied forms, which often persists even in those who imagine they have broken with Protestantism.

There are moments, however, when this grim independence becomes a great strength. At the time of the Dreyfus affair, for instance, almost unanimously and without hesitation the Protestants promptly took the side of revision.[1] Professors risked their posts, doctors and tradesmen their clients, and many families friendships which up till then nothing had shaken.

For a moment one felt that Protestantism had all at once joined company with the intellectuals, and that out of this unpremeditated meeting something new would spring.

Nothing whatever sprang from it. The only comsequence was that next day both sides asked themselves how they had managed to understand one another so well last evening, and to imagine they could continue in the same road.[2]

[1] There had been no secret understanding. Protestant personages in Paris were very slow to move ; they saw clearly how formidable was the movement of opinion that they who would go against the current must face.

[2] This situation would have greatly astonished the missionaries, philosophers, political thinkers and even economists who, about the middle of last century, counted on Protestantism for the

However, the Protestants did not lose all hope, and on the eve of the Separation one of the most sympathetic representatives of Liberalism, Pastor Wagner, whom we have already quoted and whom we shall often quote again, wrote pages of vigorous optimism.[1]

"In this labour of religious renaissance, of reconstruction on widened foundations, the advance guard of Protestantism has its place marked out. By the force of events and the laws of history, it is the heir of all the results of human toil in the religious domain. It is in its ranks, among its indefatigable thinkers, its laborious pioneers, that the questions are set and solved upon which the progress of religious ideas in the world depends. I consider it, then, as the first of spiritual potencies. Having, of all existing *milieux*, by its free and broad organisation, the greatest number of openings onto every region, and being able to exercise the widest sympathy without infidelity to its principles, it is capable of drawing towards itself, of grouping and binding into bundles, all the living forces of the past and all those of the future."

.   .   .   .   .

The uselessness of the efforts made by French Protestantism to enter into any relations whatever with its fellow-citizens has now for some time been very generally recognised by the very men who recently entertained the greatest hopes for it.

---

regeneration of France. About 1878, Émile Laveleye, the statesman Frère Orban, the writer Paul Frédéricq, and the economist Frédéric Passy, rallied to Protestantism.

[1] F. Buisson and Charles Wagner: *Libre-pensée et protestantisme libéral*, Paris, 1903, pp. 187–91.

"French Protestantism," said the Rev. Pastor Louis Lafon,[1] "is like a driving-belt which runs loose. It throws no part into gear. Intellectually, morally and socially it remains outside human action. It has not stirred for a century. And yet in that time how many things have changed!"

Nearly at the same time, another pastor, M. Paul Morize,[2] stated that Protestantism appears "to some pastors and laymen as a sort of pseudo-Catholicism, less logical, less grand than the other. . . . Its action is null: some suspect, others drop away, the greater number are indifferent. Certain strong individualities still conserve a personal influence which would always make itself felt, and after the same manner, even if they came out of very different circles from the one that formed them. They are listened to, they are loved, they are followed, not *because*, but *although*, they are Protestants. Such is the reality.

"Let us give up speaking *urbi et orbi* of the evangelisation of the French fatherland by Protestantism. It has become altogether painful and somewhat grotesque."

And still more recently, the same pastor said:[3]

[1] In the article cited (at p. 189, n. 1). He also notes a very serious fact for a world which is implacably severe on those who accept ready-made formulas without troubling themselves overmuch to ascertain their meaning. "Pastors who have, every one, repudiated the metaphysics of Calvin and the Middle Ages and the metaphysics of the Councils, preach as though they still accept them, and scatter through their sermons all the old notions which the people feel confusedly, but as time goes by, more and more clearly, to be in contradiction to the whole orientation of modern philosophy and science."

[2] *Vie nouvelle* for Nov. 26, 1910.

[3] *Vie nouvelle* for Mar. 4, 1911. This article followed and echoed a *Tribune libre* of the Rev. Pastor Néel, for Feb. 11, 1911.

" In the heart of our poor battered Protestantism there are still some imaginative men who cherish a systematic optimism. They hope thus to act by suggestion upon their co-religionists on whom they count for supplies or support.

" They do not want to see the reality, still less to allow it to be seen. . . . French Protestantism is on the way to disappearance, to decomposition, and by non-equivocal signs it may be foreseen that the succession of phenomena heralding the end will be somewhat rapid. . . . The chapels and the faculties [1] also are becoming empty. Before long the number of professors will exceed that of the students. The ministerial average is becoming lower; local churches adjust themselves with difficulty to the new conditions of their life, and each appointment of a minister becomes an occasion for division.

" . . . To this balance which is being everywhere cast upon the wrong side [2] must be added the melan-

[1] The Faculties of Protestant Theology of Montauban, Geneva and Paris, formerly recognised by the State : in which future pastors study for four or five years, after having completed a course of classical secondary studies.

A host of works, with pessimistic conclusions, might be mentioned which have appeared, and are appearing, almost everywhere. We will be content with noting that of a particularly competent man, M. Ad. Lods, in the *Journal des débats* for Nov. 22, 1910. Professor G. Bonet-Maury, on the other hand, in an article in the *Protestant*, March 11, 1911, shows himself optimistic.

[2] The material balance sheet of the Church of Rome is not more reassuring. " What statement could be more discouraging than that which has just been made in the Paris Diocesan Congress ? ' The capital lacks priests,' says the Archbishop. Last year, only sixteen ordinations took place ! This year, there will be only eleven, and next year still fewer. These are the official figures. Eleven priests only this year, still fewer next ; eight, perhaps six, for a diocese of three millions ! What a situation !

choly and humiliating enumeration of several other
causes of dissolution. . . . The poor and obsolete
formula of 1872 is supposed still, in 1911, to express
the faith of the majority of our ministers and
Churches. *Now that is not true.* As to the formal
adhesion, without introductory formula, without re-
servation and without substitutions, demanded since
1906 of pastors, professors of theology (!!) and of
the Churches themselves by the majority—is not this
the most audacious negation of all our traditions of
free examination?"

We must thank the distinguished Pastor of Ber-
gerac for his vehement candour. The situation of
Protestantism is indeed as he paints it, and each of
his assertions is supported by facts which he had no
need to recall, since these were in the memory of all
his readers.

Is this to say he is right all along the line? We
would give him pain if we consented to that. His
anger is justified; but perhaps his discouragement is
not entirely so.

Assuredly, if Protestantism should remain what it
now is : [1] for some the taking possession of the sacred

"Apart from a small number of privileged dioceses which
almost maintain their ecclesiastical effective force, there is the
same falling off, the same deficit, everywhere. In the great and
splendid diocese of Rouen, so flourishing in old times, the great
seminary scarcely counts forty-five pupils. At the last opening,
out of nine students called away to perform their military service,
only two returned. The situation is still more grievous in many
other dioceses."—Arthur Loth : *Univers* for March 10, 1911.

[1] Here is the definition of Protestantism kindly furnished me
by M. Georges Dupont, Liberal Pastor of Montpellier :

"Protestantism is a form of the Christian religion which desires

books of a Church against which one is in revolt;
for others the cohabitation in the same consciousness
of two antithetical spirits, the purely rationalistic and
the mystical, without either of the two ever being
able to act in full freedom—if Protestantism should
remain such, its position would be as seriously compromised as M. Morize sees it; and, to speak in his
language, the "house-breakers" might divide the
prize.

In any case it is noteworthy that he, the pastor of
an important parish, surrounded by the respectful
esteem of his colleagues, can speak thus, and that he
has been able to publish this painful "balance sheet"
in one of the most widely circulated of Protestant
papers, without being stoned on the morrow. Such
self-examination still indicates a certain vitality.

If Protestants could make up their minds to place
their strong individualities in touch with the contemporary social movement, which is, as we have
seen, profoundly religious in its aspirations; if they
mingled in it, forgetful of themselves, they might,
with their extraordinary richness in men, render a
priceless service to French civilisation to-day.

Can they give themselves? That is the question;
which, as I am no prophet, I will not attempt to
answer.

In any case they would do well to give up com-
plaining of each and all, and being haunted by the

---

to go back to the Gospel (the teaching of Christ and of his Apostles)
to attach itself to what is most primitive and therefore purest in
Christianity; and which, on the other hand, recognises no other
authority than the free individual conscience and, consequently,
rejects all other authority, especially that of tradition and of the
Church."

notion that they are unappreciated.[1] As soon as a
voice is raised among them which speaks the language
of life, and not that of sectarianism, Free-thinkers
and Catholics listen without asking him to disguise
his flag; I need wish for no other proof than the
apostolate and success of Charles Wagner. And
beside the name of the author of *Youth*, *The Simple
Life*, and a score of other little masterpieces impregnated with the purest religious feeling, I would like
to set that of a member of the Catholic clergy who
has had no difficulty in winning respect for his
cassock in open Parliament—the Abbé Lemire : he
also is loved and admired because, without yielding
anything of the prerogatives of his faith, he has
always shown himself full of a respectful delicacy
for the opinions of others, and because each of his
addresses seems to be introduced by the evangelical
proclamation, " Peace to men of good-will." [2]

The eager welcome given to Pastor Wagner by
Catholics and Free-thinkers is not an altogether
isolated instance. It may be said that a great part

[1] Protestants are frequently calumniated, but in our days who
is not ? They think they are caricatured in clerical journals,
and also in anti-clerical ones ; but do they spend much time in
verifying their own sources of information ? Their journals are
written in the same haste and in the same spirit of ill-will as those
of which they complain so vigorously. Yet those who make so
great a profession of criticism ought really to give the example of
introducing it a little into their daily judgments.

[2] There is, again, a resemblance between Pastor Wagner and
the Abbé Lemire, in that while both men have found ardent
affection in their respective Churches, they have also met there
with distrust, difficulty and opposition which would have wearied
men less strong than they. It was not of his own choice that
Wagner, most conciliatory of Protestants, was led to build a
church of his own.

of the importance assigned by Protestantism to the works of Dean Auguste Sabatier is due to the radiance they have shed on the world outside.

This Huguenot by race, "whose blood," as he himself said, making use of a Languedocian expression, "had to make but one turn" (*ne faisait qu'un tour*) to recall the past, found himself after a few years known, appreciated and beloved in many a country priest's house and Catholic seminary, because, showing himself the proud, uncompromising Protestant that he was, he had allowed his warm, vibrating heart to speak, and had not lowered himself to the wretched polemics, based upon pride, want of understanding and errors of fact, which too often impair the works of his co-religionists.

With him the old anti-popery, since we must call things by their proper names, was indeed not disguised; but this negative, corrosive sentiment was no longer the soul and inspiration of his whole action. His *Outlines of a Philosophy of Religion*[1] gave one a sudden sensation of being in the presence of a religious feeling which asserted itself above controversy and hatred, of a renewed Protestantism, setting forth with unexpected strength to unforeseen conquests.

And soon, outside of Protestantism, applause broke out, cries of joy echoed on every hand. It was life greeting life across the frontiers, heralding and preparing the *unum ovile* after which the present generation sighs—confusedly still, but with greater longing than ever.

The warmest encouragement came to its author

[1] *Esquisse d'une philosophie de la religion d'après la psychologie et l'histoire.*

from the Catholic clergy—encouragement which, without being in any way an adhesion,[1] while remaining on a critical basis,[2] is a communicated strength, a higher communion—communion not in results, but in an equally sincere labour, a labour equally inspired by love.

Already stricken by the illness which was to carry him off, Sabatier made a journey into Italy.

In a little town which he visited by chance an unexpected pleasure was reserved for him. With his Southern abruptness and caressing voice, he said to the friend who met him at the station, " Understand, I want to see no antiquities. You make vast promises for Italy; one would suppose you owned it. If you know two or three intelligent young fellows here who can speak French, I should like to make their acquaintance and try to find out what they think, believe and hope." " Very well," said his com-

[1] There were such, absolute and enthusiastic. Some priests came to him as to a saviour. It is greatly to be desired that this ephemeral movement—a movement so dramatic on certain sides (one cannot but think of the unhappy Abbé Philippot) might be studied with serenity.

[2] I will only cite a study by the illustrious Archbishop of Albi, Monsignor Mignot. It is included anew in a recent volume, *L'Eglise et la critique*, Paris, 1910, pp. 3–87. For others, one would have to cite nearly all the volumes of the *Revue du clergé français* for these last years.

To this review, to the works of Monsignor Mignot, *e. g. Lettres sur les études ecclésiastiques*, Paris, 1908, and to the *Annales de philosophie chrétienne*, edited by the Abbé Laberthonnière, those inquirers should turn who have no time to waste and yet are anxious to get a fairly calm and exact idea of the Catholic intellectual movement. A forthcoming volume of this Library (*Bibliothèque du mouvement social contemporain*, Armand Colin, Paris), will show the wealth of the Church's effort to win back its scientific place.

panion; "I will take you to the Seminary." "To the Seminary?" "Why, yes; to the Catholic, Apostolic and Roman Seminary. There it is in front of you." "Is this a joke or a trap? Do you forget you are speaking to the Dean of the Paris Faculty of Protestant Theology?" And his small, short-sighted eyes, still entirely young and somewhat mocking, laughed with astonishment. "No, you will only find friends there; adversaries perhaps, but adversaries one can love." "Well, let us go to the Seminary!" We rang loudly. A grating was half opened, and the porter's head passed quickly behind it. He flung open the half-door, gave a vague smile, and without a word preceded the visitors. "Why does this fellow suddenly remind me of the salads my mother used to whiten in our cellar when I was a youngster?" And answering himself, "Because it smells of the cellar. Look! all the windows are barred!" We followed, indeed, a labyrinth of entangled corridors and staircases bearing witness to hasty and provisional arrangements which had lasted for centuries.

A key grated in a lock, the porter disappeared, and the two visitors were in a large room flooded by the setting sun. Close beside us were the roofs of the cathedral, with their population of statues; beyond, but still quite close, a Capuchin hermitage with its cypresses cut out sombrely against the luminous sky.

"How beautiful!" cried Auguste Sabatier. And it seemed to the guide that his old master experienced a beneficent and ineffable æsthetic emotion.

A priest came in. His face shone with pleasure. "Is it possible? You here! You, author of *The Apostle Paul* and the *Outlines!*" And he grasped the hands of his visitor, still utterly surprised at so warm a welcome, mingled together French and Italian words, gazed at him, and drew him nearer with infinite respect and yet with familiarity, till suddenly a shadow of sadness came into his gaze : he had divined the malady which was undermining Sabatier's health.　Running to the door, he called : "To the library, all of you!"

"All" were five or six other priests, teachers in the seminary.　Forms of discipline unusual in Franciscan customs were presented there; but Sabatier's amazement redoubled when, the first curiosity appeased, it was the Professor of Physics and Chemistry who questioned him as to the differences between the exegesis of certain passages in the two editions of *The Apostle Paul*.　The conversation was lengthy.　The Ave had sounded from the cathedral *campanile*, and it still went on.　But it was time to separate.　All rose to accompany the guest : all, and he as they, assailed by sad thoughts : to love one another so warmly, almost without knowing it, then to meet, and to part for ever!　They had been enjoying one of the rarest of delights; now they paid for it in a grief they could not express.　Silent, by no choice of theirs, they descended, preceded by a young professor who, in his haste, had lit a large processional candle.　He put it out at the door, but still went forward, and it was only at the other side of the square that Auguste Sabatier, returning to actuality, realised he must take leave of the Professors of the Seminary of X.　"Gentlemen," he said, "I owe you one of the best hours of the evening of my life."

I must ask pardon for relating an anecdote at such length.　It seems to me important as symptomatic of feelings which rarely gain expression in books.　It shows also that certain prepossessions tend to dis-appear in highly evolved Catholic circles.

. . . . . .

The miscarriage of Protestant propaganda is only the more remarkable; and what renders that mis-carriage still more significant is the notable intellectual advantage of the Protestants over other groups.[1]

Their attempts to "conquer France for the Gospel" are obviously disinterested; I mean they endeavour to rob them of any narrow ecclesiasticism. It is no rare thing in ministerial gatherings, when, for the hundredth time, the causes for the unpopu-larity of Protestantism are being sought out, and the means to remedy this unpopularity, to hear some generous "social Christian" exclaim: "Let Pro-testantism perish, so only Jesus be proclaimed." But such meetings are undoubtedly ill-situated for inquiries of this kind.

If we were to interrogate those of our fellow-countrymen who are hostile to Protestantism, we should perhaps find that many of them had been shocked by the negative element in its propaganda: to a superficial gaze it may often enough appear as a rather vulgar anti-clerical effort. Reference to the crimes of the Popes excite too-ready applause. One need not be a furious Papist to feel that certain blustering lecture tours undertaken by Capuchin converts to Protestantism have a disagreeable taste.

A more important and deeper element in some "evangelising campaigns," which shocks the best of

---

[1] To be convinced of this, one has but to examine the entrance lists of the large public schools, admission to which depends upon examination.

their hearers, is the want of reticence with which the most intimate and private matters of the inner life are spoken of.

Protestants have wounded France by their theologism, their critical turn of mind, and an iconoclastic zeal that seeks everywhere for idols to destroy.[1] She reproaches them, above all, with having failed to see that she has long had her own religion : a religion to which she was not converted, and which she did not accept, for the good reason that this religion is flesh of her flesh, her creator and her creature; that she lives it and lives by it; that she has made it, and is making it every day; and that this Catholicism—for such it is—is not an administrative Catholicism fabricated in the offices of the Curia, but a living tradition wherein Roland and Charlemagne, St. Louis and Joinville, St. Geneviève and Joan of Arc, Pascal and St. Vincent de Paul, the principles of '89 and social dreams—perhaps chimerical—meet and live side by side. "I believe in the Holy Universal Church," says the French believer; and the French unbeliever and revolutionary, who has not learnt

[1] This eccentricity is fortunately recognised—and consequently half-corrected—by some very representative Protestants, e. g. the Rev. J. E. Roberty, Pastor of the Oratory of the Louvre in Paris : " Something anti-social and consequently anti-Christian, of extremely little spirituality, and I would also say of an anti-French character, this indefinable something which is called the Protestant *morgue*, still exists."—*Vers l'évangile social*, Paris, 1904, p. 15.

All the innumerable periodical campaigns for the evangelisation of France, from the efforts of individuals to those of the most general character—e. g. that of the " Commission of Protestant Evangelical Action in the moral and social sphere "—are inspired by one and the same idea : " We, Protestants, possess the truth. You, France, have it not. You have everything to learn from us, and we have nothing to learn from you."

these words, says the same thing in other words. And speaking thus, neither employs some theological formula; they chant their joy in belonging to a society which has neither beginning nor end, which plunges beyond the historic ages into the first awakening of intellect, the foolish stammerings of conscience and of will; they feel they belong to this society, but they desire more than this: they give themselves to it; with it and by it they seek to realise a dream of nobility, of beauty, of freedom, of holiness.[1]

.   .   .   .   .   .

It would be unnecessary to recount the incapacity of Protestantism to effect any continuous relation to our generation, if this aloofness were a phenomenon unconnected with the religious movement of to-day; but it illustrates and defines the orientation of the new thought. This, so far from moving in the direction of Protestant individualism, does not merely flee from it, but ignores it.

The springtime manifested in the heart of the Catholic Church has, here and there, awakened memories of the Reformation; but they alone who

[1] " For those who reject the very hypothesis of a God and only admit a Universe governed by immutable laws, prayer gives place to the patient study of these laws, and to meditations on the situation of man in the totality of things. It joins these with a fervent hope that this Universe, seemingly so indifferent to human destiny, is in process of evolution towards greater intelligence and greater justice. Prayer is the firmly taken resolve to be an agent of voluntary evolution."—Jules Payot: *Cours de morale*, Paris, 1909, p. 206. " To become a voluntary agent of the Unknowable Energy, in process of evolution toward a consciousness, toward a spiritual life, more and more intense, more and more lofty, more and more universal, this is our destiny; and our happiness will be proportionate to our efforts fully to realise it."—*Ibid.*, p. 233.

only see a few episodic details have thought of establishing a parallel between the two movements.

Catholic thought tends to renew and vivify the old ideas of authority and dogma by contact with history and life. Protestantism, on the contrary, remaining on purely intellectual ground, sacrifices one dogma and then another till sometimes only one remains;[1] but just as it accomplishes this retreat, the doctrines it allows to remain become for it more and more dull and intangible, while itself becomes more foreign to that labour of reintegrating the whole spiritual life of the past which is being accomplished by the thought of to-day. Thus it appears like some semi-rationalist, at once inconsistent and shamefaced, who, placed in the dilemma of going as far as free-thought or of retracing his steps, abruptly stands still, and will not admit it.[2]

---

[1] Dean Auguste Sabatier, in his *Esquisse d'une philosophie de la religion*, p. 83, compares the history of miracle to that " ass's skin," imagined by Balzac, which shrank as its possessor grew older. The history of dogma in Protestantism is entirely analogous.

The Protestant imagines he advances in degree as the list of his dogmas decreases. When it is empty, he fancies himself a free-thinker, without perceiving that he has been brought thither by an unbroken series of defeats. He is a vanquished man.

[2] Here, by way of documentation, is the declaration of principles voted in the Synod of Montpellier (1905) by the advanced Protestants :

" *Faithful to that spirit of faith and freedom for which our ancestors both lived and suffered :*

We assert for every member of the Church, the right and duty to draw for himself, from the Holy Scriptures and from the experience of the pious, his faith and beliefs :

We are filled with joy at the thought that we possess in Jesus Christ the supreme gift of God, the Saviour who, by his person, his teachings,

Many Protestants have imagined that if the best qualified representatives of the new spirit in Catholicism have shown but little eagerness in drawing nearer to them, this was merely precautionary and tactical. That is a gross error. Protestantism counts for nothing in the rise of the present Catholic movement; nor does this movement follow in the least the ways broken and trodden by that.

We do not say there is not here and there some ill-humour in regard to the Protestants. It would be most natural for such to exist. It is not pleasant to meet upon the road travellers of a somewhat unyielding appearance whom you do not know, but who, with fine condescension, declare themselves your relations, and do you the great honour of holding you to be their illegitimate children. Even when they find it is useless to attempt to monopolise you for their particular group, they follow you at least with their disdain! [1]

---

his holy life, his sacrifice and his victory over death, constantly communicates to the children of the Heavenly Father the necessary strength to cause justice and love to prevail even now upon the earth over every form of individual and collective evil :

And to all who seek of God in communion with Jesus Christ, pardon for their sin, the strength of the moral life, consolation in affliction and eternal hope, we fraternally open our Churches, on whose pediment we maintain the true Protestant device : THE GOSPEL AND FREEDOM."

[1] In 1910, the Protestant papers published numerous articles on Modernism, in which the almost constant conclusion was that it lacked religious value, loyalty, logic and scientific originality.

It is an unpleasant error in facts to see in the flight taken by Catholic exegesis a sort of borrowing from Protestant, and especially German, science. Those who have given this judgment show that they are scarcely cognisant of the circumstances in which the Catholic scientific stream had its source, nor the new needs to

Lofty spirits can doubtless overlook these unpleasant episodes; but they still feel, in respect to
Protestantism, a regret that it seems unable to understand that, by separating itself from the Church of
the sixteenth century, it condemned the authority of
Rome to become such as it became, and was itself
condemned to be what it has never succeeded in
ceasing to be, a sort of anti-Church.[1]

Far indeed from being a disguised Protestantism,
the movement which has manifested itself in the
heart of Catholicism is an effort of the very soul of
the Church to realise its own fruitful energies, newly
to live its own life, and to become once more for
civilisation that living synthesis wherein science,
philosophy and art, every thought and every labour,

which it answered. After a century of toil, Protestant exegesis
still remains somewhat academic. Catholic exegesis, on the
contrary, has not only given birth to a whole procession of considerable scientific works, it has had immediate practical results :
the edition of the Gospels and the Acts of the *Pia società di S.
Girolamo*, at Rome, whereof 880,000 copies have been sold in
a few years, is a little masterpiece which might be offered as a good
model to the Bible Societies.

Half-way between the labour of purely scientific criticism and
that of the popular edition, but taking account of duly acquired
conquests, there is another Catholic work, the most capable of
guiding intellectuals who are not specialists amid the labyrinth
of questions, and of putting back the whole of the Bible, as well
as each of the books of which it is composed, into its historic
framework; I mean the work entitled *Che cos' è la Bibbia*, by
Monsignor Umberto Fracassini, Rome, 1910.

[1] " Who knows if the greatest complaint of the Modernists
against Protestantism is not that it made possible by its separation,
and inevitable as a result of reaction, that regime of theological
and ecclesiastical absolutism from which they are the first to suffer
and which they have exerted themselves to amend ? "—A. Loisy,
Revue d'histoire et de littérature religieuses, Vol. I, p. 584.

may find their goal; in which each may lose itself, commingle, unite, communicate and consecrate itself, and thus prepare new resting-places for humanity. The *Letter to a Professor of Anthropology*, and the other writings of Father Tyrrell, were not Protestant works. They were the very reverse : they were the heralding token that the Church is on the point of coming out of the long nightmare which has obsessed her, during which her only purpose has been the dressing of her wounds and replying to her adversaries.

In these works, for the first time for centuries, Catholic thought affirms itself as calm and serene, sure enough of itself to be no more preoccupied with its foes, certain that it has but to reveal its nature to find itself as fully in harmony with the science as with the conscience of to-day.

.   .   .   .   .   .

This chapter has run already to an immoderate length, yet I do not wish to close it without drawing attention to the very noble effort " to come forth from the cemeteries " made by M. W. Monod in his book, *To Believers and Atheists*.[1]

Here the eminent pastor will be found proclaiming from the outset that if the Church of to-day " pretends to fulfil the mission laid upon it in the twentieth century, it must begin with an act of hope in the modern spirit." [2]

Presenting himself as " an obscure pioneer of the

---

[1] *Aux croyants et aux athées*, Paris, 1906. (What is to be done ? How is the Gospel to be read ? Is modern atheism irreligious ? An Atheist. The Problem of God.) The first page of the book associates two names hitherto rarely seen together, those of St. Paul and Guyau.   [2] *Ibid.*, p. 27.

future religion "—perhaps it would have been more accurate to say, pioneer of religious evolution, or of the religion which goes on creating itself—M. W. Monod has shown at once that in Protestantism also there is something astir. Has he truly "only said aloud what others think in their hearts"? [1] We would fain believe it, and hope that his views will spread not to become the programme of a new sect —M. Monod would be the first to regret that—but to be like an open window from Protestantism on the world without. [2]

Drawing nearer by degrees to the thoughts which stir in undenominational hearts, this minister has had the courage to conclude his book with the following page:

"Definitively, if I dare so express myself, I would say that it is a mistake to put the Almightiness of God at the beginning instead of at the end of things. There is a God who shall be, but is not yet, manifested: there is a God 'who comes' according to the formula of the Apocalypse." [3]

[1] *Aux croyants et aux athées*, Paris, 1906, p. 5.

[2] The Rev. W. Monod's effort seems to invalidate what we said at the beginning of this chapter as to Protestantism's lack of touch with the religious movement of to-day. I would I might be wrong; but the greater the moral position of the Minister of the Oratory the more striking it is to note how entirely his voice has hitherto remained isolated in Protestantism. It is, indeed, a different note which is raised by a more recent work from the pen of a young Liberal minister, the Rev. A. N. Bertrand, *Problèmes de la libre-pensée*, Paris, 1910.

As to the attempts which have been made to open the mind of Protestantism towards Catholicism, so that it may see the latter directly, and not across superficial facts, these have had no great success. [3] *Loc. cit.*, p. 193.

" . . . Indeed, unless at least we admit that God is already 'all in all,' we must acknowledge, according to St. Paul himself, that the supreme manifestation of God is yet to come. To-day, the revelation of the Eternal in history is incomplete : the present stage of cosmic evolution does not allow us to work out an adequate concept of divinity. The present world is an embryonic organism[1] which aspires to the perfect state; that perfect state is the Kingdom of God, or the City of Justice, or Humanity. We may also call it God : for God is the final cause of the world. Hence, to admit that God exists is only a first step. We must go further; we must will that God be. This affirmation and this attitude joined together constitute faith in God."[2]

" . . . To have faith in God is, then, to will God's full revelation in the future. God is not yet totally manifested. And that is why it is not strange that His existence can be doubted; that is why a modern thinker could write : 'God is the supreme decision of the soul.' That is to say, we must will that God be; we must affirm it with all the moral powers of our being; all our faculties must be accessory to His advent, allies in His cause. To have faith in God is no mere intellectual belief; it is an heroic deed, a personal enlisting in the service of truth, of justice, of beauty, of love; a free subordination of the present to the future; a consecration of our body, soul and spirit to the ideal which God pursues in humanity, by the Son of Man. Definitively, faith in God

[1] " Creation is never done : the best is to be born," Charles Wagner has said (*L'Ami*, dialogues of the inner life, Paris, 1905, p. 356).

[2] *Aux croyants et aux athées*, p. 195.

veritably *engages our faith*, in the mystical and sublime sense of the term." [1]

Then, in a kind of paraphrase of the Lord's Prayer, rising to thoughts which hitherto and upon less orthodox lips would have been regarded as blasphemous, he exclaims:

" Thy kingdom come! that is to say, may the Messiah triumph! may the Spirit of Jesus bear off the victory! May economic enfranchisement, intellectual liberation, religious redemption of the human race, become an accomplished fact and prove the divine Fatherhood! O God! achieve incarnation: after the divine Man and through Him, give us the divine Humanity!

" Thy will be done on earth! In order to conquer Thou hast need of us. 'Behold, I am here to do thy will!' Behold, I am here to suffer, love, rejoice, doubt, seek, succumb, adore! Use me! Help me to help! Not what I will, but what Thou wilt. . . . Or rather, I will what Thou willest. Thou willest what I will. Thou willest by me, Thou actest, lovest, speakest by me. Thou art the stem, I am the branch: it is by the branch that the trunk bears fruit. Ecstasy!

" Praying thus, I became an organ of the Holy Spirit: I give Him opportunity to manifest Himself here below, I enter into His compassionate insight, I subscribe to His redemptive programme; in other terms, I accede to God." [2]

[1] *Aux croyants et aux athées*, p. 195.
[2] Some day the theses of M. Monod will be set side by side with those of M. Marcel Hébert's two articles, *Revue de métaphysique*

Listening to such new accents, we no more think of allowing ourselves to be thwarted by M. Monod's Protestant phraseology than we should think of wondering at a priest who used Latin to stammer out the emotions of his soul. Borne along by his ardent mysticism, M. W. Monod has passed the point reached on a somewhat different route by Auguste Sabatier, and has attained a mountain ridge where he is met by the most living representatives of Catholicism and of Free-thought. Will this communion of feeling, effort and thought prove to be only an episode, or is it indeed a presage of a union of all the spiritual forces of France?

---

et de morale, July 1902, and March 1903, which made a great impression both on Catholicism and on the undenominational world, and led to the author's rupture with the Church.

CHAPTER XIII

ITS MANIFESTATIONS IN FREE-THOUGHT

That Free-thought is not essentially anti-religious—Free discussion according to Séailles : according to F. Buisson—Is the pessimism of Charles Péguy justified ?—Significant success of the *Cahiers de la quinzaine*—The School of Advanced Social Studies, and its section for the study of religion in its relation to society—The Union of Free-thinkers and Free-believers.

AT first sight, to speak of religious orientation in Free-thought looks like a challenge. That there may remain traces of ecclesiastical habits and a sort of religious bent among many free-thinkers is willingly allowed; but some people will find it difficult to believe that these vestiges will not in their turn be eliminated by the mere effect of time.

Is not the religious sentiment inexorably driven back by Free-thought? Has it not taken as its programme and *raison d'être* the substitution of science for religion?

Well—no! These somewhat simplistic views—very natural when the Church was setting forth to battle against all scientific freedom, when a professor of geology was denounced by the College Chaplain as teaching his pupils things which could not be made to agree with the story of Genesis—these views are everywhere outgrown. Now and again there are, indeed, attacks and fits of fury against Churches, dogmas and rites; but along with these incidents, which are often somewhat episodical and superficial, there is a very marked effort on the part of most of the authoritative representatives of Free-thought to recover the feeling which created religious institutions.

Free-thought has not always made war on religion. It has warred against certain expressions of religious feeling which, by giving themselves out to be absolute and final, not only acquired authority to be no longer living and laborious, but claimed to suppress other younger and more vigorous expressions. It is not against religious activity that it has risen up, but against idleness and pride; just as it would rise up not against science, but against the scientists who should claim that in them the human intellect had uttered its final word.

For that matter, it must be recognised that in the crisis of to-day the plain soldiers and even the non-commissioned officers of Free-thought often declare that they are following up the extirpation of all religion, and that there is no difference between superstition and religion. But if we have endeavoured to judge the Church by her best self, and not by the manifestations of the *Camelots du Roi*,[1] however noisy these may be, we ought to do as much for Free-thought, and not to judge it by the cases in which its action contradicts its ideal.

If we do so, we are soon led to state that, far from opposing science to faith, as in a kind of duel in which one or the other must give way, the men who best represent Free-thought desire for science not only a limitless freedom, including therein freedom

---

[1] Royalist partisans, literally " the king's pedlars."—Trans.

from error, but that in its efforts it should be inspired with an ardour, a patience, a heroism, which
are nothing else than faith.   They do not think of
destroying faith, but, on the contrary, of giving it
better knowledge of itself, of its strength and of the
new labours it must undertake.

    .   .   .   .   .   .

Need I say that by Free-thought I mean that in
which, according to M. Séailles' fine phrase, " there
is freedom and thought "? [1]

It is only too true that in societies of free-thinkers
a number of persons dwell side by side who understand but little of the very idea which lies in those
two words.   But is not this the fate of every human
institution?   Do not the Churches swarm with
believers whose lives are in perpetual contradiction
to the faith and morality they profess?

Even in our country districts people begin to dis-
tinguish between thought which is really free and
" Free-thought " conceived as an orthodoxy turned
inside out, which not only denies the results to which
the metaphysics of the past have led, but regards
the effort that produced them as a malady whereof
humanity has been the victim throughout the ages.
This merely negative tendency would indeed constitute a mutilation of human nature, but it is far from
being so widely represented as both its enemies and
certain of its partisans would have us believe—partisans who are, like commission agents, busy organising

---

[1] Letter to the International Congress of Free-thought at
Geneva, in 1902, reproduced at length in *La Raison* for Sept. 14,
1902, and in the volume *Les Affirmations de la conscience moderne*,
Paris, 1904, p. 225 *et seq.*

some new Church whereof they will be the high priests.

The men who are to-day most attacked as representing Free-thought—Ferdinand Buisson, Jules Payot, and Gabriel Séailles—are of quite another spirit.[1] Why, it may be asked, do they let themselves be compromised by noisy manifestations which are not always disinterested? The answer is very simple. The more Free-thought is conscious of its mission the less does it constitute a Church. Excommunication is a weapon it does not use.

The Free-thought professed by the eminent men I have just named, far from being a denial of the past labour of humanity, is an effort to continue it, and an invitation to every man to collaborate therein. It is the virile assertion that the past is neither error nor pure truth, but a dazzling series of human endeavours to conquer truth. The time has come when, for us, this idea consecrates the past with a power quite other than a kind of ritual canonisation; it makes us feel therein the life that we have received, whereby we live, and which, in our turn, we transmit. By this, Free-thought puts us into intimate and real contact with the life eternal; causes

---

[1] This spirit not merely of toleration, but of intelligence and respect, manifests itself also in the groups of young free-thinkers. Here is one declaration of many that may be read even in militant publications : "Many professed free-thinkers may be found who are nothing but fanatical sectarians. For them, Free-thought is not a method, but a doctrine, an intangible and sacred dogma. They take to themselves the Catholic formula, 'Outside the Church no salvation,' and treat with puerile contempt feelings and beliefs which their vulgar censure cannot touch."—*Annales de la jeunesse laïque*, the organ of the Federation, in the issue for Sept. 1910, p. 123.

us to touch it in some way; constitutes it a fact of
experience which goes beyond us in every direction,
and becomes as real to us as our own personality.

It is said in the Churches that " Man can only
attach himself with love to that which is eternal " :
and, in answer to this desire, the old metaphysics
offer intellectual constructions which have only this
defect—they lack a fulcrum, unless there comes an act
of will to offer them one by a kind of *coup d'état*.
Free-thought, on the contrary, by setting us before
the stream of life whose momentary expression we
are, presents this eternity to us as an elementary fact
to be ascertained. Free-thought awakens in us the
sensation which, for long ages before Christ, was
preparing his spiritual cradle—the sensation enunci-
ated by the prophets of Israel in the phrase which
dominates all the Old Testament—" God lives," and
which forms, as it were, the leitmotiv of the early
Christian preaching.[1] *Quærere Deum si forte attrec-
tent eum aut inveniant, quamvis non longe sit ab
unoquoque nostrum. In ipso enim vivimus et
movemur et sumus; sicut et quidam vestrorum
poetarum dixerunt: Ipsius enim et genus sumus.*

The French language, even at its most flexible and
finely shaded, lends itself but ill to render what in
the original Greek, and in the Latin of the Vulgate,
is here so living and dramatic. How splendid

[1] Acts xvii. 27–9, Paul's address on the Areopagus. " [It was
God who planted in the nations the instinct of] seeking after
God to see if they might find Him [which they have not been able
to do] though He be not far from each one of us. For it is in
Him we live, and move, and have our being; as some of your
poets also have said : . . . Of His race are we."—After Renan's
translation, *Saint Paul*, p. 196.

and moving is this advance of humanity towards a divine it does not see—a divine it forebodes and creates!

It is an experimental philosophy of life that Free-thought brings us—a philosophy which brings us into communion of feeling and action with all the past.

"Free examination," writes M. Séailles,[1] "is not the right to decree one's opinion, to proclaim one's infallibility; it is the duty of doubting where one must; of avoiding precipitation; of curbing one's passions and prejudices; IT IS THE MERITORIOUS EFFORT TO OBEY GOD BY REDISCOVERING HIS THOUGHT.[2]

"But in obeying God, we submit ourselves to our own reason, for our reason is joined to the divine thought; truth is not imposed upon us from without; it is within that we discover it as our law, as our good, as that which realises us, fulfils us, gives us veritable existence.[3]

[1] *Les Affirmations de la conscience moderne*, Paris, 1904, p. 185.

[2] The capitals are ours.

[3] Is not this, in a way, the theory of religious experience as William James has summarised it ?

"The individual, so far as he suffers from his wrongness and criticises it, is to that extent consciously beyond it, and in at least possible touch with something higher, if anything higher exist. Along with the wrong part there is thus a better part of him, even though it be but a most helpless germ. With which part he should identify his real being is by no means obvious at this stage. But when stage two (the stage of solution or salvation) arrives, the man identifies his real being with the germinal higher part of himself; and does so in the following way. *He becomes conscious that this higher part is conterminous and continuous with A MORE of the same quality, which is operative in the universe outside of him, and which he can keep in working touch with, and in a fashion get on*

" If by reflection we perceive ourself, not as a being of desïres and sensations, a solitary individual opposed to all that is not he, but as a *person*, made that he may think and will the universal, and thus join himself with all reasoning beings in the truth and good which are their law and their common reality, we shall come forth from among the contradictions that render us unintelligible to ourself. We have not to choose between anarchy and despotism, to sacrifice one of the two terms which all true life ought to reconcile—order and liberty, free examination or harmony of mind, the individual or society. We are not forced to submit to an outer authority without discussion, our only chance of agreement lying in silence : we may hope that through many mistakes and momentary divisions, from the progress of thought, from the provisional contradictions it implies, unity of spirit will, little by little, disengage itself. Free examination does not condemn us to reject tradition with scorn, because tradition expresses an instant of that pious effort whereby men strive towards a truth they will never possess save under imperfect symbols."

Is not this, indeed, the sequel to St. Paul's address on the Areopagus, which we quoted above? Are not those who, after reading such pages, can treat their authors as sectarians, atheists, and anti-religious persons, the heirs and successors of those heathen who accused the first Christians of atheism?

In a little volume which marks an epoch in the

---

board of and save himself when all his lower being has gone to pieces in the wreck."—*Varieties of Religious Experience*, London and New York, 1903, fifth impression, p. 508. [M. Sabatier quotes from the French translation of M. Abauzit, Paris, 1908.]

history of French Protestantism,[1] Ferdinand Buisson, another of the masters of present-day Free-thought, wrote in the same spirit, recalling Marcel Hébert's words : "'The ideal God of the good and the true,' far, indeed, from being a vain and shallow conception of the human spirit, is the supreme reality—it is force and being *par excellence*. Is there anything more alive than the laws of the spirit which are the very soul of our soul—those laws of nature which are the most eternal and eternally active things in the universe, infinitely more existent than our paltry and ephemeral existences?"

Ferdinand Buisson notes the tendency and policy of the Churches to identify themselves with religion, and then adds :

"Yet we need not let religion be thus indefinitely confiscated by the religions.

[1] *Libre-pensée et protestantisme libéral*, by F. Buisson and Charles Wagner, Paris, 1903, p. 54.

The book was written under the following circumstances : Ferdinand Buisson, having accepted the presidency of the National Society of Free-thought, and participated in various anti-clerical ceremonies, many Protestants, of various tendencies, blamed him strongly for it. The honourable member for Paris seized the opportunity for an explanation with his co-religionists ; and, in four letters written to the paper *Le Protestant*, advised them with great energy to become more open towards Free-thought. He showed them that they are free-thinkers without knowing it, and that for them to meet their unsectarian fellows would lead these to correct certain faults of theirs, while giving themselves a chance of acquiring new vigour in actual life.

The paper charged Pastor Charles Wagner with drawing up a reply; it is enough to say that it was worthy of the speaker.

It constitutes a conclusion of non-acceptance very dignified and even amiable, but categorical. The whole is collected in the volume cited.

" There is only one religion; there has ever been but one under the numberless forms corresponding to the different ages of human civilisation. This is the religion of goodness : or, to analyse it more deeply, the religion of the spirit aspiring to fulfil its function of spirit; to know the true, love the beautiful, and do the good, the last term summarising the two others. It is the effort of the human soul to realise its law, to live its normal life, to attain its natural purposes. Religion, which is nothing else than the instinct and urge of humanity pursuing its destiny; religion, which man draws out of the depths of himself, and which he represents to himself as coming to him from the deep of heaven, so authoritatively does it command him, so much does it appear to him as the supreme law of the universe.

" It takes more or less long to disengage itself in its purity and simplicity, to avow that it is the voice of his conscience, and that all its majesty comes precisely from its being Nature herself—his own nature —that which is at once most familiar and most mysterious in his being."

Did not the author of the Fourth Gospel catch a glimpse of some analogous truth when he put into the mouth of Jesus, as he talked with the Samaritan woman by the well of Sychar, the words, " Woman, believe me, the hour cometh when neither in this mountain nor in Jerusalem shall ye worship the Father. Ye worship that which ye know not; we worship that which we know, for salvation is from the Jews. But the hour cometh and now is, when the true worshippers shall worship the Father in spirit and truth; for such doth the Father seek to be his worshippers. God is a Spirit, and they that worship him must worship in spirit and truth."? [1]

.   .   .   .   .   .

The great crisis through which the Church is passing at this moment does not arise out of the incredulity of a few men, nor even from I know not what plot concocted by secret societies—a puerile explanation which one wonders to see put forward so often [2]—but from the fact that the official morality

---

[1] John iv. 21–24.—R.V.

[2] The notion of a plot does not cease to haunt the mind of some members of the clerical party, and perhaps it is this that renders them most alien to contemporary life and thought. Dangerous in their natural *milieu*, they are infinitely more so if by misfortune they leave it and go over to Free-thought, for then they carry over with them this unwholesome habit of mind.

Even a man of the intellectual and religious worth of the Comte de Mun writes that " Universal Free Masonry, whereof formerly *philosophy* was the intellectual cloak as *science* is to-day, exerts its powerful influence upon governments. Master of all the forces that shape *the world's opinion*, it pursues the same object, the annihilation of the Church, her organisation and social influence; and to attain this, makes war on the Papacy, the head, heart and intelligence of the Church. To separate the Catholic peoples from the Papacy by denouncing its blindness and intransigence, and by this means to lead them into apostasy, such is the plan followed with untiring perseverance, sometimes openly, sometimes by crooked paths. Thus the drama which is now beginning in Spain reproduces even in detail the one whose melancholy scenes we have known, and whose obscure vicissitudes are not yet unfolded." —*Gaulois*, Aug. 13, 1910.

Elsewhere, a bishop, Monsignor Touchet, Bishop of Orleans, recounts unhesitatingly strange stories which make one think of Leo Taxil and certain veiled women of sad memory. See *Univers* for Oct. 12, 1910, article on " A Masonic Plot." (Cp. in *La Croix* for Aug. 21, 1910 : " Free Masonry against Canada. History of a conspiracy and its original discovery.") The scholastic laws are also the result of a plot, and *L'Entente cordiale*, Jan. 8, 1911,

of the Churches has suddenly found itself lagging behind that of men's consciences.

It is true that pessimistic voices make themselves heard here and there. M. Charles Péguy, for instance, wrote not long ago : [1]

" We do not yet know whether our children will knot together again the thread of tradition, of republican conservation; whether, joining themselves across the intermediate generation, they will maintain and rediscover the sense and instinct of republican mysticism. What we know, what we see, what we perceive with absolute certainty, is that we are for the moment the rear-guard.

" Why should we deny it ? The whole intermediate generation has lost the republican sense, the taste for the Republic : the instinct surer than any knowledge—the instinct of republican mysticism. It has grown totally foreign to this mysticism. The intermediate generation—and that makes twenty years. Twenty-five years of age, and at least twenty years of duration.

" We are the rear-guard; not only a rear-guard, but a somewhat isolated, sometimes even an abandoned rear-guard. An unsupported troop. We are

---

writes : " What is moving and dramatic in the last plot concocted by the sect against the French soul is that it will inevitably drive Catholics into prison and to the shedding of blood." See also in *La Croix*, Jan. 28, 1911, under the heading " Certain Plot."

We have felt it necessary to give a few recent and precise examples of this curious mental attitude, less to show how distressing it is in men who have a great influence over Catholic opinion than to indicate how difficult it is for Free-thought to maintain discussions in the serene region of ideas and of deep personal respect.

[1] *Notre jeunesse*, p. 13.

almost *specimens*. We are about to be, we ourselves are about to be archives, archives and tables, fossils, witnesses, survivors from these historic ages, tables which will be consulted.

" We are extremely ill situated in chronology and in the sequence of the generations. We are a rear-guard badly connected, unconnected with the bulk of the troop, with former generations. We are the last of the generations that retain the republican mysticism. And our Dreyfus affair will be the last performance of republican mysticism.

" We are the last. Almost the leavings (*les après-derniers*). Directly after us begins another age, an entirely other world—the world of those who no more believe anything, who make that their glory and pride.

" Immediately after us commences the world we have named, and will never cease to name, the modern world. The world that wears a knowing look. The world of the intelligent, the advanced, of those who know, of those who have not to be shown anything, of those who cannot be imposed upon. The world of those to whom one can teach nothing. The world of those that look knowing. The world of those who are not dupes or imbeciles, as we are. *That is to say:* the world of those who believe in nothing, not even in atheism : who devote themselves to nothing, who sacrifice themselves to nothing. *Precisely:* the world of those who have no mysticism, and who boast of it. Let us not be deceived thereby, and let no one in consequence rejoice either on one side or on the other. The movement of the *de-republicanisation* of France is, in a profound sense, identical with the movement of

de-Christianisation.   It is altogether one and the
same profound movement of *de-mysticisation*.   It is
because of the same profound movement, because of
the one sole movement, that this nation believes no
longer in the Republic and believes no longer in
God; that it wishes to lead the republican life no
longer, and that it wishes no longer to lead the
Christian life (as it has done tolerably); it may almost
be said that it wishes no longer to believe in idols,
and wishes no longer to believe in the true God.
The same unbelief, *one sole* unbelief, affects the
idols and God together, affects the false gods and the
true God, the antiquated gods, the new God, the
ancient gods, and the God of the Christians.   One
and the same sterility dries up the city and Christianity.   The political city and the Christian city.   The
city of men and the City of God.   That is, properly,
the modern sterility.   Let no man, then, rejoice,
beholding the misfortune which befalls his foe, his
adversary, his neighbour.   For *the same* misfortune,
the same sterility befalls him."

The considerable sensation caused by this *Cahier*
proves, if I am not mistaken, that M. Péguy was the
interpreter of preoccupations more widespread, perhaps, than he supposed.   One is grateful to him for
having spoken of republican mysticism and for
having related it to Christian mysticism, for having
shown the thread which joins the republican tradition to the entire historical evolution of our country.

This self-examination of our generation, in which
the passage from mysticism to politics is illuminated,
in which the author shows with so candid a severity
how, " by the swing and history of events, by the

baseness and sin of man, mysticism has become
political "—this self-examination marks a new
moment in the history of our ideas, and the influence
won by M. Péguy shows that if our most undenominational society appears to have lost interest in
synagogues, chapels and churches, it can thrill profoundly the moment a disinterested inspiration
appeals directly to its conscience.

It is a common feature among the prophets that,
being laborious workers, they rarely see the work
already done, and only think of that which remains
to do.   M. Péguy is no exception to this rule.
Hence the pessimism which makes him fancy he
belongs to a rearguard when he is a forerunner.

But this pessimism which, in the prophet, is a
homage to God, to the perfection remaining to be
realised, would, in an historical essay, constitute an
error.

The greater part of those who talk of the spiritual
condition of France only know Paris, only think of
Paris, and are ceaselessly tempted to give an importance to the manifestations of our national life
proportioned to the stir they make in the capital.
Partisans [1] of every shade naturally ask no better
than to think the nation is behind them, and attribute
an historic importance to themselves.   They only
possess what one gives them : and it would be better
to count them quietly before getting agitated as to
their number.

The Paris of manifestations, even the Paris of the
people who hang about ministerial ante-rooms,
editors' offices, the purlieus of the Bourse, the draw-

---

[1] *Camelots*, see 217 n.

ing-rooms of men in power, and even sometimes of
their hoydens—the Paris that Edouard Rod [1] and
Paul Seippel [2] show us suffocating between two
dogmatisms, is not the whole of Paris, still less is
it the whole of France.

Facing his little sanctum, [3] the centre of such virile
and noble endeavour, M. Péguy sees the old temple
of science rebuilt by a Republic which never thought
—let us do it this justice—of blotting from men's
minds either Robert de Sorbon, the confessor of the
King St. Louis, or Cardinal Richelieu. The day
will soon come when our politicians and gamblers,
our mystification-mongers and their dupes, our
charlatans and our deluded ones, will have disappeared : when one will go to the Sorbonne and the
Pantheon to meditate before Puvis de Chavannes'
frescoes; when one will think that the people from
among whom such creations sprang—they, too—had
an artistic and mystical ideal which did not yield to
that of any age.

Around this same Sorbonne, grouped close about
it, at the same time attracted by its prestige and eager
to communicate to it a little of their faith, spring up
various institutions; and these, also, are manifestations of the new orientation of men's minds. " The
School of Advanced Social Studies " [4] and " The

---

[1] *L'Indocile*, Paris, 1905.

[2] *Les deux Frances et leurs origines historiques*, Paris, 1905.

[3] *Les Cahiers de la quinzaine* are published at 8 Rue de la
Sorbonne.

[4] *L'École des hautes études sociales*. Since 1903 this school has
had a department " for the study of religions in their relation
to society."

Some of the lectures given in 1903–4 were collected in a volume
entitled *Religions et sociétés*, Paris, 1905. In 1909–10, the pro-

Union of Free-thinkers and Free-believers for moral culture " [1] are due to different initiative and inspired by different preoccupations. Yet they have common

---

gramme of this department was entirely occupied by the course of M. Edouard Le Roy, Professor at St. Louis College, who studied " the Catholic attitude and affirmation."

M. Théodore Reinach, Member of the Chamber of Deputies, and Director of this department, has published a remarkable summary of its work from the commencement (*La Religion dans ses rapports avec la société*, Paris, 1911, 12-page pamphlet). " By turns entrusted to free-thinkers and believers, to believers of all denominations, our teaching aims above all at reflecting as faithfully as possible, the varied manifestations of contemporary religious thought, at connecting them with their sources, and determining their social effect. . . . To follow so complex an evolution with an attentive eye, without prejudice but with sympathy (for it is as impossible to write sound religious history without religious feeling—I do not say faith—as sound musical criticism without an ear) to catch a glimpse across the gropings, the storms, the obscurities of the present hour, of the rays that herald the smiling and quiet dawn : such is the task we have set ourselves. Though we may have filled but an insignificant part, we yet feel we have merited well of science and of the consciences of our contemporaries, we have taught them to know and tolerate one another better."

[1] Honorary Presidents : Messrs. Hyacinthe Loyson ; Frédéric Passy, Member of the Institute ; Gabriel Séailles, Professor at the Sorbonne. Standing Committee : Messrs. Leclerc de Pulligny, Chief-Engineer of Roads and Bridges ; Chairman : G. Belot, Professor of Philosophy, Member of the Higher Council of Public Instruction ; Wilfred Monod, Pastor, Lecturer to the Faculty of Protestant Theology ; Vice-chairman : Jean Kaspar, former Missionary in Madagascar, Barrister at the Court of Appeal ; General Secretary : J. Anglas, Teacher in the Alsacian School ; Assistant General Secretary : H. Fillot, Deputy Head Clerk in the Bank of France ; Treasurer : Ch. Berthomieu, Secretary to the Editorial Board of the *Annales de la jeunesse laique* ; Jacques Marty, Student of Theology ; Wautier d'Aygaliers, Pastor ; Secretary : E. Gounelle, Pastor ; P. Felix Pécaut, Professor of Philosophy.

features : the worship of truth ; absolute respect
for all those who seek it, whatever their flag; and,
finally, a continual effort to require that science
should translate itself into the reality of life. Is
there not something religious in this faith and
effort?

.   .   .   .   .   .

The spirit of reciprocal goodwill so strongly
marked in the constitution of the " Union of Free-
thinkers and Free-believers " is, perhaps, more widespread than is supposed. What it especially lacks
is the opportunity to manifest itself.

There is a multitude of Catholic believers who are
profoundly respectful toward Free-thought, and who
do not dream of its according them any favoured
treatment. One feels they are wishful to see, hear,
understand every sincere voice, even those most
opposed to their views.

The allusion to men of goodwill will at once have
brought one name to the minds of many readers—
that of M. Léon Chaine, author of the fine book
French Catholics and their Present Difficulties.[1] The
success of this work has made it clear that the theory
of the two " *blocs*," in which our contemporary
history is generally summed up, is far from being
always accurate.

M. Chaine is by no means an isolated individual.
His voice continues to arouse an ardent sympathy in
every land and in the most varied circles. The
religious activity of this undenominational soul sets

[1] *Les Catholiques français et leurs difficultés acteuls*, Lyon, 1904.
See, by the same author, *Menus propos d'un catholique libéral suivi
des commentaires de la presse*, preface by Pierre Jay, Paris, 1910,

one dreaming of the Christmas bells; as also do the efforts of another Lyonnais, the poet and philosopher, M. Joseph Serre.[1] He, too, is indeed a man of that passionate race "whose high moral instincts," as Renan said, "derive not from the reason, but from the very heart and bowels."

.   .   .   .   .   .

To return to Free-thought and its recognised representatives, if we were briefly to summarise their attitude in regard to the various religions—which must not be confused with clericalism—we should say it was a very marked and persevering effort to do justice to all those manifestations of thought and conscience.

These are not formal principles, but ideas which men who are every day denounced as odious sectarians are seeking to propagate. Not to remain among generalities, this is how one of them, M. Ferdinand Buisson, spoke on August 22, 1903, to M. Aulard in *L'Action:*

"I say that in every age there is, in humanity— variable as it is, and passing through all the stages of its development—a phenomenon essentially human, natural and normal, and, consequently, legitimate—the religious phenomenon—one of the characteristic traits of man in distinction from the animal.

"I say that this phenomenon may be manifested

[1] See especially, among his works, *La Religion de l'esprit large,* Paris, 1908, *La Lumière du cœur,* Paris, 1910. Always preoccupied with synthesis, conciliation and harmony, he has devoted his latest work to an endeavour to draw together *Les Sillons et l'action française,* Paris, 1911,

under three forms : the religious *idea;* the religious *emotion;* the religious *act.*

" The religious idea is, at the outset, the confused intuition and, later, the clear affirmation that we do not know all, and cannot do all; that man is the merest particle of this vast universe; that he is neither the author nor the master of his life; that around him, outside him, there are forces, laws and powers upon which he depends, and which do not depend on him; that in the heart of this infinity he is infinitely small, and that, nevertheless, it is from this imperceptible point that the light leaps forth which shall illumine the rest of the world—the light of the spirit, of reason, of conscience.

" The religious emotion is the rebound of this idea in our feelings. By turns, it is a sentiment of terror before the vastness of the unknown, before the infinite that overwhelms us; and then, in the opposite direction, a feeling of faith in the universal order, of confidence in the supremacy of the spirit which is the basis of ourselves and, doubtless, of the universe. It is the feeling of our relation with those mysterious forces that rule the worlds, of our participation in the life universal; the feeling of the nothing we are, and yet of the infinite value of the reason that is in us; the feeling of the Beyond which escapes our grasp; the ideal we are so unhappy never to reach, and which we should be more unhappy yet not to pursue for ever.

" Finally, religious action is that in which man forgets himself and sacrifices himself to an invisible law that no one imposes upon him, that no one shows him. It is the impulse of devotion, whereby, without hesitating, he joyfully abandons his interests, his instincts, his happiness, his life, braves every affliction, endures every torment, to give satisfaction to an idea which he believes to be just, to a dream he judges beautiful, to a commandment of the spirit, to an order of conscience.

"Which of these three roots of the religious fact do you, my dear friend, believe it your duty absolutely to extirpate from the human soul, as a parasitic and noxious weed?" [1]

[1] We wanted to give the essential part of this article without omission to show that free-thinkers do not hesitate to take views which are full of respect for religion before the most popular audiences. Many analogous facts might be cited. We will only mention one : the fine address on "The scientific Spirit and the religious Spirit," given on Nov. 11, 1906, in the great amphitheatre of the Sorbonne, by M. Paul Painlevé, of the Institute, socialist Deputy to-day for Paris. It was published in the *Revue du mois* for Dec. 10, 1906, Vol. II, pp. 658-68.

In it he said : "It is then by no means absurd to foresee an epoch, less distant perhaps than we think, when these two tendencies of man, instead of hurling themselves against one another, will collaborate as they collaborated in the dawn of civilisation : the religious spirit always preceding science in the domains the latter cannot yet reach, stimulating its discoveries, but always ready to yield to the latter with a good grace each new position it becomes able to occupy. In return, science owes it to itself not to exceed in its assertions the limits of truly acquired knowledge, leaving to each scientist the responsibility for his individual opinions on questions which still elude positive research.

"But if all conflict between the real scientific spirit and the real religious spirit be impossible, there may be—what do I say ? there will necessarily, there will always, be conflict between science and the men who exploit the religious spirit, claiming, instead of allowing, it to evolve freely to the rhythm of life, to give it style and stiffen it into an artificial rigidity in conformity with their interests, their habits or their prejudices. There will necessarily be conflict between science and all religion which claims to impose on it by virtue of I know not what revelation, an absurd and puerile astronomy, geology and cosmogony ; in a word, there will always be conflict between science and all domineering religion, which having formerly invaded the ground open before it, refuses to abandon any parcel of it.   It is the inevitable and permanent character of such a conflict which renders the conviction so general that there is an irreducible antinomy between the scientific and the religious spirit."

CHAPTER XIV

THE CREATION OF THE UNDENOMINATIONAL SCHOOL

If the war of 1870 influenced our scholastic organisation, the soul
of the undenominational school has a more distant and a loftier
origin—Our undenominational school is the new incarnation
of an age-long religious effort—In 1882 it was far from being
anti-clerical—Crusade against it preached by the Conservative
parties : the result—It is now compelled to give the children
the spiritual nurture they would otherwise lack.

WE come now to the heart of our subject.

For contemporary France the creation of the undenominational primary school has been no mere
episode; with the organisation of her military defence
it has been her constant preoccupation.

We must here set these two questions side by side,
for so they stand in reality. But we must not
exaggerate their relationship. After the war, when
we were still hypnotised by defeat, many of those
who strove the most ardently for the diffusion of
instruction found an argument, both too ready and
too oratorical, in the notion that it was the Prussian
schools that beat us, and that by reorganising public
instruction on new foundations we were organising
revenge.

The argument was not a happy one, for it tended
to give a merely occasional aspect to a movement
which had long occupied France and was leading her
towards a renovation of teaching in every grade.

It was a singular mistake to make of patriotic claims, however just, the soul of the school. Accordingly, this mistake was of short duration. Little by little, whatever was transplanted into our soil from an orientation, from methods and customs, contrary to our proper genius, was naturally eliminated.[1] To-day, the school no longer dreams of becoming a barracks: it is the barracks that is getting ready to become a school, wherein all citizens will not only learn to handle weapons, but will become conscious of national solidarity and the duties imposed thereby. A more considered bravery upon the battle-field will be yet more brave and more efficacious. The audacity of our aviators has sufficiently shown how naturally, without the support of mass-enthusiasm, our soldiers can face death.

The country has made sacrifices for its schools with an ardour and perseverance which have not flagged for forty years. *Sacrifices*—the word has here its original sense, for those sacrifices, accorded with extraordinary joy at so difficult a moment, are the manifestation of a faith which is ignorant of itself and finds such expression as it may.

That is a social phenomenon of great import, whose intensity and direction must be grasped if we are not to misunderstand contemporary history.

For it is by the undenominational school that our country has sought to conquer herself and has striven to realise her new dreams. That is why the word "creation" comes naturally to our pen, and not "organisation" or some other similar term. The

[1] We have not forgotten the ephemeral existence of the " school brigades "—*bataillons scolaires*.

undenominational school, without intending it, without even thinking of it, has become something other and more than the dispenser of elementary knowledge, and also something other than a government organ whose function was to prepare future subjects.

The present religious movement has found in it both a field for experiment and its own concrete manifestation. In and by it, all the tendencies which in preceding chapters we have seen somewhat scattered abroad, tend to unite, to embody themselves and become the generators of a new civilisation.

The adversaries of the undenominational school are not mistaken when they denounce it as the bulwark of the new ideas, and concentrate their strength on attacking it. Where they are completely mistaken is in failing to see the roots which so formidable an institution thrusts down into the political, intellectual, moral and religious life of the whole country, and in imagining that it is the result of some international conspiracy.[1]

If they had eyes they would perceive that in spite of all its imperfections the undenominational effort is the sequel and heir to the tradition, at once Christian and French, which revealed itself so characteristically in the thirteenth century.

Dogmatic formulas did not create ogival architecture : it was the faith of the Middle Ages that found this means of expression. Each of our Gothic cathedrals sings of God, the desire for the divine and the beautiful, the city's dream as it sought to unite hands and hearts, and to partake in an ever-loftier labour.

[1] See p. 225, n. 2.

Under another form, the undenominational school is an analogous endeavour to express an analogous faith; and they are but superficial observers who can recall on this occasion the famous formula : *ceci tuera cela*—this will slay that.

Our primary school itself is far from knowing what it is doing and whither it goes. It develops as an adolescent develops, amazed to note the changes in itself whereof it is both the witness and author, and over which it has but slender influence.[1]

It was shaped by circumstances, and we should be much mistaken if we supposed it to be definitively constituted; its adversaries, attacking and striving to suppress it, are as maladroit and unwise as those who think to suppress a lamentable event by causing the disappearance of the messenger who brings the news.

It is incontestable that in 1880 no one could foresee what the undenominational school was about to become. At that time effort was especially directed to gratuity and compulsion. The idea of undenomi-nationalism, when then it began to be defined, was sometimes inspired by the ready and rather superficial

---

[1] It is somewhat difficult to-day to realise that the school code of Aug. 17, 1855, in force till June 7, 1880, devoted seven articles (20–26) to the duties of the teacher in respect to the Churches. Here is the last : " Religious teaching comprises the reading of the Catechism and the elements of sacred history. Every day there must be added a part of Sunday's Gospel, which shall be repeated entire on Saturday. There shall be a catechism lesson every day, even for the children who have taken their first communion. The lessons in religious instruction shall be arranged according to the instructions of the parish priest."

The catechism was then, in the full meaning of the expression, " the foundation of national instruction."—Father Lecanuet, *L'Église de France sous la Troisième République*, 1870–1878, p. 352, Paris, 1907.

eclecticism of Victor Cousin, sometimes by pragmatist views much akin to those which seem to inspire the Government of the United States in its relation with the Churches : it was most desirable explicitly to recognise their distinguished collaboration in the social task, and to treat them with abundant deference.

This attitude was perfectly sincere. Nothing permits us to suppose that it was a hypocritical and provisional manœuvre to facilitate the spread of the new educational theories.

The Government and the Houses of Parliament had only one wish : to forward the reform of public instruction without disturbing any one's conscience. The school must cease to be a kind of branch of the Churches and become wholly independent; but far from making an anti-Church of it, they were obviously studious to avoid every occasion for conflict. In the circular of November 2, 1882, the Government concluded its instructions to the Prefects by announcing " the pretension, while making the law respected, to make it also understood and beloved."

" The teacher," ran the official instructions for July 27, 1882, " has not to teach at every point a theoretic morality followed by a practical morality, as though he were addressing himself to children destitute of any previous idea of good and evil; on the contrary, the vast majority come to him having already received, or now receiving, a religious instruction which familiarises them with the idea of a God, the Author of the universe and the Father of men, and with the traditions, beliefs and practices of a Christian or a Jewish worship. By means of this

R

worship, and under the forms proper to it, they have already received the fundamental ideas of eternal and universal morality; but these ideas are still, for them, in the state of a naissant and delicate germ; they have not penetrated deeply into them : they are fleeting and confused, rather caught sight of than possessed, entrusted to the memory rather than to a conscience, scarcely as yet exercised. They wait to be ripened and developed by suitable culture. It is this culture that the public teacher is about to give them.

" His mission, then, is well defined : it consists in strengthening and rooting into his pupils' hearts for their whole lives, by causing them to enter into daily practice, those essential ideas of human morals which are common to every doctrine and necessary to all civilised men. He can fulfil this mission without having personally to adhere to or oppose any of the various denominational beliefs with which his pupils associate and mingle the general principles of morality. He takes the children as they come to him, with their ideas and their speech, with the beliefs they derive from their families, and he is only anxious to teach them to draw from these what is most precious in them from the social point of view; that is to say, the precepts of a lofty morality.

" Undenominational moral teaching is, then, distinct from, but not contradictory to, religious teaching. The teacher neither takes the place of the priest nor of the head of the family; he joins his efforts to theirs to make a good man of each child. . . . All theological and philosophical discussion is manifestly forbidden him by the very character of his functions, by the age of his pupils, by the trust of their families and of the State. All his efforts are concentrated on a problem of a different nature, not less arduous, though its nature is exclusively practical : to give all these children an emotional apprenticeship to the moral life. Later, when they have become citizens, they may be separated by dogmatic opinions; but in practice they will at least be agreed to set the end of life as high as possible; to have the same horror for everything base and vile, the same admiration for what is noble and generous, the same delicacy in the appreciation of duty; to aspire to moral perfection, whatever efforts it may cost; to feel themselves united in that general worship of the good, the true and the beautiful which is, moreover, a form, and not the least pure, of religious feeling."

This long quotation was necessary in order to recall the intentions of the legislators of 1882 to those who have forgotten them.

We need not here describe the attitude of hostility and challenge adopted by the party which at that time claimed to represent the Church of France. Any weapon was good wherewith it might fight what it called "the School without God." Jules Ferry, Ferdinand Buisson, Felix Pécaut, Jules Steeg—all those who actually collaborated in the organisation of primary education—were first attacked before Parliament with unheard-of violence; then, frank and direct legal opposition failing to prevent the voting of the new laws, a desperate resistance was organised, even in the smallest hamlets, against their application. No means was rejected which might serve what was called the cause of God. The new schoolmistresses were coming out of the Normal College, and were specially attacked. When, despite the threats with which they were assailed, they went to fill their posts, they were subjected in "Christian" villages to a formidable quarantine. Not only would no one speak to them or respond to their greeting, but often the baker and grocer refused to sell them anything what-ever. Hostile shouts and base abuse broke out when they went by; and for months, sometimes for longer, the undenominational school remained absolutely deserted.

We must in a few words recall these manœuvres and persecutions, for we are tempted to forget them. We have good reason to do so from the point of view of morality and national reconciliation; but from the point of view of history and of our public conduct we should be absolutely wrong if we did not profit by the lesson of these events, for therein lies one of the factors which have envenomed the present situation. By organising against the undenominational school manifestations which did not stop at any vulgarity, by subjecting to the punishment of isolation and of the vilest calumnies young women who were often most religious, certain ecclesiastics not only lowered themselves to a rôle foreign to their part; they created against the Church, and against all it represents and teaches, stores of hatred and desires for retaliation, and precisely among the whole lower middle-class and the small landed proprietors, that is to say, in those circles which are like a nursery for the Normal Schools, and which had till then remained wholly refractory towards anti-Catholicism.[1]

[1] The Church was not content with organising obstruction against all the laws which organised the school. When it saw the uselessness of its efforts, it created a whole network of institutions from the infant school to the industrial school and the university. In other lands one is acquainted with denominational schools,

Here, then, is something of which we must not lose sight when we want to understand the disaffection evidenced by France towards her clergy when the law of Separation was being voted.

If, instead of declaring war on the undenominational school, the Church in France had acted as it did in the United States, and generally in countries where it has felt it must accept circumstances in place of claiming to impose its own control, the enormous majority of the country, which only wished for peace with the Church, would have been infinitely grateful for its collaboration, and probably the orientation of the nation's life would have been very different. The Conservative Republic would have entered into our customs; France would have regarded her rank of eldest daughter of the Church as a precious title, and it is difficult to imagine what a Pope as clever as Leo XIII might not have made of the situation.[1]

---

but I do not think that there has anywhere been the systematic effort which has been made in France to take the child from his cradle and keep him through all his studies from any contact with thought not strictly denominational.

The Catholic University stands opposite to the University without an epithet. Abroad it may be imagined that the latter gives in France a kind of anti-Catholic official education. That is a gross error. A very large majority of the professors of our universities are, naturally, of Catholic derivation, and if some among them do not hesitate to manifest their anti-clerical opinions, there are others, and a great number, who are very orthodox Catholics, and speak and behave as such.

[1] For the rest it must be recognised that if under Pius X's pontificate the crusade against undenominationalism was organised at Rome, under Leo XIII it was somewhat otherwise : the Crusade was then organised in France by the remains of the old parties, and was far from receiving all the encouragement it desired from Rome.

The pacific attitude of the Church would doubtless have produced results similar to those which it has produced in America; and in this country it would have been assured an incomparable position, because of the profound roots it thrusts down into the soil of our history.

.   .   .   .   .   .

Those who represented it in fact rather than by right [1] commenced the desperate and often odious struggle of which we have been spectators, less to defend the rights of conscience and liberty, as they professed, than because they hoped to be victors and seize upon power.

Not only was the attempt little worthy of those who made it or of the cause they desired to serve; it was ill calculated, and has not ceased to sustain the most grievous rebuffs; moreover, its organisers seem to have profited nothing by the lessons of defeat.

By refusing such honourable conditions of peace as were offered them in the law of 1882, the representatives of the Church have obliged France to reopen the era of hostilities and to go to the very limits of undenominational claims.   To the Government and the country, which desired an indefinite truce, the answer was a formidable mobilisation in which genuine Conservatives and the sharpshooters of subversive parties were soon seen fighting side by side.

By this struggle, devoid of wisdom or dignity, the

[1] Then, as to-day, the Clerical Press, while protesting its absolute respect for hierarchical authority, did not cease to force its directions upon the episcopate.

Church lost a great part of its prestige in the social strata in which its moral and religious influence had been the most considerable.

Certainly it was not wrong in declaring that the neutrality established by the law of 1882 was impracticable, provisional and precarious; a kind of compromise which could satisfy neither the Church nor the State. But is the educational situation so different in many countries where the Church has completely accommodated itself to the various enactments? If at the time the task of collaborating in the work of Parliament had been permitted, we should have continued to see what we saw in the first years—I mean the law yielding to circumstance, and accommodating itself to local environment and traditions. Long after 1882, and even after 1900, teachers have been known to sing in the choir, to accompany on the harmonium, to take their scholars to Mass and supervise them there.

The Church did not choose to accept this *modus vivendi* without basis in the text of the law, this situation which varied from commune to commune, from teacher to teacher: it thought to serve its cause better by compelling the country to evolve rapidly towards complete neutrality.

This policy was obviously inspired by the notion that neutral teaching, being impracticable, would soon degenerate into anti-religious teaching, and that this official anti-religion would result in such a decline in public morals that the nation would be obliged to cast itself anew into the arms of the Church to escape final dissolution.

The success of this calculation was not improbable, for in the least religious quarters many representative men were of opinion that, as a measure of public hygiene, a form of worship should be retained at the base of public education which they would not choose either for the financial aristocracy or for the intellectuals.

This homage by the comfortable to the Church deeply shocked the working classes, and is perhaps one of the major causes for the depreciation of religion in our country.

The famous phrase : *Il faut une religion pour le peuple*—The people requires a religion—has done more harm to the Church than all the attacks of her foes.

. . . . . .

At the present time, educational neutrality, attacked with equal heat by the clerical and the anti-clerical parties, is only defended and observed by a part of the primary teaching body. Setting aside an insignificant minority of teachers, of whom some would give a clearly anti-religious character to their lessons, while some would make them foreign to any philosophical or ethical outlook, it may be said that, little by little, the great majority has arrived at a very clear desire to strengthen undenominational moral teaching and to give it an unshakable basis. They want it to possess an efficacy whereto it has not yet attained; partly, as they think, because it derives more or less from the morality of the Churches. It is an imitation without force or originality. Hence they are seeking for the new soul of the new school.

These aspirations harmonise with the great bulk of public opinion. On the one side, this expects and

mouth, reaching our young people and even the peasants of our country-side, as though to persuade them that in these days corruption is everywhere, virtue and devotion nowhere. Much has been said of late about the deleterious influence exerted on the people by various judicial cases and criminal stories. It is perfectly true. Yet in the Press of to-day there is a corrupting influence still more immediate and powerful, the senseless accusations circulated by partisans against their adversaries : against men whose life is public and may be followed, so to speak, from hour to hour, the silliest legends are invented in the assurance that their victims have something else to do than to reply; and it is not recognised that, though of all this nothing may remain of a nature to injure the slandered man, yet something of it will always remain in the minds of those who read the slander. They fancy themselves knowing, and succeed in persuading themselves that whoever is invested with any social charge, and even any man in the public eye, is in some way enrolled in the army of corruption and venality.

Calumnies do not generally strike those against whom they are launched, but they suggest to the mass of the people that the social staff is filled with men capable of committing any crime in order to enrich themselves. Those who profess by such means to avenge public morality could act no otherwise if they wished to persuade our people that, since governments have no ideal save their own passions and interests, the governed would indeed be foolish to show themselves more virtuous.

But if corruption is much greater in appearance and in the columns of the Press than in reality, it is no less true that it is formidable, and that in many quarters there exists real moral anarchy. Whose is the fault? On every hand the representatives of tradition are violently attacking those who strive to put an end to the confusion of conscience.

Is it really undenominational morality that is here at fault? Would it not rather be right to accuse ecclesiastical morality?

.   .   .   .   .   .

We cannot in these pages examine all the essays which have been made to satisfy the new needs. They are too many. We shall only mention two or three among the more recent : either because they are attempts at organic synthesis, or because, having aimed at the establishment of moral teaching in the schools, they have not remained in the region of philosophic speculation, but have been widely experimented in, and in the primary school exert already a real influence over conduct.

J. M. Guyau's views have only had an indirect influence; but still they have here and there awakened the reflections of teachers seeking a new basis for moral education. The influence of Felix Pécaut—and, later, that of Charles Wagner—has, perhaps, been more general, because the ideas of these two eminent moralists are presented under a more simple practical aspect, and as though bathed in that mystical poetry and feeling whose absence is too often felt in the manuals of undenominational morality. But these remarkable and felicitous efforts correspond rather to the situation of 1882 than to that of to-day. They are not positively systematic, and suppose an intellectual and moral synthesis already made outside the school.

Now it is evident that, for divers reasons, a great number of children—even, perhaps, a majority—have come to school during the last few years without having been brought into explicit, or even implicit, contact with any religious or moral synthesis whatever.[1]

This state of things has been keenly felt by some of the leaders of contemporary thought and pedagogy. They have seen clearly that if the school has no right to replace the family and Church for those who have one, it can no longer ignore the fact that many children have neither a family nor a Church. To give them scattered moral precepts without giving them wherewithal to bind the sheaf together, to surcharge their memories with special precepts without preparing their conscience to act and find in its own depths the solution of the unforeseen and formidable questions life will set them, is a moral impossibility.

We must repeat: the undenominational school did not desire to erect itself into an institution of moral education; it has been driven by circumstances to accept this function. It can no more refuse its duty, under pretence of neutrality, than it can neglect the physical health of its scholars.

This is what M. Jules Payot, the well-known author of the *Education of the Will*, felt deeply.

---

[1] Monseignor Dadolle, Bishop of Dijon, could tell Pius X that the number of practising Catholics [in France] did not exceed four or five millions. There must, then, at this moment, be about thirty millions of our fellow-citizens living outside all ecclesiastical influence. This is an important historical fact, and one can understand the irresistible pressure exerted on the undenominational school to demand a programme of ideal life from it.

S

His *Ethical Course* [1] is a living effort to find a synthesis which may be offered to the child, not as a sort of temporary scaffolding to serve him for a few years and be abandoned the moment reason awakes, but to cause him to find within himself a guide and intelligence which is, indeed, a categorical imperative, but which is more, because, while it brings the precept it brings also the justification. This eminent thinker saw clearly that one of the chief causes of the moral anarchy of our age is the singular attitude of many parents, who profess to have their children taught a morality they themselves do not observe— one based upon dogmas to which they refuse any consideration or credence. To destroy the canals and aqueducts, and then go to quench one's thirst at the fountains they should feed—what strange inconsequence is this!

Yet it is that of a notable fraction of the most civilised peoples. This initial falsehood vitiates a part of our present education : the child, more alert and attentive than is usually supposed, perceives the difference between that which is inculcated upon it and that which is believed, and early comes to regard morality as a sort of traditional etiquette, like that of fine manners.

There are parents, and even elementary schoolmasters, who, in face of this danger, have valiantly essayed to return not only to the religious ideas but to the practices of such and such a Church. Could many cases be cited in which this attempt has suc-

---

[1] *Cours de morale*, seventh edition, Paris, 1909 (the first edition was published in 1904). This book, intended for teachers, is complemented by another, specially intended for scholars : *La Morale à l'école* (first edition, 1906), fourth edition, Paris, 1910.

ceeded, in which the existing Churches have given the individual the help and illumination of which he stood in need not merely for his personal life but for his function as an educator?

Many of those who turn towards Protestantism— and in particular towards liberal Protestantism— taste the rather negative delight of prisoners whose bonds have been broken; but this sensation very soon grows thin, and there are those who never succeed in finding the inward discipline they sigh for.

M. Jules Payot, therefore, sought the basis and starting-point for the moral initiation of the child into life in individual experience, corroborated by that of society as a whole, in so far as we can grasp it. The child is called on to discover within himself the idea of "rational life in which the highest freedom is included." [1] He ascertains promptly that this national life is only possible in and by human co-operation. Thus, appeal is only made to experience and its organic growth. The child habituates himself to an idea of knowledge which is wholly living and true, very different from the notion given by intellectualism. Moral instruction, thus conceived, is "a force directive of thought and action," setting the entire individual in motion and achieving in him, with his collaboration, a work of creation, of evolution, and of the building up of the individual, in and for that society which is, as it were, the essential basis of man's life.

In other words, for M. Payot, as for a whole group of thinkers who, in these last years, have set themselves to the remoulding of undenominational moral

[1] *Cours de morale*, p. xi.

instruction, the starting-point and fulcrum is sought in the life of the individual regarded at the very out-set as a member of society; the idea of progress won from the historical view of facts is invoked to deter-mine the individual will and to bring it to constitute itself " an agent of voluntary evolution." [1]

This point of view is lofty enough not to come into collision with the moral instruction of the vari-ous Churches. The ground on which M. Payot moves is that of experience, that of the Churches is revelation : and a child can be imagined receiving both forms of instruction at the same time without finding them contradictory. Naturally, the *Ethical Course* does not speak of the various positive religions from the standpoint of the Churches; but it is an entire stranger to polemics, and finds a lesson of toleration and spiritual labour in the historical statement of the extreme diversity of religions.

We have taken this book as a type of the moral instruction given to-day in the elementary school, not merely because of its intrinsic value, but also because it has seemed to us the most representative

[1] *Cours de morale*, p. 206. With M. Dürkheim (*Bulletin de la société française de philosophie*, April and May 1907) the notion of society's authority is asserted with such vigour that one cannot help thinking—*mutatis mutandis*—of the views of certain Catholics concerning the Church, the perfect society ; for whom, moreover, the idea of the Church, experimentally fixed, becomes both the source and goal of every action.

See also, Léon Bourgeois, *Solidarité*, Paris, 1900 ; Levy-Brühl, *La Morale et la science des mœurs*, Paris, 1901; Belot, *Études de morale positive*, Paris, 1906 ; *L'Éducation morale dans l'Université* (Collection of lectures by Messrs. Levy-Brühl, Malapert, Belot, etc.), Paris, 1901 ; *Morale sociale* (similar collection of lectures by Messrs. Belot, Brunschwicg, Buisson, Darlu, etc.), Paris, 1903 ; B. Jacob, *Devoirs*, Paris, 1908.

of the present tendencies.   Besides, its author is now
the man most widely attacked by the Press hostile
to undenominationalism in France.   And with good
reason.   By neglecting the blustering manifestations
of a sectarian anti-clericalism which dreams of restor-
ing the doctrinal unity of the country to the advantage of a new orthodoxy, and by attacking with a
kind of frenzy the men who have no more hatred
on their lips than in their hearts, this part of the Press
has shown that it discerns clearly enough on which
side the great force of the future lies.

Is this to declare that M. Payot's views are final?
He himself would not claim that; and now and again
there are pages one would like to discuss with him; [1]
but precisely this is one of his great merits, that he

[1] For example (p. 190), the notion that religions " have had
a common origin in the fear of hostile forces and in a naïve
interpretation of death."

This discussion would bring us to ask if we knew the savage
races well enough to be able to study in them the birth and evolution of feelings very difficult to follow even among civilised peoples
speaking the same language as ourselves.   I am tempted to think
that we often class under the heading of religions, phenomena
entirely heterogeneous.   One of the first questions explorers put
is of the religion of the tribes they are studying.   Is not this a
mistake in method, a manner of questioning which modifies
reality in advance ?

Is it really in conformity with the truth of facts, that wherever
man is found, some features of religion are met with ?   Even in
our actual society, are there not beings in whom the religious
initiation to which they have been subjected has aroused nothing,
changed nothing, created nothing ?   Is there not sometimes in
the look of a dog, a language in which emotions may be read never
to be met with in the eyes of some men whose moral consciousness
—the life of the heart and of the spirit—does not seem to exist ?

Does the idea of good and evil, of moral discipline, which to-day
would seem to be the heart of all religious faith, exist among all
our contemporaries ?

creates in his readers, both great and small, the impression of views long meditated upon but presented without any kind of dogmatism. He is a traveller who points out to others the way he has just travelled after having first surrounded himself with every means of investigation in his power. He does not claim that no one can find another way.

.   .   .   .   .   .

The same spirit of good-will towards the past, the same endeavour to seek in historic and present experience the plan for an efficacious moral instruction, is found in M. Jean Delvolvé's essay entitled, *Rationalism and Tradition. An Inquiry into the Conditions of an Efficacious Undenominational Morality.*[1]

It is, unfortunately, impossible to pause as long as we would wish over this book—a specially important contribution not only to the pedagogic history of the Third Republic but to the moral ideas of the present time.

First, the writer studies the present organisation of moral and religious instruction with an elevation of view which can only be reproached for one thing— if, indeed, it is a subject for reproach—an excess of generosity which makes him credit the moral instruction dealt out by the Churches with an efficacy beyond what it possesses.

Over against this optimistic picture he has painted the attempts of undenominational moral instruction in colours whose accuracy makes one think of a man who sees the spectacle he is painting at too short a

---

[1] *Rationalisme et tradition. Recherches des conditions d'efficacité d'une morale laïque*, Paris, 1910.

range. I do not wish to exaggerate the contrast in pointing it out; it is obviously disinterested and un-intentional, and springs out of a very noble and rare anxiety to cherish a kind of prejudice in favour of those whose ideas one does not share.[1]

The repugnance which it notes among a great number of schoolmasters in what concerns the teaching of morals, and the eagerness with which they seek to get rid of this part of their task, have very various causes.

---

[1] M. Delvolvé notes rightly that " among the picked individuals who come to the higher schools of Paris, there is a purely verbal memory of rational principles, a feeble understanding of the simplest duties, and a singular aptitude for retaining the anecdote while forgetting its moral significance " (p. 17). He might have made exactly the same observations if he were studying the young Catholics or Protestants who have had an entirely religious education. Save in exceptional cases, it has inculcated in them ecclesiastical or moral customs which remain for a very long time external and superficial. It is only later on, and often very slowly, that they become interior, root down to the conscience, form an integral part of the individual's life.

The reports on moral instruction in primary schools are of very slender historical value. They belong to official literature. That of M. Frédéric Lichtenberger for the Exhibition of 1889, teaches us more about its writer's mentality than about the subject studied. It was he who—before Jules Ferry, at the inauguration of the Paris Protestant Theological Faculty—launched the formula : " If France had had a Luther, she would have had no Sedan." His report naturally insinuates—with all the reserve and moderation that become a man occupying a high University post—that un-denominational moral instruction was incomplete and destitute of solid basis ; and this with a hope that the services Protestantism was prepared to undertake if called upon to educate the Democracy, would soon be recognised.

Was it not singularly premature to think of drawing up a sort of balance-sheet of undenominational moral instruction within ten years of the first attempt to organise it ?

It must be recognised that here and there some failures, having painfully gained their certificates, and obtained posts after urgent political manœuvrings, imagine that the advent of the republic has sanctioned the disappearance of all religious and moral authority, and that the master's sole business is to prepare children to get the certificate for elementary studies; but these cases are very rare, and frequently the experience of life, the pressure of public opinion and the counsels of their colleagues suffice to correct their errors.

The truth is, the masters often find themselves but ill prepared for moral teaching because in their own education morality and religion were not separated. Now they are legion whose faith—or rather whose attachment to the Church—has suffered wreck without their moral conscience having been touched. But when it comes to leading the children whom they direct to moral initiation, they cannot take as their basis the dogmas or the revelation they no longer believe, and they have no idea at all how to find another way.

This is an actual condition much more frequent than is supposed; it is one, moreover, that exists in numberless families belonging to the moral *élite* of our country. The parents no longer feel they have a right to bring up their children in absolute submission to a Church in whose divine authority they themselves have ceased to believe; yet they have not found outside it the moral foundation they require.

Hasty and ingenious people get out of the difficulty by a kind of *coup d'état;* some of them behave as though they still believed in dogma; others, as though the theological disorder had brought about complete moral anarchy. In both cases there is indolence, falsehood and cowardice. Wherefore, we ought to be thankful to many an insignificant teacher, to many a humble schoolmistress, for their courage in remaining in this state of waiting and uncertainty, for acknowledging to themselves what is precarious in this situation, and even for acknowledging it to others.

Thus, in many instances, the very real insufficiency of moral instruction is due to scruples most honourable in those who entertain them. These feelings are entirely new, and a sign of singularly lofty pre-occupations, which ought, indeed, to be described as religious, even if they seem to manifest themselves in actions hardly pleasing to the Churches.

The Churches—and the anti-Churches just as much—will exclaim, "But you have no right to disturb the child with your hesitations; he expects Truth from you, and to be shown the Way to follow!" "Have I the right to point it out when I do not know it myself, just in order to keep him tranquil? He would not credit my intended assurance, and the lesson in scepticism I had thus given him might poison his whole education."

These are considerations not to be lost sight of, if one would be just to undenominational teaching. Much is said of its failure, and quite wrongly; for it was really too puerile to fancy it was going to be established in ten or twenty years! Such an illusion could only be cherished by incorrigible doctrinaires, who never lower their eyes to the reality which is in a perpetual labour of bringing forth.

There would have been real failure if the obvious good-will of the Government had triumphed over all obstacles, and in a few months in all the schools in France a sort of undenominational catechism had been taught with as complete indifference as the diocesan catechism had been taught before. If this had occurred, the enemies of the new ideas might, perhaps, have thought the undenominational triumph complete, but the very absence of every difficulty would have been a sign that all life and energy had disappeared.

The resistance, hesitation and groping about of many schoolmasters are a token of an anxious integrity, virility and dignity.

The vigour with which they perceive that their mission is changing its character, and that the country expects them to play a part for which they have not been prepared, reveals, in its way, their moral worth. Hirelings pure and simple would have been at no pains to conform to the new requirements.

Returning to M. Delvolvé's book, one could wish it might be slowly read and re-read by all who are interested in the moral situation of our country. Its survey of Catholicism is animated by so real an *intelletto d'amore* that this Free-thinker reveals surely to his Catholic readers some of the most admirable features of their faith, and will keep non-Catholics who understand him from unjust judgments, and the habit of summary condemnation. The author does not hesitate to enter into details, and to show, for example, the rôle of the Sign of the Cross with a clearness and certainty of observation [1] to be found with difficulty among the most popular of orthodox writers.

[1] *Loc. cit.*, p. 36.

He notes, as he proceeds, the deficiency of certain attempts which have thought to imitate the Churches from outside : " the imitation of Christ [1] is, in reality, obsession by the divinity. To seek to supply it by multifarious human examples shows that one has missed its meaning and force. Nothing is more distressing than these superficial counterfeits of an ill-grasped system."

The great merit of the moral teaching given by the Churches in general, and by the Church of Rome in particular, is that of being " organicist " ; [2] they tend to build the entire moral life upon the spiritual foundation of faith. On the other hand, undenominational teaching is depicted as " essentially theoretical and analytic." [3]

If it seems to us that M. Delvolvé is wrong in

---

[1] *Loc. cit.*, p. 34, note 1.   [2] *Ibid.*, p. 39.

[3] These assertions appear disputable. M. Payot and the sociological school, for instance, set out from no *a priori*, but from individual and historical experience, around which the whole moral edifice takes form.

Similarly, one might question whether the fundamental notion with which Catholicism imbues the soul is really that of God, or if it does not rather arouse an experience of the Church idea, which leads us to a basis very similar to that of the sociological school. I think I am not mistaken in saying that as a matter of fact it is faith in the Church which is the basis of the Catholic life, and that faithful union with the Church is the supreme goal. It is the Church that leads to God, not *vice versa*. Thence there comes to Catholicism, as compared with other Christian communions, a basis of experience often unsuspected by those who only see in faith an intellectualist act.

M. Dürkheim says somewhere (*Bulletin de la société française de philosophie*, 1906, p. 129) : " In divinity I only see society transfigured and symbolically conceived." Many Catholics who cannot analyse their intellectual life have experiences entirely analogous.

opposing traditional religious ethics to undenominational ethics—as the eminent thinkers whose works
we have only been able to indicate seek to constitute
the latter—and if it really seems to us that this undenominational ethics is also—to use M. Delvolvé's
own expression—"organicist," we think, nevertheless, that his endeavour to give greater unity, cohesion and efficacy—or, as he calls it, "motricity"—
driving force—to undenominational moral instruction is entirely justified. But again we must not
mistake the facts that unfold before us. The increase of criminality proves nothing against the substitution of undenominational moral instruction for
the other, since this increase is manifested throughout the whole world, and especially in countries
where undenominationalism is far from being the
rule. Unsectarian moral teaching lacks, of course, the
prestige of tradition—that patina of time which at
sunset gilds the façades of our cathedrals and gives
us the illusion of their being wrought out of a single
piece : it is as yet at the stage of preparation and of
groping about; but the present crisis of morals,
far from proving the "motricity" of traditional instruction, shows that it is high time to put another
more efficacious in its place.

But M. Delvolvé really continues the effort of
those whom he has just criticised, and moves in full
intellectual and moral harmony with the most universal preoccupations of contemporary life, when he
inquires how the new moral instruction may win the
motor value essential to it without having to seek
a fulcrum in dogmas no longer ours, to which, if we
would, we cannot return.

When our legislators decided that traditional

religious instruction should cease in the State schools, they really only marked a disappearance which was already accomplished, since for a long time this instruction had been nothing but an exercise in memorisation.

It was not slain: it died of languor; it died inglorious.

On the other hand, nothing seems to foretell an intellectual and religious development which will allow members of the teaching profession of every rank to inculcate—sincerely—the chief doctrines of Catholic morality upon future generations.

But what has been abandoned—and probably for ever—is only a path, not the idea and desire of the ascent to be achieved. There are religious and moral foods which we can no longer assimilate, but the religious hunger, the ideal thirst has not disappeared, it has simply become more exacting and more delicate.

M. Delvolvé, for instance, far from denying all value to the efforts of the schools of philosophy or of the Churches, sees in them a work to be taken up and pushed forward in the same spirit and often with similar methods. He would have the child brought to a feeling of the divine that should become for him, if I rightly understand, a kind of experimental sensation, forming part of his individuality at its profoundest, most instinctive and most efficacious; he would create in him a state of soul in which intellect and will should become co-ordinated and strengthen one another.

These are supremely mystical ideas, which make one think of St. Paul's teaching in the epistles of his captivity [1]—it matters little to us here whether they are his or another's—when his thought divests itself of its first theological precision, and essays to take flight outside the Judaic world to which it had clung so closely even when he struggled with the Synagogue.

" *Social life*," [2] says M. Delvolvé, " offers a means not only for the contemplation of universal unity and finality, but also—and this is what gives it its pre-eminent interest—of universal action. Society presents itself to us under the form of a whole, whereof we are parts; of a whole which is not merely a collection of parts, but a high reality, which we participate in without adequately understanding. It exerts an authority over us which determines—whether we are aware of it or no—the moulds into which our action flows : it evolves according to a finality to which our individual finalities know themselves intimately bound. In a word, society is a real form of *communion*. Now the sense of human communion being incomparably the richest form of the sense of the unity of being, human society becomes, for the mind that contemplates it, the most suggestive symbol of, and approximation to, the divine. It is even much more : in society we are not merely the spectators but the actors of the divine unity and finality."

All these pages must be read in order to see how far the youngest among contemporary philosophic minds returns toward mystical views.

Tendencies such as these are the more striking as they are more universal, and correspond to an

---

[1] For instance, *Colossians* i.   [2] *Loc. cit.*, p. 148.

analogous movement manifesting itself among the
working classes. "There seems to me no doubt," [1]
M. Delvolvé rightly says, "that contemporary
Socialism lives by an ideal which presents the most
immediate affinity with religious forms of thought,
and consists in replacing individual finality by the
finality of a *greater* unit (class, socialised humanity)
marked by qualities of perfection in which the individual is deficient—a finality whose fulfilment is,
moreover, certain and inevitable (Hegelianism, historic materialism) : this is why the most brilliant
representatives of our theoretic and practical Socialism are—I say it without irony—almost theologians.
Outside the religious forms (in the broad sense) of
the social ideal there are only the doctrines and facts
of social dissolution. Change the vocabulary, and
the hero of social devotion remains accurately depicted by the words of the *Imitation:* ' *He who
possesses the true and perfect charity seeks nothing
for himself, but his single desire is that God's glory
may be wrought in all things.*' Rare are the hearts
wherein this fire of charity is alight, but only they
have real social value in whom a spark of it is
hidden."

Thus this movement—which, by a path other than
that of the Churches, rediscovers for undenominational moral teaching foundations, a goal and a spirit
very similar to those of religious education—has in
this Montpellier professor become completely conscious, avowed and accepted. It dates from far back,
and would be more quickly affirmed if the ecclesiastical polemics, who have dominated our national

[1] *Loc. cit.*, p. 151.

life, had not carried on a nefarious agitation, wherein the most peaceable people were obliged to become combatants, and in which it was most difficult to collect oneself in order to take bearings and search the far horizon.

Deeply religious people who will read M. Delvolvé's work in a spirit of goodwill, far from discovering in it the corrosive acid that would gradually annihilate their faith, will find therein, on the contrary, a pilgrim of the ideal, who, reaching their road by another way, meets them suddenly and shows them they had not wandered from the path.

If one thinks of the Jew meditating on Abraham's submission as he raised his hand to sacrifice his son to the Eternal; or of the Christian on Good Friday, losing himself in contemplation of him who, at Gethsemane, found himself alone in his struggle against the instinctive rebellion of the flesh, and was nevertheless obedient unto death, even unto the death of the Cross, one perceives that between them and M. Jules Payot, when he speaks of " the firmly-taken resolve to be an agent of voluntary evolution," or M. Delvolvé when he reaches " our voluntary adhesion to the life universal " (p. 165), the identity of direction is complete. These latter give the general definition of actions meditated upon in a concrete and symbolic instance by the former.

Perhaps peace will never be signed between undenominational morality and the traditional morality of the Churches, but, virtually, that unproclaimed peace is already made. This is because the school feels itself henceforward independent, and, above all, because it has attained to views which embrace and surpass those of ecclesiastical morality, and which are, one may say, more catholic, more universal.

There is no contradiction between the efforts of dogmatic morality and those we make now we no longer deny mystery: nature becomes the point of view from which we regard mystery.[1]

Traditional principles were like prophecies and anticipations: their perfect realisation cannot be seen from their starting-point—which was itself prepared by a labour of unimaginable deliberation—nor at such and such a point in their development; but, just as all the results of science would vanish in the twinkling of an eye if the scientific spirit were to disappear, so is it with religion and morals, wherein it is not the results that matter, but the spirit that engendered them.

This is why the resurrection of the religious spirit, which is asserting itself so vigorously and under so novel an aspect in such a number of publications not originating under the shadow of the Churches, constitutes the most important event for centuries in the spiritual evolution of France.

[1] Cp. *loc. cit.*, p. 157.

T

CHAPTER XVI

SCHOOL AND CHURCH

Neutrality impracticable—Place and part of the history of religions in education—New conception of history—Attitude of our contemporaries toward religious questions—The Bible again taken possession of—Return of admiration for the Churches and monuments of the past—A non-Catholic historian at Mass in Notre Dame.

IN the preceding chapter we have seen the attitude the school tends to take towards morality and religious effort. We must now inquire as to the attitude it is prepared to adopt toward the religious institutions existing under the children's eyes. If we have succeeded in grasping the new orientation, we shall have perceived the fertile germ which the undenominational movement brings to the country, and shall understand that, far from being a revolt against the past, or being inspired by an anti-historic, anti-social spirit, it aims, on the contrary, at bringing forth the new city out of the old.[1]

It cannot, however, be denied that, from one end of France to the other, the conflict is now in the acute stage. In a very great number of our villages, war is declared anew between the priest and the school-

[1] Read, *e. g.*, the articles in *Le Peuple,* a Brussels socialist paper, devoted several years ago, by Marcel Hébert, to religious questions, and see how a violent and merely negative anti-clericalism has to-day been left behind. The collection of the *Annales de la jeunesse laïque*, in many of its articles, authorises a similar statement.

master, and when they are not actually in combat these two essential moulders of the child's individuality profess to ignore one another.

But this ignorance is either a fiction or an illusion. In reality, each of the two adversaries is haunted by the thought of the other.

How may this problem be solved?

Neutrality, always so difficult when it was a matter of moral instruction, here becomes impracticable. The child puts a hundred and one questions which the schoolmaster cannot evade. Let us admit he should say nothing as to the actual Church; he is obliged to speak of the Church of the past. Now the Catholic child has scarcely any ecclesiastical furniture save two or three prayers, the *Pater*, the *Ave Maria* and the *Credo*, with a few phrases about God, the dogmas and the sacraments—phrases he has learnt by heart without ever attaching anything definite to the words. He fires them off at the call of certain syllables mechanically, because, in his little head, associations are rather of sound than of sense.

But the intonation of litanies and of the rosary, and the worship which surrounds so many saints, both men and women, whom he sees all about him, and who, moreover, speak to him of a long past, while they create in him no intellectual notion of the Church, inoculate him with a feeling of it that little by little becomes an integral part of his vision of things, and of what is most intimate in his thought.

Without rendering account of it, he already has a non-individualistic vision; he has the instinct of the whole to which he belongs: and from that moment every judgment of the Church, every criticism passed upon it, sets mysterious chords vibrating within him. The Fatherland is much less present to him than the Church.

The teacher supposes that by abstaining from any judgment as to dogmas he observes neutrality; he does not perceive that for his impressionable audience the Church has neither beginning nor end, and that centuries do not count. To rise against the Church of the sixteenth century is to rise against that of to-day. The child feels hurt: and either reacts against the undenominational teacher who has wounded his feelings, or rebels against the priest and religious instruction.

Real neutrality is impossible to keep; since everything is in everything, and it is impossible to give a lesson in history, or even in literature, without voicing judgments dependent upon the speaker's philosophic synthesis.

But since neutrality is impossible, and since the State cannot think of handing back its schools—all its schools, from universities to infant schools—to the tutelage of the Church, what is to be done? [1]

[1] To get an idea of what the theorists who speak in her name claim for the Church, see, in the *Etudes* of July 5, 1911, M. Cyprien Macabiau's article: *École laïque, école neutre, école confessionelle.*

One forgets to take a certain kind of orthodoxy into account; *Les Annales politiques et littéraires* have recently had experience of this.

M. and Mme. Adolphe Brisson, editors of this publication, banish from it everything that might wound the beliefs of their readers. At the close of 1910 they asked the Archbishop of Paris to charge an ecclesiastic with reading their publications attentively in order to point out to them, if there should be occasion, whatever might be of a nature to shock Catholic ears.

Here, then, is a paper, purely undenominational, which not only abstains from all religious polemics, but conforms to the regulation

There were those who dreamed of a logical solution of the difficulty : the State would fight the Church, and have its own undenominational catechism in harmony with the latest results of science. It would oppose Scientific Truth to the unverifiable dogmas of the Churches.

But scarcely had these notions been formulated, when the impossibility of realising them became manifest to their most enthusiastic apostles. To-day, there are scarcely any but village wise-heads to repeat them. If science has not gone bankrupt, to employ a famous expression, it is beçause it does not think of decreeing definitive and absolute truths. The very notion of dogma is entirely foreign to it. Its most recent and representative interpreters proclaim at once its prodigious power and the modesty from which it cannot dream of deviating.

What, then, is the right attitude toward this Church, so many ages old, which has forged our conscience and furnished our imagination, which

---

decreed by the Encyclical *Pascendi*, and asks for an " official censor."

On June 23, 1911, Canon Lesêtre, priest of St. Étienne-du-Mont, Paris, who had received the mission of examining the *Annales* from the Ordinary, gave testimony " to the perfect loyalty of the editor . . . to the conviction and firmness with which he pursued immorality . . . finally, to his sympathetic and sincere respect for the Catholic religion and its teaching."

This approval, delivered by the man who had received a definite mission from his superior, did not suffice to assure the tranquillity of the *Annales ;* and the journals which boast their absolute submission to the hierarchy carried on a campaign against M. and Mme. Adolphe Brisson's publication, wherein, in their out-biddings of orthodoxy, they will certainly have the last word. The documents cited are to be found in the *Foi catholique* for Aug. 15, 1911, article by Father Bernard Gaudeau, S.J.

penetrates our being to the uttermost, and to which
we belong whether we will or no, even when we
rebel against it, then—sometimes—most of all?

The great mass of the country is not wrong to
hesitate, to seek its way, now hurrying forward along
paths it scarcely knows, now pausing abruptly when,
of a sudden, it finds itself astray.

To submit to the Church is no longer possible,
since to do so would be false and hypocritical: to
rebel against it would be absurd, since that obliges
us to pursue it on its own ground, and induces us
to oppose dogma with dogma, an ecclesiastical with
a rationalistic infallibility.

It is very natural that members of the teaching
body feel themselves derelict before this alternative.
Hesitation may become a real moral torment to men
and women—and such cases are not rare—who owe to
the Church the best of their emotional and spiritual
life, their radiant memories, their beneficent moments
of contact with the ideal, and, it may be, their heroic
inspirations. If they can no longer believe, how can
they forget?

" Time is a good fellow," says the Roman proverb
truly: little by little it clears up the most difficult
situation. Its success comes from this: Time takes
as chief collaborator neither logic nor force, but life.

And it may be the great ecclesiastical problem which
dominates contemporary life will be solved by unexpected ways.

Since the teacher can no more teach the divinity of
the Church than ignore its existence, why should he
not act accordingly?

.   .   .   .   .   .

The error of confusing a people's history with the

recital of its wars and the lives of its monarchs has often been remarked. But is not history also distorted by eliminating from it religious thought and evolution? The history of religions is not to be separated from the history of civilisation : it is not a heading along with other headings, it is the germ of all the rest. By placing it at the very centre of historical teaching one returns to actuality. True, this is a complete revolution, but a revolution which is on the point of being quite peacefully achieved, because all things concur in and prepare for it.

We move towards a solution which is neither submission to Catholic dogmas nor rebellion against them, and which is still less the adoption of an opportunist *via media*, without method and without dignity.[1]

When a man of some intelligence visits countries whose civilisation is quite different from his own, he is greatly astonished when his guides seek to draw him into the orbit of their special preoccupations, and monopolise him to the advantage of their social, political or religious ideas. When he is told, " Those are good men, these bad : truth is on this side, falsehood on that," he is inclined to kick and retort, " I have not come to take a side, but to observe and

[1] Many ideas which we only mention here have been set forth at length by M. Alfred Loisy in the articles first published in the *Correspondance de l'union pour la vérité*, 1909-10 (21 rue Visconti, Paris, VI), which have since been gathered into a volume under the title, *À propos d'histoire des religions*, Paris, 12mo, 1911. The illustrious exegetist has there expounded in detail the spirit in which this history must be regarded in order that it may become an integral part of public education. These strong, noble pages will be, as it were, the initial syllabus which will inspire the coming generation for this delicate question.

study. All I see interests me not from the stand-point of its results, but as an aspect of life, thought and effort. Without being anything of a sceptic, I neither dream of bringing you absolute and final truths nor of asking such from you : I neither want to steal your institutions nor to make you a present of mine.

" Allow me to commune with you not by adopting your vestments, formulas and rites, but by walking beside you and sharing to some extent in your efforts. I have not come to you either to furnish my memory with picturesque images, to surprise secrets or dis-cover treasures, but urged by a mysterious instinct of love and solidarity."

Why should we not cherish the same sentiments towards our fellow-citizens and towards the past, the whole past? If many among us have had crises in their lives which have changed the direction of their activity, what matters is not their present programme —no more final than its predecessors—but rather the toil it manifests. And does not the collective life, with its revolutions and its apparent breaks, present the same unity? In this the individual beholds his own story, objectified and enlarged, and grasps at once the humility and dignity of the function assigned him.

This new thought embraces even those who sup-pose they live farthest from it : little by little, for the ideas of the transcendent and the absolute, it substi-tutes those of evolution and of immanent activity. It does not set us before creation—an initial and unique miracle—but before the mystery of ceaselessly creating life, of life calling all that exists to exist yet more, and to create.

Under this influence history has been completely transformed. It is no longer a mass of recollections preserved pell-mell in man's memory. It is no longer a gallery of portraits or of splendid actions wherein a nation seeks patterns and inspirations; nor a morality wherein one may always see vice being punished and virtue rewarded : it is not even the scientific reconstruction of the past—we perceive that of all illusions the most dangerous are those which have an apparently scientific basis—it is the study of life in the past; not of a dead past, but of a past whence we are come, from which we proceed, which has begotten us. The sensation of tradition, of the interdependence across time and space of thousands of generations, opens horizons to the historian vaster than the immense spaces, with the worlds that people them, of the astronomer's contemplation. What interests us now is the mystery of mysteries : man, gradually realising his existence as a free personality, a collaborator in creation, capable of intervening in the mechanism of the universe, and bringing into it ameliorations or disorders whose author, at once free and responsible, he feels himself to be.

In modern thought the importance of a fact is measured by no mechanical dynamometer; the convulsions of a great empire may count for less than the words of a single individual. There is no history save of living, of willing, of conduct. There is no history from which the idea of progress can be absent, and that idea of itself involves a whole religion; for to say " progress " is to proclaim that there is good and evil, a duty, an ideal; it is to affirm the responsibility of the individual, the bonds which attach him to a society whereof he is an integral

part, by which and for which he lives; it is at once
to humble oneself and to be exalted before the
mystery that envelopes us.

In all this there is nothing but the data of daily
experience. To remain strange to it one must dis-
tract or forget oneself, refusing to see or to think.

A Church needs an historical fulcrum to serve it
as a basis. The moral life, on the other hand, has
much deeper and anterior bases : it does not separate
itself—normally, and for civilised humanity—from
existence. When he thinks, man implicitly asserts
the good, duty, a finality in regard to which he feels
himself under obligations.

These ideas are in the air, and by their means a
certain number of the teachers of contemporary
pedagogy succeed in finding entirely solid foundations for undenominational morality. By taking
one's stand on constant individual experience one
has nothing to fear from science, and one prepares
a kind of justification for the various religious
systems, since by showing their source in relation
to the deepest needs of man's soul one saves the
children for ever from superficial incredulity and
cheap scepticism. He who, from the awakening of
his thought, has been led to realise his inner life, to
penetrate into the seclusion wherein it elaborates
itself, can never suppose that all religious institutions
are societies cleverly organised by priests in order
that they may live at the expense of their innocent
parishioners. He is forearmed both against shallow
ecclesiastical undertakings and against summary judgments on the great currents of religious thought and
effort.

Our primary school in France has a notable origin-

ality in this respect; more than any other it reverences
the child and his personality : it aims far less at
running the young life into a uniform mould supplied
by a Church or a Government, than at leading it to
unfold harmoniously and to give out its own note.

By teaching the child to know himself, to seek
himself, it rallies to no metaphysics and to no
theology; it directs its gaze toward the central reality :
it does not take the place of Nature, but serves her
with that feeling for life which is indeed the most
fruitful conquest of contemporary thought.

The undenominational school is orientated towards
science, that is to say, toward the study of facts and
realities—and what is more real than the moral life?
—but not at all towards science conceived as the
working out of an intellectualist mentality such as
was pursued by the scholasticism of the Middle Ages
or the superficial rationalism of the eighteenth century. A complete revolution in popular thought is
being realised around us.

.   .   .   .   .   .

Religious history, far from being foreign to public
or undenominational teaching, on the contrary is
called to become in fact and by right its essential
element.

Nothing human is foreign to history. Least of all
can the unbroken effort by which man transforms and
creates himself be foreign to it.

It is true the historical spirit is, before all, a spirit
of goodwill towards everything that exists : irrecon-
cilable enemies will therefore agree in reproaching it
with justifying all the errors of man's mind. Let us
say it makes them understood and shows their inner
value. It no more proclaims them eternal than

astrological formulas. Science sees everything from the standpoint of reality, which is that of life.

The historical spirit accustoms us to regard every act and thought of man as a phenomenon that is not isolated, but joined—like the leaf which flutters in the wind at the top of the aspen tree, and lives by the essences extracted by innumerable roots out of the bowels of the earth—to a mysterious effort whose origin and end are alike unknown to us.

But in thus ceaselessly awakening in us the idea of life, the historical spirit, with the same persistence, awakens that of death, or rather of becoming. It accustoms us to regard nothing under a static aspect. The mere assertion that there is a history of morals, implies and involves the conviction that little by little, by incessant struggle and in spite of all contradictions, man pursues an ever more efficacious and more harmonious idea of good.

Yesterday's truth has not become false, but yesterday's truth was only the germ of to-day's. Progress does not demonstrate itself. We believe in it with the same instinctive faith as in our own existence. It does not demonstrate itself, because it seeks itself, feels itself, above all, because it is alive, and so there is no instrument which can measure it or make a schematic plan of it.

The potency of the most highly evolved religions comes from their uniting individual efforts for a better future. No doubt they almost always flatter themselves that they set out from an initial revelation; but in declaring that that revelation was made to some intermediary, charged with its transmission, they soon come to leave it in the background, to speak above all of its messengers, and so, after a slight detour, to exalt the labour whereby truth must penetrate into the world.

For those more and more numerous persons who have reached this point of view, religious history is the history *par excellence*, since it recounts to us the essentially human work. They approach this history with the precautions, the attention, the ardour which the true savant brings to the study of the most complex, subtle and potent phenomena.

.   .   .   .   .   .

We live at the precise moment when history definitely claims the right to study every religion without exception. It is a great event in the annals of civilisation. A few years ago there appeared a valuable work in which the history of every religion but that of the Christian Church was studied. To-day such an omission would be impossible.[1]

Doubtless there is still a certain number of priests and believers who are disposed to set a protective hedge about the history of their Church, but such pretensions become rarer and rarer; and even among those who formulated them a few years since, many are now anxious that savants should approach religious evolution with the same methods as the rest of history.[2]

[1] Chantepie de la Saussaye : *Manuel d'histoire des religions*, Paris, 1904.

[2] It is interesting to note the simultaneous existence of the two tendencies even in the organisations most recently created for the defence of pure orthodoxy.

The writer of these lines was privileged to be present at the Vatican, on May 31, 1911, when Père Buzy, of the Sacred Heart of Bétharram, sustained his doctor's thesis before the Biblical Commission presided over by Cardinal Rampolla. One does not

Corresponding to this movement in the heart of the Churches is a parallel movement among the Churches' adversaries.

---

forget that the Pontifical Commission for Biblical Studies are parties to the decretals which greatly astonished most exegetists. So it may well be imagined that the discussions which take place there are entirely formal and formalistic. Now at the sitting of which I was just speaking, if one closed one's eyes, one might have imagined oneself at the Sorbonne or the *École des hautes études*, so great was the freedom, sincerity and scientific value of the debate. The names of Messrs. Jülicher and Loisy were repeatedly mentioned without embarrassment, or the least deprecation.

The discussion turned especially on the interpretation of the saying attributed to Jesus by the Synoptics (Matt. xiii. 14; Mark iv. 12; Luke viii. 10): "I speak unto them in parables that hearing they may not understand." The consultors who conducted the discussion were Dom Laurent Janssens, O.S.B., Father Giovanno Genocchi, M.S.C., and Father J. B. Frey, of the Congregation of the Holy Spirit.

When one or other of the examiners, abandoning patristic arguments, appealed to common sense, the whole audience burst into wholesome, vigorous, and quite undenominational laughter.

The Cardinal alone did not laugh; but neither did he frown; he had the air of being wholly aloof from all that passed before him. He might have been taken for the statue of the dogma which is supposed to be outside of history.

The contradiction between certain decisions of the Biblical Commission and discussions such as that in question is easily explained. Only their Eminences the Cardinals have a voice in the decisions.

After having been present—mute—at discussions in which the consultants have studied a question with a quite scientific freedom, they formulate replies which might just as well have been dictated before any discussion took place.

Is not this juxtaposition of two organisms, apparently so opposite, worthy of note? Logical minds rebel and find this contradictory. They are not wrong. Only we ought to find out whether this contradiction is not a condition of life. Does not every individual carry about two men within him?

The result of it all is a profound change in the attitude of our contemporaries toward religious questions. The day is not far off when, leaving the theologians to their debates about revelation, every one who cares about the formation of his mental and moral being, as also for that of those who belong to him—from the members of his family to his fellow-citizens and the generality of men—will desire to take possession of the religious patrimony bequeathed to him by the past, not to live on it as a spiritual *rentier*,[1] but in order to make it fruitful.

Thus, for example, science, having passed the Bible through the sieve of criticism, is about to give it back to us at the moment when it might have been supposed that, after scattering every one of its pages to the winds, it was going to blot out its very memory.

History has not even to discuss the theses of the dogmatism that affirms the supernatural character of this collection. It has neither to defend nor to attack; its part is easier and more modest—to study the formation of each of the books which form the collection; to reconstitute the crises of social consciousness whereof they are the expression; to mark the obscure, age-long labour which brought them into juxtaposition, the stages of man's thought and consciousness whereof they are the milestones. It has also to observe the editings and rehandlings to which they have been subjected, to study the interpolations and falsifications.

Thus one gradually reaches a singularly different notion of the Scriptures from that which theopneusty

[1] One, *i.e.* who lives on unearned spiritual income.—TRANS.

would impose. The Bible is no longer a book which has fallen from heaven, written under God's dictation : it is the road-book of humanity, starting from the idolatrous worship of the teraphim [1] to rise little by little to the idea of a just and good God, and attaining to the pages of the New Testament, wherein Jesus, far indeed from closing the book with an announcement that henceforward no one should write in it, promised, on the contrary, to those who should love him, new and ampler knowledge.[2]

Protestants continue to call the Bible "the Word of God," but will they still behave as though it were so ? Who will open it at random as they did in old times, in order to find, in the first passage that met their eyes, the oracle's response to their preoccupation ?

The Bible is banished to-day from almost every hearth because a multitude of its pages are devoid of any present and obvious interest; many offer a notion of the Deity far inferior to that of the most blunted conscience, while some are even revolting and immoral.

But consider the collection from the historical point of view, and all immediately lights up. It is the word of Man, lifting himself with difficulty above material preoccupations in order to create a moral consciousness, taking perhaps thousands of centuries to stammer the words of good and evil, to create myths that may appear infantine and incoherent, but are nevertheless the preface to the greatest of humanity's achievements.

In this advance toward the best, Man does not

[1] Genesis xxxi. 19.   [2] See, e. g., John xiv.

pause. The patriarch, asleep in the desert, has visions of the future : he awakens to strive with the mystery, demands its name of it, and concludes by imposing one upon it.

Jacob's ladder had no objective existence; yet to banish it from education under the pretext that it does not correspond to any historical fact is to rob us of an image which, if it is doubtless very imperfect, is singularly useful.

There are but few attentive pedagogues who have not noted the void left in education by the absence of Biblical myths; for the complete and harmonious shaping of consciousness requires the individual to pass rapidly through the stages which it took the race ages to traverse. He can only continue the ancestral labour on condition of knowing it and of having partaken of it. Every child should, in some fashion, live over again the whole life of its race. This necessity is more and more vividly perceived in every region, and those who regard progress as a break with the past become rarer and rarer.

It is far from being mere snobbishness that leads so many people to fall in love with cathedrals : it is true lovers of the Gothic are usually very devoid of architectural knowledge; but what interests them is far less the building, strictly speaking, than the feelings of those who constructed it. They only admire the stones so much because they see in them the expression of an effort, an ineffable yearning after the ideal and—to tell all—a creation of faith. They are moved at the thought of the innumerable processions of artists and craftsmen who only lived that they might write these anonymous pages scattered over the whole of Europe; and it may be that their

U

admiration, more than they themselves suspect, is like a participation of desire in an ideal and disinterested work.

.   .   .   .   .   .

A few years ago, on one of the chief holidays, a professor charged with the teaching of history in one of our great scientific institutions took his place in the ambulatory of the choir of Notre Dame, opposite the Archbishop's throne. At the same moment a very short-sighted young man sat down beside him, and, raising his eyes to his neighbour, whose umbrella he had awkwardly knocked down, was stupefied to recognise his former professor, of well-merited anti-clerical fame, holding a fat and brand-new Prayer-book.

The master shook his pupil warmly by the hand. "Fancy," he said, " I have never exactly realised what the Mass is. I have often been present at marriages and burials, but naturally, like the majority of those present, I was entirely aloof from the religious side of the ceremony. I know the purpose of this office is transubstantiation, but there my knowledge ends. So I have come to-day to try and see whether, with goodwill, I can succeed in being interested in it. I have armed myself with a Prayer-book, and have studied it somewhat to try and follow the various phases of the ceremony." So speaking, he showed that he had already opened the volume at the Ordinary of the Mass and at the Office for Easter-day.

In the meantime a chant arose in the choir. "It is the canons singing tierce," the young man answered to a mute question; and during nearly the whole of the Mass he had to continue giving explanations.

From the *Sanctus* on, his teacher left him to his reflections and prayers, somewhat astonished to see him absorbed in them.

They came out together, equally embarrassed, not knowing how they should separate.

When they were come into the square, the young man said, to shelter his master : " Forgive my being of so little use. Did you find any interest in it?" "Not a bit. . . . But now we stand no longer in the relation of master and pupil, will you allow me to ask you a quite personal question? If it is indiscreet do not answer it. Have you faith?"

" Your question takes me at unawares : but since it was no more prepared than my reply can be, I do not want to evade it. . . . Yes, I think I can say with a good conscience I have faith. It is true I ought to have begun by begging you to define what you mean by faith. Under the same word each man means a different thing. Who could give a perfect definition of love? Now faith is still love—love triumphant over time, space and matter, and creating the future." " But it seems to me the theologians——" " I beg you, do not speak to me of the theologians. I scarcely have occasion to frequent them. You put me a personal question, which I answered personally. I think I have understood, from certain of your lectures, that for you, faith is the act whereby the faithful give adhesion to the dogmas defined by the Church. But that is only a very small fraction of the reality, and by isolating it one alters and distorts it. Adhesion to dogma is but one of the manifestations of faith. It is an external and, in a way, a juridical sign of it, but is neither its beginning nor its end. For me it is a kind of *joie de vivre*, which finds extraordinary exaltation in communion with the Church. When I sing the *Credo*, and when I kneel to worship the Holy Sacrament, I join myself to the Church with a kind of luxury, with the glorious certitude that without her I should be nothing but a waif : that yet she has need of me, and that with her my life lays hold of meaning and import."

There was a pause. The young man reproached himself for his volubility and presumption. He had a singular esteem for his master, and did not wish to seem to be giving him a lesson. On his side, the professor feared he had been wanting in reserve and perhaps in tact. All at once he felt awkward and embarrassed. Instead of continuing the conversation, he asked his companion to come and see him.

They returned three or four times to Notre Dame. The master went alone much oftener. He also went to other churches. He strove to understand what the faithful put into or find in so many acts of worship that formerly appeared to him mere empty forms.

His convictions have not changed, but he feels his life enlarged and beautified by the new sentiment he entertains for his Catholic fellow-citizens. He has not become a Catholic, but he understands that one could; and if he notes that many people are so by chance and not by choice, he also sees that the Church has members who live by her and by whom she lives.

.   .   .   .   .   .

A similar work is being wrought in many minds. If the Separation of the Churches and the State has encroached upon the material resources of the Church in a degree that it is hard to estimate, if it has taken from her the mighty prestige of an official institution, and caused many candidates—whose vocation was scarcely more than a lively desire to become officials —to desert the avenues of the sanctuary, it has drawn to her a sympathy and aid which in the near future may well compensate, and more than compensate, her for the losses sustained.

If Catholicism could succeed in separating its cause from that of a political, aggressive, violent and intolerant Clericalism, the awakening of idealism which is everywhere astir, both in our country and elsewhere, would quite naturally translate itself into a Catholic religious spring. Who lives will see.

What is certain is that at this moment the need is imposed on every mind to revise those summary judgments on religion which were the very natural reaction from the persecutions to which free-thought had been subjected.

The success of William James's works is a characteristic proof of this. People are grateful to him for having shown how the religious life may be the object of scientific study; in Latin countries they have been especially grateful to him for being an American, and for having said all he has without being, strictly speaking, a believer. If his *Varieties of Religious Experience* had had a Latin author, it would have had far less importance on this side of the Atlantic; people would have been tempted to see in it an indirect essay in apologetics.

.   .   .   .   .   .

We are at the precise moment when psychological and religious science have just joined hands to make the religious life their favourite study.

What will be the result of the action of these two sciences on the evolution of ideas, feelings and convictions? It is difficult to foresee. But it would seem to be already certain that, after having momentarily disconcerted old customs, they are renovating this region by rendering it wholesome. They cannot sow other seed in it than that which exists already; but this seed, scattered over well-tilled ground, where, above all, the wind and sun have free play, will yield harvests of unexpected beauty.

The study of religious experience and of the history of religions is about to transform our teaching and profoundly to modify our political, moral and social ideas.

The unheard-of progress made by the sciences during the last half-century has created among many savants, as also among thinkers and even among statesmen, the nostalgia for progress of a spiritual order.

CONCLUSION

In order to recapitulate our country's present religious situation, two facts, apparently contradictory, must be noted: the rapid advance of indifference, and an unexpected awakening of religious aspiration. This double phenomenon may often be observed in one and the same individual.

At bottom this is not so strange as at first sight it would appear: the Churches treat alike as unbelievers those who have no religious life, and those in whom it is too young and too intense to find full and entire satisfaction in the formulas of the past.

Now it really seems as though we had reached an era of reconstitution, and one might say of religious vindication, somewhat similar to that of the beginnings of Christianity. If the Church of Rome appears to have been more affected than any other by the political and intellectual crisis, it may, nevertheless, be said that, in the midst of the spiritual debris that surrounds us, the thought of to-day is seeking out, for the foundations and columns of the new temple, ideas and feelings whose Catholic origin is unquestionable: the sentiment of the mystery that envelops and embraces us; of the unity and the solidarity of all beings throughout time as throughout space.

The ensemble of confused impressions that leads

295

us to the great law of tradition: the certainty that
there is a duty for man, and that this duty is to utter
his harmonious note in the eternal concert wherein he
participates for a moment only, but of which he
glimpses the meaning and, as the philosophers say,
the finality; the conviction that every effort avails
only in so far as it is disinterested, and that the most
vital man is he who gives himself, forgets himself,
sacrifices himself; the sensation that he, in appearance
an ephemeral being, will leave an ineffaceable trace of
his passage, and may associate in the labour of eternal
life—a labour which he dominates and may, in a
measure, direct: all these feelings are emphatically
those of the present generation,[1] and it is emphatically the Church which has sown their seed in its
heart.

The Church of Rome, despite its failures and in
spite of all appearance, keeps thus a unique and peerless place in the heart and conscience of the flower
of the coming generation, because it alone has realised the unity and eternity of its life. As to other
ecclesiastical institutions, they do not even perceive
that the greater part of the advantages they pride
themselves on offering are, on the contrary, incurable
vices. How many intelligent people fail to understand that the notion of a national Church is a mutilation which takes the meaning and value from the
very idea of a Church!

Pius X and his predecessors may, indeed, have
been far from exceptional men; but the idea whereof
they are the precarious and fragile symbols is one of

---

[1] M. Delvolvé expresses this in other words when he says that
" the finality of the conscious ego is only one with a universal
finality."

the greatest and most fruitful humanity has caught sight of, and all the living forces of democracy push on towards its realisation. To those who observe it, this idea is perceived to be first-cousin to that which was the soul of our country during the period so ill-named the revolutionary. For many a Frenchman, that wholly superficial appellation still conceals the real character of a crisis which was, before all else, the outcome of an age-long effort.

Our contemporaries often find no answer to the simplistic minds who make a pretext of the mistakes, weaknesses or crimes of the popes for cursing the Papacy; but there are also those among them who feel the vanity of such arguments. They divine that when it created the expression " the Chair of Peter," and the notion which it represents, and even when it served ambitions which were not always ideal, the genius of man groped its way forward towards infinitely grand ideas, stammered prophecies of whose realisation we scarcely catch a glimpse, but whose realisation has, nevertheless, begun.

The Church has, indeed, traced out paths whereby to ascend toward the heights. It must, of course, be expected that not one of them is definitive, and that along each one discouraged and wounded pilgrims are sure to be met, reproaching their illusions; but evidently many of our contemporaries perceive that to put forward these disappointments and failures as a pretext for not advancing toward the heights is as mistaken as to give up eating for fear of adulterated foods.

If, whether we will or no, "we live and move and have our being" in the Church, it is certain she, in her turn, receives something from us, and is

gradually transformed, while remaining ever the
same.[1]

[1] When M. Dürkheim says, "In divinity I only see society
transfigured and symbolically conceived," he formulates a notion
near akin to the fundamental Catholic thought, according to which
the experience that the faithful have of the Church is the basis of
all else.   That experience leads to God, and becomes the constant
inspiration of life.   Hereby Catholicism, apparently based upon
doctrinal theses considerably remote from our preoccupations,
may have roots in the individual life, unsuspected by its adversaries.

The Catholic says to God, "Our Father," but when he speaks
of the Church he says, "Our Mother"; and it is she whom, from
his first glance, he sees leaning over his cradle; she who teaches
him to lisp the name of the Heavenly Father.   The Communion
of the Catholic with the Church is not the result of an act of will,
or of reasoning, it is the initial fact of his moral life.   He believes
in her as naturally as the new-born babe believes in his mother.
The Church takes possession of his soul so quickly and entirely
that, in his experience, the Church and his soul are not merely
inseparable, but, in a sense, they have one and the same being.

Ignorance of this fundamental fact explains the failure of anti-
Catholic propaganda.   It is not very difficult to draw individuals
or groups of individuals away from all ecclesiastical influence;
but so far as I know the attempt to provide them with a new spiritual
milieu has been no more successful than attempts to provide
orphan children with a mother.

INDEX OF NAMES

Richard Clay & Sons, Limited, London and Bungay.

OTHER BOOKS
BY PAUL SABATIER

Vie de saint François d'Assise. 38e tirage. In-8º de cxxvi–420 pages.
Paris, 1912.

Speculum perfectionis seu *sancti Francisci Assisiensis legenda antiquis-sima, auctore fratre Leone.* Nunc primum edidit Paul Sabatier. In-8º
de ccxiv-376 pages.

*Fratris Francisci Bartholi de Assisio tractatus de indulgentia S. Mariae
de Portiuncula.* Nunc primum integre edidit Paul Sabatier. In-8º de
clxxiv-204 pages.

Actus S. Francisci et sociorum ejus. Edidit Paul Sabatier. In-8º de
lxiv-272 pages.

*Floretum S. Francisci Assisiensis, liber aureus qui Italice dicitur
Fioretti di san Francesco.* Edidit Paul Sabatier. In-8º de xvi-250 pages,
2e édition.[1]

A-propos de la Séparation des Églises et de l'État. 6e édition. In-12
de lxxxiv-216 pages.

Lettre ouverte au Cardinal Gibbons. In-12 de xx-84 pages.

Les Modernistes. Notes d'histoire religieuse contemporaine. Avec le
texte intégral de l'Encyclique *Pascendi*, du Syllabus *Lamentabili* et
de la Supplique d'un groupe de Catholiques français au Pape Pie X.
6e édition. In-12º de liv-258 pages. Paris, 1909.

[1] In 1905, the Institute awarded the decennial Grand Prix Lefèvre-Deumier to M. Paul Sabatier for his Franciscan works.

A CENTURY
OF EDUCATION

By HENRY BRYAN BINNS

Being the Centenary History of the British and
Foreign Schools Society

Large Crown 8vo.   Illustrated

APPENDICES

ELEMENTARY EDUCATION
By T. J. MACNAMARA, M.P.

SECONDARY EDUCATION
By SIDNEY WEBB, LL.B.

THE TRAINING OF TEACHERS
By PROFESSOR FOSTER WATSON

THE FUTURE OF ENGLISH EDUCA-
TION IN THE LIGHT OF THE
PAST
By GRAHAM WALLAS

J. M. DENT & SONS, LTD.
ALDINE HOUSE, BEDFORD STREET, W.C.